$25.00 JCP

GENETIC PROGRAMMING AND DATA STRUCTURES:
Genetic Programming + Data Structures = Automatic Programming!

THE KLUWER INTERNATIONAL SERIES
IN ENGINEERING AND COMPUTER SCIENCE

GENETIC PROGRAMMING AND DATA STRUCTURES:
Genetic Programming + Data Structures = Automatic Programming!

by

W. B. Langdon
The University of Birmingham
United Kingdom

KLUWER ACADEMIC PUBLISHERS
Boston / Dordrecht / London

Distributors for North America:
Kluwer Academic Publishers
101 Philip Drive
Assinippi Park
Norwell, Massachusetts 02061 USA

Distributors for all other countries:
Kluwer Academic Publishers Group
Distribution Centre
Post Office Box 322
3300 AH Dordrecht, THE NETHERLANDS

Library of Congress Cataloging-in-Publication Data

A C.I.P. Catalogue record for this book is available
from the Library of Congress.

The publisher offers discounts on this book when ordered in bulk quantities. For more information contact: Sales Department, Kluwer Academic Publishers, 101 Philip Drive, Assinippi Park, Norwell, MA 02061

Printed on acid-free paper.

Printed in the United States of America

Contents

Foreword

This book, Genetic Programming and Data Structures, is the first book in the Kluwer series on genetic programming.

Genetic programming addresses the problem of automatic program synthesis and automatic programming, namely the problem of how to enable a computer to do useful things without instructing it, step by step, how to do it. Genetic programming accomplishes this by breeding a population of computer programs over many generations using the operations of Darwinian natural selection, crossover (sexual recombination), and mutation. The publication of more than 800 papers by some 250 authors since 1992 attests to the wide range of problems that can be solved with this biologically inspired metaphor.

However, early work on genetic programming was largely confined to evolving computer programs with either rudimentary forms of memory (such as named memory, indexed memory, and matricial memory) or, in many cases, no memory at all.

It was at this point that Bill Langdon, a professional software engineer, entered the fray and showed how the lessons of software production and the essential role of abstraction can be advantageously used in the context of genetic programming. In particular, Langdon demonstrates in this excellent volume how a large arsenal of familiar and useful data structures (such as stacks, queues, lists, rings, etc.) can be implemented in genetic programming. In fact, this book can be summarized by what should be called Langdon's equation:

Genetic Programming + Data Structures = Automatic Programming.

John R. Koza, Consulting Professor,
Computer Science Department

Preface

Computers that "program themselves" has long been an aim of computer scientists. Recently genetic programming (GP) has started to show its promise by automatically evolving programs. Indeed in a small number of problems GP has evolved programs whose performance is similar to or even slightly better than that of programs written by people. The main thrust of GP has been to automatically create functions. While these can be of great use they contain no memory and relatively little work has addressed automatic creation of program code including stored data. It is this issue which this book addresses.

Motivated by the observation from software engineering that data abstraction (e.g. via abstract data types) is essential in programs created by human programmers we will show that abstract data types can be similarly beneficial to the automatic production of programs using GP.

We will show how abstract data types (stacks, queues and lists) can be evolved using genetic programming, demonstrate GP can evolve general programs which solve the nested brackets problem, recognise a Dyck context free language and implement a simple four function calculator. In these cases an appropriate data structure is beneficial compared to simple indexed memory. This book also includes a survey of GP, including a critical review of experiments with evolving memory and reports investigations of real world electrical network maintenance scheduling problems that demonstrate that Genetic Algorithms can find low cost viable solutions to such problems.

The subtitle of this book is initially derived from the famous expression by Niklaus Wirth *Algorithms + Data Structures = Programs* used for the title of his book [Wirth, 1975] and subsequently rephrased by Zbigniew Michalewicz to *Genetic Algorithms + Data Structures = Evolution Programs* as the title of his book [Michalewicz, 1994]. With *Genetic Programming + Data Structures = Automatic Programming!* we continue the common thread. All three books share a common idea. "To build [or evolve] a successful program, appropriate data structures should be used together with appropriate algorithms (these correspond to genetic operators used for transforming individual chromosomes [or programs])", [Michalewicz, 1994, page xi]. It would unfair to the reader to mislead them into thinking it is possible at present to automatically evolve every program. The subtitle reflects the hope that this book will be a step towards automatic programming.

This book is an updated version of my thesis which was submitted as part of the requirements of the degree of Doctor of Philosophy in the University of London in September 1996 and obtained in December 1996. The thesis was written at the Computer Science Department of University College, London, which is part of the University of London.

W. B. LANGDON

Acknowledgments

My thesis was primarily funded by the EPSRC via a PhD quota award and The National Grid Company plc. via a CASE award.

I would like to thank my supervisors (M. Levene and P. C. Treleaven), Tom Westerdale, and Mauro Manela for their critisims and ideas; UCL Computer Science department for not minding too much me using their machines and Andy Singleton for the initial version of GP-QUICK on which much of my code was implemented.

My thanks to John Macqueen and Maurice Dunnett who introduced me to the NGC maintenance planning problem. Mike Calviou, Ursula Bryan, Daniel Waterhouse, Arthur Ekwue and Helen Cappocci for much practical assistance such as fitness functions, installing SDRS2, fast DC loadflow code and reviewing various draft papers (often to unreasonably short deadlines). To Laura Dekker for assistance with setting up QGAME.

Lee Altenberg (of University of Hawai'i) for directing me to the work of George Price (of UCL) and helpful comments and suggestions on this work.

I would like to thank the following Howard Oakley, Suran Goonatilake, Lee Spector, Maarten Keijzer, Thomas Haynes, Frederic Gruau, Peter Angeline, Riccardo Poli, Justinian Rosca, Hitoshi Iba and various anonymous reviewers who all helped me by reviewing my work and making suggestions for its improvement and supplying references to existing work.

I would like to thank Julia Schnabel for reading and constructively criticising the many drafts of my thesis.

And thanks to Dave Lawrence (of Digital Equipment Corp.) for inspiring conversation in Richard Head's (Houston).

1 INTRODUCTION

In both natural evolution and human endeavour, complex problems are solved by assembling solutions to parts of the problem into a complete solution. Whilst this is highly successful, it requires limited interaction between components. The building block hypothesis [Goldberg, 1989] states the same is true for artificial evolution. While doubts concerning the building block hypothesis have been expressed in general (e.g. [Beyer, 1995]) and for genetic programming (GP) in particular [O'Reilly and Oppacher, 1995], if complex solutions are to be evolved then it must be possible to assemble complete solutions from program fragments which solve parts of the problem. Where program components have complex interactions progress is more difficult, since improvement in one aspect will affect many others in an unpredictable and so usually negative way. Global memory allows such complex interactions. In software engineering complex interactions via global memory can be tackled by controlling programmers use of memory with scoping rules and abstract data types, such as stack, queues, files etc.

The thesis is that data structures can be used within the automatic production of computer programs via artificial evolution and that appropriate data structures are beneficial.

1.1 WHAT IS GENETIC PROGRAMMING?

Genetic programming [Koza, 1992] is a technique which enables computers to solve problems without being explicitly programmed. It works by using genetic algorithms to automatically generate computer programs.

Genetic algorithms (GAs) were devised by John Holland [Holland, 1992] as a way of harnessing the power of Darwinian natural evolution for use within computers. Natural evolution has seen the development of complex organisms (e.g. plants and animals) from simpler single celled life forms. Holland's GAs are simple models of the essentials of natural evolution and inheritance.

The growth of plants and animals from seeds or eggs is primarily controlled by the genes they inherited from their parents. The genes are stored on one or more strands of DNA. In asexual reproduction the DNA is a copy of the parent's DNA, possibly with some random changes, known as *mutations*. In sexual reproduction, DNA from both parents is inherited by the new individual. Often about half of each parent's DNA is copied to the child where it joins with DNA copied from the other parent. The child's DNA is usually different from that in either parent.

Natural evolution arises as only the fittest individuals survive to reproduce and so pass on their DNA to subsequent generations. That is DNA which produces fitter individuals is likely to increase in proportion in the population. As the DNA within the population changes, the species as a whole changes, i.e. it evolves as a result of selective survival of the individuals of which it is composed.

Genetic algorithms contain a "population" of trial solutions to a problem, typically each individual in the population is modelled by a string representing its DNA. This population is "evolved" by repeatedly selecting the "fitter" solutions and producing new solutions from them (cf. "survival of the fittest"). The new solutions replace existing solutions in the population. New individuals are created either asexually (i.e. copying the string, possibly with random mutations) or sexually (i.e. creating a new string from parts of two parent strings). The power of GAs (to find optimal or near optimal solutions) is being demonstrated for an increasing range of applications; financial, imaging, VLSI circuit layout, gas pipeline control and production scheduling [Davis, 1991].

In genetic programming (GP) the individuals in the population are computer programs. To ease the process of creating new programs from two parent programs, the programs are written as trees. New programs are produced by removing branches from one tree and inserting them into another. This simple process, known as *crossover*, ensures that the new program is also a tree and so is also syntactically valid (see Figure 1.1). Thus genetic programming is fundamentally different from simply shuffling lines of Fortran or machine code.

The sequence of operations in genetic programming is given in Figure 1.2. It is fundamentally the same as other genetic algorithms. While mutation can be used in GP, see Section 2.4.6, often it is not. For example it is only used in Appendix C in this book.

GP has demonstrated its potential by evolving programs in a wide range of applications including text classification or retrieval [Masand, 1994; Dunning and Davis, 1996], performing optical character recognition [Andre, 1994c], protein classification [Handley, 1993], image processing [Daida et al., 1996], target identification [Tackett, 1993], electronic circuit design [Koza et al., 1996a] and car monitoring for pollution control [Hampo et al., 1994]. At present published applications in everyday use remain rare, however Oakley's [Oakley, 1994] use of evolved medical signal filters and the BioX modelling system [Bettenhausen et al., 1995] are practical applications.

Parents

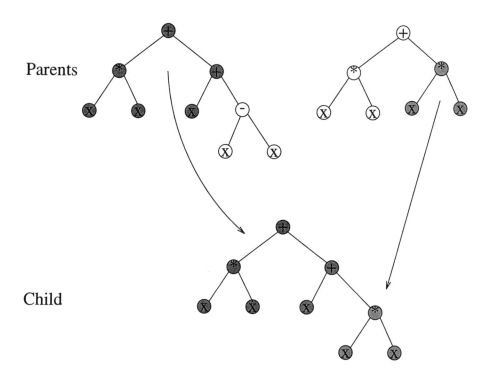

Child

Figure 1.1. Genetic Programming Crossover:
$x^2 + (x + (x - x))$ crossed with $2x^2$ to produce $2x^2 + x$.

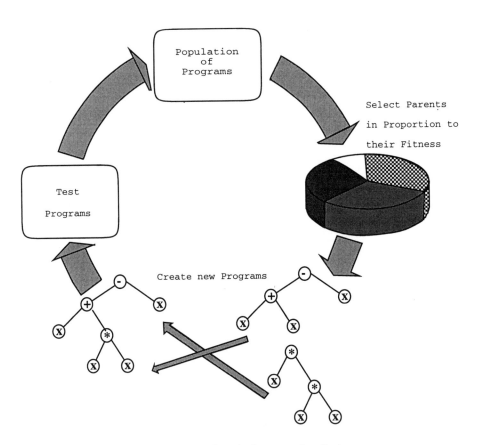

Figure 1.2.   Genetic Programming Cycle

1.2   MOTIVATION

There are three main goals of this work. Firstly to show that data structures, other than simple random access indexed memory, can be used within genetic programming. Secondly to show that appropriate data structures can be beneficial when evolving programs and finally to show that appropriate data structures can be evolved as needed. As we shall see, the first two goals have been achieved. While we shall show it is is possible to evolve data structures on their own, and it is believed evolving them as needed is achievable (Section 7.5 offers some support) this has yet to be demonstrated. We will show:

1. that abstract data types (stacks (Chapter 4), queues (Chapter 5) and lists (Chapter 6)) can be evolved using genetic programming,

2. on a number of different problems, an appropriate abstract data type is beneficial (Chapter 7),

3. GP can evolve general programs which solve the nested brackets problem (Section 7.1), recognise a Dyck context free language (Section 7.2) and evaluate Reverse Polish Notation (RPN) expressions (i.e. evolve a four function calculator, Section 7.3).

4. Chapter 2 contains a survey of GP, while a critical review of experiments with evolving memory is presented in Section 7.4).

5. Finally Appendix C describes investigations of real world electrical network maintenance scheduling problems that demonstrate that Genetic Algorithms can find low cost viable solutions to such problems.

1.3   OUTLINE

Following this introductory chapter, Chapter 2 describes in general terms the genetic programming technique and then Chapter 3 covers in some detail the specific techniques used in the remainder of the book. The next four chapters describe experiments. The knowledgeable reader may wish to commence with the experimental chapters, i.e. Chapter 4, and follow the references back to sections within Chapters 2 or 3 as necessary.

Chapter 4 describes in detail an experiment which shows it is possible to automatically generate programs which implement general stack data structures for integers. The programs are evolved using genetic programming guided only by how well candidate solutions perform. NB no knowledge of the internal operation of the programs or comparison with an ideal implementation is used. The two trees per individual in the population introduced by [Koza, 1992, Sections 19.7 and 19.8] is extended to five trees, one per stack operation. Chapters 6 further extends it to ten trees plus shared automatically defined functions (ADFs). Chapter 4 concludes by considering the size of the test case (in terms of its information content in the [Shannon and Weaver, 1964] sense) and the size of the evolved programs. The general solutions evolved are smaller than the test case, i.e. they have compressed the test case.

Chapter 5 describes a series of experiments which show genetic programming can similarly automatically evolve programs which implement a circular "First-In First-Out" (FIFO) queue. Initially memory hungry general solutions evolved but later experiments show that adding resource consumption as a component of the fitness function enables memory efficient solutions to be evolved. The final set of experiments show FIFO queues can be evolved from basic primitives but considerably more machine resources are required. Mechanisms are also introduced to constrain the GP search by requiring evolving functions (ADFs) to obey what a software engineer would consider sensible rules.

In Chapter 6 the last data structure, an integer list, is evolved. A list is a generalisation of both a stack and a queue but more complex than either. A controlled iteration loop and syntax rules are introduced. The evolution of the list proves to be the most machine resource intensive of the successful experiments in our book. Chapter 6 also describes a model for the automatic maintenance of software produced by GP. In one experiment considerable saving of machine resources is shown.

Chapter 7 is the crux of the book. It shows in three cases GP can beneficially use appropriate data structures in comparison to using random access memory. The three problems are the balanced bracket problem, a Dyck language (i.e. balanced bracket problem but with multiple types of brackets) and evolving a reverse polish expression calculator.

Chapter 8 stands back from the experiments and considers in some detail the dynamics of GP populations using the runs from Chapter 4 as an example. Chapter 8 starts by considering the application of results from theoretical biology. It concludes Price's theorem of selection and covariance can, in general, be applied to genetic algorithms and genetic programming but the standard interpretation of Fisher's fundamental theorem of natural selection cannot. The remainder of Chapter 8 investigates the reasons behind the small proportion of successful runs in the stack problem. It concludes the presence of easily found "deceptive" partial solutions acts in many cases via fitness based selection to prevent the discovery of complete solutions. Partial solutions based upon use of memory are readily disrupted by language primitives which act via side-effects on the same memory. This leads to selection acting against these primitives, which in most cases causes their complete removal from the population. However where complete solutions are found, they require these primitives and thus in most runs complete solutions are prevented from evolving by the loss of essential primitives from the population. While the details of the mechanism are specific to the stack problem, the problem of "deceptive" fitness functions and language primitives with side-effects may be general.

The stack populations are also at variance with published GP results which show variety in GP populations is usually high (in contrast to bit string genetic algorithm populations which often show convergence). With the stack populations in many cases there are multiple identical copies within the population. This is due to the discovery of high fitness individuals early in the GP run which contain short trees. With short trees many crossover operations produce offspring which are identical to their parents and these tend to dominate the population so reducing variety. This effect may be expected in any GP population where high fitness solutions contain short trees but are fragile, in that most of their offspring have a lower fitness. The presence of code within the trees which does not affect the trees performance (variously called "fluff", "bloat" or "introns") may conceal this effect as trees need not be short and many offspring may be functionally identical to their parents (and so have the same fitness) but not be genetically identical. Should these dominate the population then it will have high variety even though many individuals within it are functionally the same.

The concluding chapter, Chapter 9, is followed by an extensive bibliography and then appendices. Appendix A tabulates the resources consumed in terms of number of trial solutions processed by the previous experiments. Appendix B contains a glossary of evolutionary computation terms. This is followed by Appendix C which details experiments using a permutation based genetic algorithm and others using genetic programming, to produce low cost schedules for preventive maintenance of the high voltage electrical power transmission network in England and Wales (the National Grid). The final appendix contains notes on the code implementation and network addresses from which it may be obtained.

2 GENETIC PROGRAMMING – COMPUTERS USING "NATURAL SELECTION" TO GENERATE PROGRAMS

Computers that "program themselves"; science fact or fiction? *Genetic Programming* uses novel optimisation techniques to "evolve" simple programs; mimicking the way humans construct programs by progressively re-writing them. Trial programs are repeatedly modified in the search for "better/fitter" solutions. The underlying basis is Genetic Algorithms (GAs).

Genetic Algorithms, pioneered by [Holland, 1992], [Goldberg, 1989] and others, is the evolutionary search technique inspired by natural selection (i.e survival of the fittest). GAs work with a "population" of trial solutions to a problem, frequently encoded as strings, and repeatedly select the "fitter" solutions, attempting to evolve better ones. The power of GAs is being demonstrated for an increasing range of applications; financial, imaging, VLSI circuit layout, gas pipeline control and production scheduling [Davis, 1991]. But one of the most intriguing uses of GAs – launched by Koza [Koza, 1992] – is automatic program generation.

Genetic Programming applies GAs to a "population" of programs – typically encoded as tree-structures. Trial programs perhaps in LISP, or even C, are evaluated against a "fitness function" and the best solutions selected for modification and re-evaluation. This modification-evaluation cycle is repeated until a "correct" program is produced. GP has demonstrated its potential by evolving simple programs for medical signal filters, modelling complex chemical reactions, performing optical character recognition and for target identification.

This chapter surveys the exciting field of Genetic Programming. As a basis it reviews Genetic Algorithms and automatic program generation. Next it introduces Genetic Programming, describing its history and describing the technique via a worked example in C. Then it surveys recent work with sections on each of the six GP steps (Terminals, Functions, Fitness measure, Control Parameters, Termination criterion and Architecture), new genetic and search operators and lists some of the GP development tools. Finally we survey pioneering GP applications with sections on Prediction and Classification, Image and Signal Processing, Optimisation, Trading, Robots, Artificial Life and Artistic uses of GP. ([Langdon, 1996a] contains an extensive bibliography of GP).

2.1 INTRODUCTION

Genetic programming is a technique which enables computers to solve problems without being explicitly programmed. It works by using genetic algorithms to automatically generate computer programs.

Genetic algorithms were devised by John Holland as a way of harnessing the power of natural evolution for use within computers. Natural evolution has seen the development of complex organisms (e.g. plants and animals) from simpler single celled life forms. Holland's GAs are simple models of the essentials of natural evolution and inheritance.

The growth of plants and animals from seeds or eggs is primarily controlled by the genes they inherited from their parents. The genes are stored on one or more strands of DNA. In asexual reproduction the DNA is a copy of the parent's DNA, possibly with some random changes, known as *mutations*. In sexual reproduction, DNA from both parents is inherited by the new individual. Often about half of each parent's DNA is copied to the child where it joins with DNA copied from the other parent. The child's DNA is usually different from that in either parent.

Natural evolution arises as only the fittest individuals survive to reproduce and so pass on their DNA to subsequent generations. That is DNA which produces fitter individuals is likely to increase in proportion in the population. As the DNA within the population changes, the species as a whole changes, i.e. it evolves as a result of selective survival of the individuals of which it is composed.

Genetic algorithms contain a "population" of trial solutions to a problem, typically each individual in the population is modelled by a string representing its DNA. This population is "evolved" by repeatedly selecting the "fitter" solutions and producing new solution from them (cf. "survival of the fittest"), the new solutions replacing existing solutions in the population. New individuals are created either asexually (i.e. copying the string) or sexually (i.e. creating a new string from parts of two parent strings).

In genetic programming the individuals in the population are computer programs. To ease the process of creating new programs from two parent programs, the programs are written as trees. New programs are produced by removing branches from one tree and inserting them into another. This simple process ensures that the new program is also a tree and so is also syntactically valid.

As an example, suppose we wish a genetic program to calculate $y = x^2$. Our population of programs might contain a program which calculates $y = 2x - x$ (see Figure 2.1) and another which calculates $y = \frac{x}{x - x^3} - x$ (Figure 2.2). Both are selected from the population because they produce answers similar to $y = x^2$ (Figure 2.4), i.e. they are of high fitness. When a selected branch (shown shaded) is moved from the

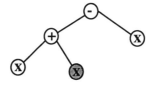

Figure 2.1.   Mum, fitness .64286, $2x - x$

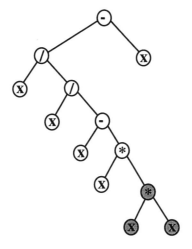

Figure 2.2.   Dad, fitness .70588, $\dfrac{x}{\frac{x}{x - x^3}} - x$

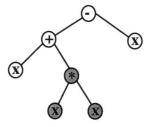

Figure 2.3.   Correct Program, fitness 1.0, $x + x^2 - x$

father program and inserted in the mother (displacing the existing branch, also shown shaded) a new program is produced which may have even high fitness. In this case the resulting program (Figure 2.3) actually calculates $y = x^2$ and so this program is the output of our GP.

The remainder of this chapter describes genetic algorithms in more detail, placing them in the context of search techniques, then explains genetic programming, its history, the six steps to GP, shows these steps being used in our example and gives a survey of current GP research and applications, which are presented in some detail.

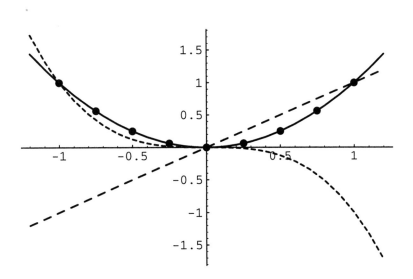

Figure 2.4. x^2 (solid), test points (dots), values returned by mum ($2x - x$, dashed) and dad ($\frac{x}{\frac{x}{x - x^3}} - x$, small dashed)

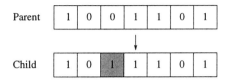

Figure 2.5.   Genetic Algorithms - Mutation

2.2 GENETIC ALGORITHMS

Genetic algorithms are perhaps the closest computation model to natural evolution. Their success at searching complex non-linear spaces and general robustness has led to their use in a number of practical problems such as scheduling, financial modelling and optimisation.

The inventor of genetic algorithms, John Holland [Holland, 1992], took his inspiration for them from nature. Genetic algorithms contain a population of individuals, each of which has a known fitness. The population is evolved through successive generations, the individuals in each new generation are bred from the fitter individuals of the previous generation. The process continues through successive generations until we decide to stop it. As with the breeding of domestic animals, we choose the individuals to breed from (using a *fitness function*) to drive the population's evolution in the direction we want it to go. As with domestic animals, it may take many generations to produce individuals with the required characteristics.

Inside a computer an individual's fitness is usually calculated directly from its DNA (i.e. without the need to grow it) and so only the DNA need be represented. Usually genetic algorithms represent DNA by a fixed length vector. Where a genetic algorithm is being used for optimisation, each individual is a point in the search space and is evaluated by the fitness function to yield a number indicating how good that point is. If any point is good enough, the genetic algorithm stops and the solution is simply this point. If not then a new population, containing the next generation, is bred.

The breeding of a new generation is inspired by nature; new vectors are bred from the fitter vectors in the current generation, using either asexual or sexual reproduction. In asexual reproduction, the parent vector is simply copied (possibly with random changes, i.e. mutations). Figure 2.5 shows a child vector being created by mutating a single gene (in this case each gene is represented by a single bit). With sexual reproduction, two of the fitter vectors are chosen and the new vector is created by sequentially copying sequences alternately from each parent. Typically only two or three sequences are used, and the point(s) where the copying crosses over to the other parent is chosen at random. This is known as *crossover*. Figure 2.6 shows a child being formed firstly by copying four genes from the left hand parent then the three remaining genes are copied from the right hand parent. Figure 2.7 shows the genetic algorithm cycle.

Holland in his paper "Genetic Algorithms and the Optimal Allocation of Trials" [Holland, 1973] shows, via his schemata theorem, that in certain circumstances genetic algorithms make good use of information from the search so far to guide the choice

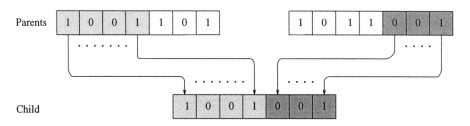

Figure 2.6.   Genetic Algorithms - Crossover

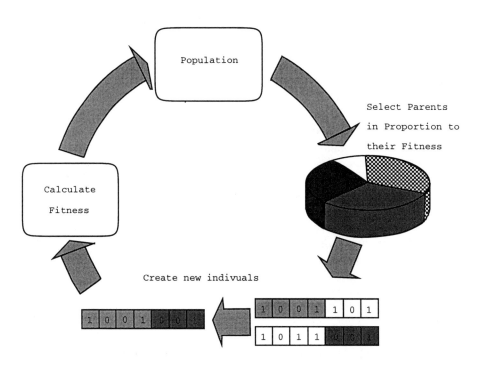

Figure 2.7.   The Genetic Algorithm Cycle

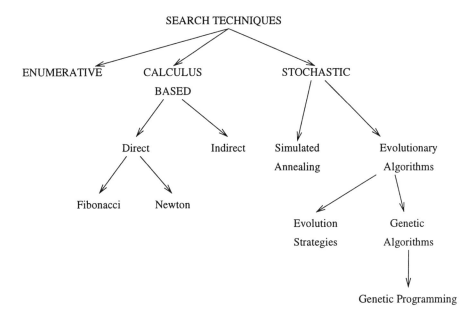

Figure 2.8.   Search Techniques

of new points to search. [Goldberg, 1989] gives a less mathematical treatment of the schemata theorem.

Holland argues that the elements of the vector should be as simple as possible, in many cases single bits are used. Nature seems to agree, as it constructs DNA from only four components (the four nucleotides: adenine, guanine, cytosine and thymine).

The schemata theorem requires the vector representation and fitness function be designed so that the required solution can be composed of short fragments of vectors which, if present in a vector, give it a relatively high fitness regardless of the contents of the rest of the vector. These are known as *building blocks*. They can be thought of as collections of genes which work well together.

Given building blocks exist, genetic algorithms, even starting from a random collection of vectors, can progressively select the vectors with building blocks and using the crossover operator gradually splice these together until the population contains vectors which are substantially correct.

2.2.1 Search Techniques

There are a large number of well established search techniques in use within the information technology industry, Figure 2.8 categorises them.

Enumerative techniques, in principle, search every possible point one point at a time. They can be simple to implement but the number of possible points may be too large for direct search. In some cases, e.g. game playing [Uiterwijk et al., 1989], it is possible to curtail the search so that points in regions which cannot contain the solution are not checked.

Calculus based techniques treat the search space as a continuous multi-dimensional function and look for maxima (or minima) using its derivative. **Indirect** methods use that fact that at the extrema the function's derivative is zero. Where the function is smooth the volume of space where its derivative is zero can be a very small sample of the whole search space.

Direct calculus techniques such as **Fibonacci** and **Newton** use the gradient/function values to estimate the location of nearby extrema. These techniques, and others, are known as *Hill Climbing* techniques because they estimate where a maximum (i.e. hill top) lies, move to that point, make a new estimate, move to it and so on until they reach the top of the hill. These techniques can be used upon "well behaved" problems or problems which can be transformed to become "well behaved".

Stochastic search techniques use information from the search so far to guide the probabilistic choice of the next point(s) to try. They are general in their scope, being able to solve some very complex problems that are beyond the abilities of either enumerative or calculus techniques. **Simulated annealing** searches for minimum energy states using an analogy based upon the physical annealing process, where large soft low energy crystals can be formed in some metals (e.g. copper) by heating and then slow cooling [Kirkpatrick et al., 1983].

Evolutionary algorithms are based upon Darwin's Natural Selection theory of evolution, where a population is progressively improved by selectively discarding the worse and breeding new children from the better. In **Evolutionary Strategies** points in the search space are represented by a vector of real values. Each new point is created by adding random noise to the current one. If the new point is better search proceeds from it, if not the older point is retained. (Historically Evolutionary Strategies search only one point at a time but more recently they have become more like genetic algorithms by using a population of points [Back et al., 1991]). In contrast, a **genetic algorithm** represents points in the search space by a vector of discrete (typically) bit values. Each new child is produced by combining parts of the bit vector from each parent. This is analogous to the way chromosomes of DNA (which contains the inherited genetic material) are passed to children in natural systems.

While any of the above search algorithms may be well suited to a particular problem, the No Free Lunch (NFL) theorems [Wolpert and Macready, 1997] show averaged over all possible problems they are all equivalent. I.e. if well suited to a particular problem, there exist other problems which they perform badly upon. Of course these other problems may not be of interest. In other words averaged over all possible problems any search algorithm (including genetic algorithms and genetic programming) performs as badly as random search. The time taken by random search is $O(\frac{\text{Size of search space}}{\text{Acceptable solutions}})$. With GP we are interested in very large search spaces. For example in the case of the stack problem described in Chapter 4 there are in excess of $1.4\ 10^{262}$ possible trees. The number of acceptable solutions is more difficult to calculate but we expect it to be relatively small and so are not surprised that random search has never solved the stack problem ($1.4\ 10^{262}$ mS is a very long time!). In contrast Chapter 4 will show it can be readily solved by GP. The NFL theorems give a formal way to argue that our search techniques (such as GP) must match the search problem and show that can be no universally good algorithm for all possible problems.

2.2.2 Automatic Program Generation

A computer program can be thought of as a particular point within a search space of all such programs and so computer programming can be thought of as searching this space for a suitable program. Human programmers exercise their skills to direct their search so they find a suitable program as quickly as possible. There are many tools (such as high level languages and code generators) which transform the search space to make it easier for the human navigator to find his goal.

When programming neural networks, calculus based search techniques such as back propagation are often used. (Simulated Annealing, Evolution Strategy and Genetic algorithms have also been used to program artificial neural networks). Calculus based search techniques are possible because the search space has been transformed (and simplified) so that it is smooth. When the search has succeeded the neural network is said to have been trained, i.e. a suitable combination of connection weights has been found. Note that a program (a neural network) has been automatically generated by searching for it.

An alternative to implementing a general transformation that converts the vast discrete space of possible programs into a continuous one (which is sufficiently well behaved as to allow it to be searched by calculus based techniques) is to search the original space itself. The discrete nature of this space prevents the use of calculus based techniques and the vast number of possible programs make enumerative search infeasible, however there has been some success with some stochastic search techniques.

Table 2.1 lists the stochastic search techniques used with the classes of programming languages. It appears work has been concentrated on using genetic algorithms. The remainder of the chapter concentrates on the recent success achieved by combining genetic algorithms with traditional programming. The term *genetic programming* was suggested by David Goldberg to describe the automatic production of programs by using a hierarchical genetic algorithm to search the space of possible programs.

2.2.3 Representation and Execution

The normal use of the term genetic programming implies the data structures being evolved can be run as computer programs. The term has also been applied to using a genetic algorithm to evolve data structures which must be translated into another form before they can be executed. Both linear and tree (or hierarchical) data structures have been used. This process can be likened to an individual (the executable program) growing according to the instructions held in its DNA (the genetic algorithm's data structures).

The final form is often a neural network. Many ways of representing a network using a genetic algorithm have been used [Polani and Uthmann, 1993; Romaniak, 1993; Zhang and Mühlenbein, 1993b; Harvey et al., 1993]. An especially powerful way of representing a network is cellular encoding [Gruau, 1993]. [Gruau, 1993] shows cellular encoding, inconjunction with a hierarchical genetic algorithm, can automatically produce complex neural networks with a high degree of modularity. Cellular encoding has also been used to specify finite state automata [Brave, 1996b]

Table 2.1.   Automatic Programming using Stochastic Search

		Class of Programming Language		
Search Technique	Traditional	Logic (e.g. Prolog)	Expert Systems (Rule based)	Finite State Machines
Simulated Annealing	1.			
Evolution Strategy				Evolution Program
Genetic Algorithms	Genetic Programming	2.	BEAGLE Classifiers 3.	4.

While the above table shows most work on automatically producing programs by applying stochastic search to programming languages has been on genetic programming, classifiers or evolutionary programming, some work has been carried out in other areas. The numbers in the following list refer to those in cells in the above table.

1. [Andrews and Prager, 1994; O'Reilly and Oppacher, 1994] show some problems can be solved using simulated annealing (SA) and stochastic iterated hill climbing search techniques with a GP (i.e. tree) representation. While [O'Reilly, 1996] suggests SA can be advantageous in program search, [Sharman and Esparcia-Alcazar, 1993] suggest a hybrid where SA is used to tune numerical constants within GP programs.

2. Nachbar has demonstrated evolving programs written in Mathematica [Nachbar, 1995] and some work has been done on using genetic programming with Prolog [Nordin, 1994b].

3. In Classifiers [Holland et al., 1986] a genetic algorithm, plus other techniques, is used to automatically generate both a rule base and its interconnections. [Feldman, 1993], amongst others, has used genetic algorithms to evolve aspects of Fuzzy Logic systems.

4. [Dunay et al., 1994] evolved finite state automata which recognised simple regular languages. Later work [Dunay and Petry, 1995; Petry and Dunay, 1995] evolved Turing Machines which recognised simple regular and context free languages, while [Zomorodian, 1995] evolved push down automata for recognising the balanced bracket context free language. Self demonstrated a genetic algorithm evolving a Turing Machine which recognised three bit even parity but had less success with other more complex problems [Self, 1992].

and electronic circuits [Koza et al., 1996a; Koza et al., 1997]. [Kodjabachian and Meyer, 1994] summaries various approaches to evolving artificial nervous systems.

2.3 GENETIC PROGRAMMING

2.3.1 History

The idea of combining genetic algorithms (GAs) and computer programs is not new, it was considered in the early days of genetic algorithms. However John Holland's work on combining genetic algorithms and production languages, rather than tradition computer languages, was more actively pursued. This work led to classifiers.

Richard Forsyth's BEAGLE [Forsyth, 1981] evolves programs (rules) using a (GA like) algorithm. The rules are tree structured boolean expressions, including arithmetic operations and comparisons. BEAGLE's rules use its own specific language, however Forsyth did suggest at some point in the future Lisp might be used. BEAGLE is now commercially available as an expert system (see Section 2.5.1).

Nichael Cramer also applied genetic algorithms directly to special computer programming languages [Cramer, 1985] but it was John Koza [Koza, 1992] who successfully applied genetic algorithms to Lisp and showed that in this form genetic algorithms are applicable to a range of problems. Techniques like his have come to be known as "genetic programming". Koza claims [Koza, 1992, page 697] genetic programming to be the most general machine learning paradigm. Interest in the subject has grown rapidly since [Koza, 1992] and the number of papers published concerning GP has grown exponentially. Recently the first GP text book [Banzhaf et al., 1997a] has been published.

A simple approach of breeding machine code and even FORTRAN source code which ignores the syntax fails because the programs produced are highly unlikely to compile or run, let alone approach the required solution [De Jong, 1987] (however see Section 2.4.1). There are countless examples of apparently minor syntax errors causing programs to misbehave in a dramatic fashion. These two facts foster the common belief that all computer programs are fragile. In fact this is not true; many programs are used and yield economic benefit despite the fact that they are subject to many minor changes, introduced during maintenance or version upgrades. Almost all programs are produced by people making progressive improvements.

Genetic programming allows the machine to emulate, to some extent, what a person does, i.e. to make progressive improvements. It does this by repeatedly combining pairs of existing programs to produce new ones, and does so in a way as to ensure the new programs are syntactically correct and executable. Progressive improvement is made by testing each change and only keeping the better changes. Again this is similar to how people program, however people exercise considerable skill and knowledge in choosing where to change a program and how; genetic programming, at present, has no such knowledge and must rely on chance and a great deal more trial and error.

Many variations of the basic genetic algorithm have been tried; in genetic programming the fixed length vectors are replaced by programs. Usually, a tree (or structured or hierarchical) representation of the program is used and individuals in the population are of different sizes. Given the new representation, the new genetic operators such as tree crossover must be used. As Figure 1.1 (page 3) shows tree crossover acts within branches of the tree to ensure that the the programs it produces are still trees and have a legal syntax. Thus genetic programming is fundamentally different from simply shuffling lines of Fortran or machine code. The sequence of operations in genetic programming is essentially as that for other genetic algorithms (see Figure 1.2 on page 4).

2.3.2   Basic Steps

[Koza, 1994] says there are six preliminary steps to solving a problem using genetic programming. These are choosing the terminals (1), the functions (2), the fitness function (3), the control parameters (4), the termination criterion (5) and determining the programs' architecture (6).

In Koza's terminology, the terminals (1) and the functions (2) are the components of the programs. In Figure 1.1 (page 3) the junctions (or internal nodes) in the tree are formed from the functions $+$, $-$ and $*$. In Figure 1.1 the tree leafs (or end nodes or external nodes) are formed by the only terminal, x. The connections between the terminals and functions indicate the order in which operations are to be performed. For example the top left tree in Figure 1.1 shows a program which calculates $(x * x) + (x + (x - x))$. Note how the brackets, which denote the order of evaluation, correspond to the structure of the tree.

The choice of components of the program (i.e. terminals and functions) and the fitness function (3) largely determine the space which genetic programming searches and consequently how difficult that search is and ultimately how successful it will be.

The control parameters (4) include the size of the population, the rate of crossover etc. The termination criterion (5) is simply a rule for stopping the GP run. Typically the rule is to stop either on finding a program which solves the problem or after a given number of generations.

In the final step the evolving programs' architecture (6) is chosen. In Koza's work this means defining the number of automatically defined functions (ADFs), the number of arguments they take, and which may call which and which may be called by the main program (see Section 2.3.2). More recent work [Koza and Andre, 1995a] has shown the architecture itself can be evolved during a GP run. The choices involved with multi-tree program architectures (cf. Section 3.6) are analogous to step (6).

Choosing Terminals (1) and Functions (2)

The first requirement when deciding the terminals and functions that the evolved programs will be composed from, is to ensure that they are capable of expressing the solution to the problem. Koza [Koza, 1992, page 86] calls this the *sufficiency* property. Having ensured it is possible to express the solution, the next task is far harder. We want to choose them so that it is likely that a solution will evolve.

The terminals and functions form the language which represents the trial solutions. The genetic operators (crossover, mutation etc.), ADFs, fitness function and selection scheme combine to form a transmission function which transforms the population of individuals written in the representation language. Over successive generations we want the transmission function to evolve the population towards, and eventually to reach, an acceptable solution. Design of a successful (let alone optimal) transmission functions is not trivial. [Kinnear, Jr., 1994c, page 12] advises "always pick the most powerful and useful seeming functions from the problem domain that you can think of". However it would also seem wise to avoid complicated primitives, e.g. with side-effects or that have complicated special cases.

Closure   Koza [Koza, 1992, page 81] defines closure as being satisfied when each of the functions is able to accept as its arguments any value or data type that might possibly be returned by any function (including itself) or be taken by any terminal. If the terminals and functions have this property then new offspring trees can be created by crossover inserting arbitrary subtrees at arbitrary points and the result will be both syntactically correct and executable. In traditional GAs, closure is not needed as the chromosome is not treated as an executable program.

Closure is often achieved by requiring all terminals, functions and function arguments to be of the same type, e.g. integers. However special cases may also need to be considered. For example divide by zero is not normally defined, but if closure is to be satisfied, a divide function must still return a valid value even if the divisor is zero. (In this book DIV returns 1, if its second argument is zero). In special cases, we could define a particular primitive to evaluate to a special value, such as "bad", but then all functions would need to be able to process "bad" values. Functions which trap illegal argument values and return valid answers are known as *protected* functions.

An alternative to closure which allows GP to manipulate trees containing a mixture of types is Strongly Typed Genetic Programming (STGP), discussed in Section 2.4.1.

In our experiments the terminals, functions' arguments and functions' return values are all of the same type. This is in keeping with almost all genetic programming. In most GP experiments there is an "obvious" way of achieving closure for the particular problem. However this may not be true for more complicated programs. Closure influences the choice of terminals and functions and so the problem representation and thus problem difficulty. Little work has been reported on this important aspect of closure.

Fitness Function (3)

Ultimately the fitness function drives the evolution of the GP population. It is vital that the fitness function not only gives a high reward to the correct solution, but also it preferentially rewards improved solutions throughout the GP run, from the creation of the initial population to the discovery of the final solution. To some extent preferential rewarding is easier if the fitness function has a small grain size, so any small improvement in solution is rewarded on average by some non-zero improvement in fitness.

It is possible to design a combination of fitness function and representation that is deceptive [Goldberg, 1989]. That is, together they drive the population away from optimal solutions, towards local optima, i.e. towards programs of relatively high fitness that do not solve the problem. While "deception" has been studied in linear genetic algorithms [Goldberg, 1989; Whitley, 1991; Grefenstette, 1993; Goldberg et al., 1992] it does not appear to have been generally recognised as a problem in genetic programming (exceptions are [Tackett, 1995a, page 286], [Banzhaf et al.,

1996, page 308] and [Taylor, 1995]). Unfortunately it has been encountered in several experiments described later. Where detailed analysis was performed (Chapter 8) the problem seems to have been associated with the choice of language primitives, i.e. the representation rather than the fitness function.

In most cases determining the fitness of trial solutions consumes the vast proportion of the GP's run time and so the efficiency of the fitness function is also important. Run time may become excessive if the evolved programs can use either iteration or recursion.

In many cases the fitness function is based upon executing the evolved programs on one or more prescribed test suites. In principle the test suites can be devised in the same way as those used when testing traditional manually produced programs. So techniques such as, regression testing, "special case" tests (such as data points at ends of legal ranges), code test coverage metrics and performance testing, might be used. However it is recognised that exhaustive testing of man made programs is impossible and there is always a risk, no matter how clever the tester is, that a program which passes all its testing will still contain errors. In the case of evolving programs even more care is needed. GP is guided only by the fitness function and GP population are adept at exploiting deficiencies in the test suite. The situation is made worse by the volume of testing that is being attempted. In most GPs, every new individual is run on the complete test suite. I.e. instead of running a few hand built programs, thousands or even millions of programs are run. Usually this has the effect of requiring all testing to be automated and secondly, to ensure GP run time remains feasible, the size of the test suite is severely restricted. [Kinnear, Jr., 1994c, page 9] describes some pit falls to avoid when creating the fitness function.

Fixed Fitness Cases   Except in a few special cases, in the experiments presented in the following chapters, the fitness of each individual within the population is determined when it is created by running it against a fixed test case. In Chapter 4 experiments were initially conducted using random test sequences, however there were problems with this approach:

- The random nature made it difficult to spot bugs.

- It was difficult to design random test cases which adequately tested the trial solutions.

- It was relatively easy to score well with some cases but harder with others. This caused the fitness of individuals to depend dramatically upon the tests being run. When these were changed, the fitness of programs which have already been tested was not directly comparable with that of new programs.

For these reasons all fitness testing has used fixed fitness test cases. This is not to denigrate work using variable test cases but this is a research topic in its own right (cf. Section 2.4.2) and so better not mixed with investigations into data structures.

Control Parameters (4)

There are many control parameters, however the one of most interest is the population size. Whilst [Goldberg et al., 1991] give a population sizing rule for certain genetic algorithms, it would appear that most GP populations are smaller than their optimum being constrained by the available machine resources [Koza, 1994, page 617] [Kinnear, Jr., 1994c, page 14].

The default values for parameters used in our experiments are given in Section D.3. Where non-default parameter values are used, the actual values are given in tables with each experiment (for an example, see Table 4.2 on page 66).

Termination Criterion (5)

The most common termination criterion is to stop the evolution of genetic programs when either an exact or approximate solution is found or 50 generations (or generation equivalents, cf. Section 3.3) is reached. The motivation for this follows from the observation that on many problems the GP seems to "run out of steam" before generation 50. So that continuing the GP run only marginally increases the chance of a solution being found. [Koza, 1992, page 564] argues that in many cases it is more effective to run a GP several times rather than increase the number of generations used by any one run.

Most runs in this book terminate either when an individual passes the whole of the fitness test case or the maximum number of individuals have been created. (This is usually either 50 or 100 times the population size. I.e. 50 or 100 generation equivalents). In a few experiments, the GP does not stop once the whole test case has been solved but continues until the limit on number of individuals is reached. This allows the possibility of evolving improved solutions (e.g. faster or more general) to be investigated.

Automatically Defined Functions (6)

"An automatically defined function (ADF) is a function (i.e., subroutine, procedure, module) that is dynamically evolved during a run of genetic programming and which may be called by a calling program (e.g., a main program) that is simultaneously being evolved" [Koza, 1994, page 1]. Koza and Rice introduced ADFs in order to tackle the scaling problem, i.e. to help GP scale up to and solve more complex problems. [Koza, 1994] contains many examples where GP with ADFs solves problems faster than plain GP or is able to solve bigger problems than plain GP. ADFs are used in many of the experiments from Chapter 5 onwards.

The ADFs used in this book are of the first type introduced by [Koza, 1994], i.e. they have a fixed (rather than evolvable) architecture and crossover only moves code between the same ADFs or between main programs (result producing branches). That is, crossover between different ADFs and between ADFs and main programs is forbidden ([Koza, 1994] calls this branch typing). Thus in terms of genetic operations and representations, ADFs are identical to the multi-tree architecture to be described in Section 3.6.

In this book evolved program are executed by a high speed interpreter (GP-QUICK [Singleton, 1994]). The basic implementation of GP-QUICK was extended in several ways, in particular so that it supports ADFs. It treats ADFs as (imperative language) function calls. On encountering an ADF function, the interpreter evaluates the ADF's arguments (if any) and passes these to the ADF as it starts interpreting the ADF. (This is the standard way ADFs handle arguments, [Spector, 1995] describes an alternative

("Automatically Defined Macros", ADMs) in which the arguments are passed uneval-uated to the evolving module. The ADM evaluates the arguments as it needs to). When the interpreter has finished interpreting the ADF, it returns the value it has calculated for the ADF to the point it had reached when it called the ADF and continues execution from that point. This calling mechanism supports recursion but recursion is not used in this book. Details of the argument passing mechanism are given in Section 5.6. (Other forms of encapsulations are described in Section 2.4.5).

2.3.3 Example

In this subsection we will outline a very simple example of genetic programming. We will use it to perform symbolic regression on a set of test values. That is we will find a formula (symbolic expression, program) whose result matches the output of the test values.

One use of symbolic regression is prediction, for once such a formula has been found, it can be used to predict the output given a new set of inputs. E.g. given a history of stock prices, symbolic regression may find a formula relating the price on the next day to earlier ones, so allowing us to predict the price tomorrow.

In our very simple example the test values are related by the formula $y = x^2$. (The C code for this example is available via anonymous ftp. Section D.9 contains the network address. The interested reader is invited to copy this code and try their own examples. Similar polynomials e.g. x^3, $x + x^2$, $x^4 - x^3 + x^2 - x$ may be produced by changing the test values and possibly population size).

Following the six steps outlined in the previous section:

1. The leafs (terminals) on our programming trees will be the input value, x.

2. Our program will use the four floating point arithmetic operators $+$, $-$, $\div$ and $\times$.

   Our choice is guided by the expectation that output will be a simple polynomial of x. If we guess wrongly then it may not be possible to devise a correct program given our functions and terminals. We can add others but this will increase the number of possible programs to search, which might slow down the search.

   The terminals and functions are chosen so that any function can have as any of its arguments any terminal or any function call. This allows programs to be assembled from any mixture of terminals and functions (this property is known as closure, see also Section 2.4.1). In our case all terminals and functions are of type "float". To avoid divide by zero errors, we define divide by zero to be unity. Note as all the functions have two operands, the programs evolved will each have the form of a binary tree.

3. Fitness is calculate by executing each program with each of nine x values and comparing each answer with the corresponding y value. The nine (x, y) pairs are chosen so that $y = x^2$. They are shown as dots in Figure 2.4. To yield a number which increases as the program's answer gets closer to the y value, 1.0 is added to the absolute difference between the programs value and the corresponding y and the result is inverted. (Adding 1.0 avoids the possibility of divide by zero). The final fitness is the mean of all nine calculations.

If the program is within either 0.01 or 0.01 × y we call this a hit, indicating that this is close enough.

4. We chose control parameters so that:

   - there are 16 individuals in the population;
   - on average 60% of new individuals are created by crossover;
   - of the other 40%, 99% are direct copies from the previous generation and
   - 1% (i.e. .004) are mutated copies;
   - our programs contain no more than 25 nodes (i.e. no more than 12 functions and 13 terminals).

5. We stop when we have a found a program that correctly matches all nine test points (i.e. there are nine hits) or when we reach 50 generations.

6. We choose an architecture consisting of a single tree, i.e. without ADFs.

On one run the following 100% correct code was generated:

```
float gp( float x )
{
  return ((x+(x)*(x))-(x));
}
```

By noting x-x is zero and removing excessive brackets it can be seen that the return statement is equivalent to return (x*x); i.e. C code to calculate x^2.

This 100% correct program is shown in Figure 2.3. It was produced by crossover between the two programs shown in Figures 2.1 and 2.2, both of which were of above average fitness. The subtrees affected by the crossover are shown shaded. It can be seen that the net effect of crossover is to replace the middle x with a subtree which calculates x^2 and this yields a program which is exactly equivalent to x^2.

Figure 2.4 shows the values calculated by the two parent programs against the test points (which their offspring calculates exactly).

2.3.4   Taxonomy

Table 2.2 shows how the field of genetic programming is expanding. Several strands can be seen:

1. Various changes to the representation of the programs to be evolved (Section 2.4.1).

   - Reducing memory requirements and reducing runtime using Directed Acyclic graphs (DAGs)
   - Linear rather than tree representations
   - Representing programs with graphs
   - Using trees to specify how to grow another structure (such as an artificial neural network [Gruau, 1996a], an electrical circuit [Koza et al., 1997] or simulations of flowering plants [Jacob, 1997])

- ■ Including semantic information via type systems
- ■ Incorporating state or database information within a genetic program (cf. also Section 7.4).

2. Investigation of better ways to assess program fitness (Section 2.4.2).

- ■ Dynamic fitness such as LEF, RAT and co-evolution
- ■ Measures aimed at either reducing the size of the evolved programs or
- ■ Iteration and Recursion

3. GP control parameters (Section 2.4.3)

4. Termination criterion (Section 2.4.4)

5. Measures to allow programs to be evolved from program modules and to simultaneously evolve the modules (Section 2.4.5).

- ■ Automatically defined functions (ADFs)
- ■ Module Aquistion (MA/GliB) and
- ■ Adaptive Representations through Learning (ARL)

6. Search operators and algorithms (Section 2.4.6) such as

- ■ Mutation
- ■ Context preserving crossover (SCPC/WCPC)
- ■ One-point Crossover
- ■ Non genetic algorithm methods of searching the space of programs

7. The adoption of exotic genetic algorithm techniques by genetic programming (Section 2.4.7).

8. An increasing number of implementations, many of them in the public domain (Section 2.4.8).

9. An increasing number of applications (Section 2.5).

Section 2.6 draws together some conclusions and guesses as to where genetic programming may lead.

2.4 GP RESEARCH

2.4.1 Program Representation

In most genetic programming work the programs being evolved are represented using trees [Koza, 1992]. Originally most work used the LISP language however C and C++ are increasingly used.

[Keith and Martin, 1994] considered prefix, postfix and hybrid (mixfix) languages but conclude that their linear prefix language and its jump table interpreter are the

Table 2.2.   Taxonomy of Genetic Programming

Active Topics in Genetic Programming						
Represent-ation	Fitness Function	Control	Search Operators	Exotic GA	Imple-mentations	Applic-ations
		Termin-ation				
		Architec-ture				
DAG Linear	Dynamic Program size	ADF GliB	Mutation 1-point	Table 2.3	Tables 2.4 and 2.5	Modelling Image Processing
PDGP STGP Memory	MDL Iteration	ARL	SCPC PIPE			Optimise Trading Robots A Life Artistic

more efficient. (The GP-QUICK interpretter used in this work, implements their linear prefix jump table approach).

Trees can also be represented using directed acyclic graphs (DAGs). As GP populations contain many individuals which are descended from the same or similar parents they contain a lot of common code. By using a single DAG to hold the whole population the common code need only be stored once resulting in considerable reduction in memory needed [Handley, 1994a; Keijzer, 1996]. Further [Handley, 1994a] has shown that where GP primitives do not have side effects considerable reduction in run time can be achieved by the use of caches of partial fitness evalutations within the DAG which readilly allow partial fitness evaluation information to be inherited and shared throughout the population. (Section D.5 describes how caches can reduced run time in the presence of side effects). [Keijzer, 1996] also considers using a DAG with multi-tree programs. The remainder of this section describes experiments with other syntax.

[Perkis, 1994] uses a linear postfix language and claims some advantages over the more standard tree approach. [Banzhaf, 1993] also uses a linear approach but various operations convert this to a tree shaped program which is executed. However of the linear chromosome approaches perhaps the most surprising and successful is [Nordin, 1994a] in which the representation is a small (up to 1000 bytes) machine code program. Enormous (more than thousand fold) speed ups in comparison with LISP are claimed. The success of Nordin's approach may be due to the use of a simple machine architecture (SUN RISC) which is further restricted so only some machine operations are allowed. In [Nordin, 1994a] there was considerable loss of generality: there is no branching or looping, the program is of fixed length (12 instructions), the program is specific to the SUN SPARK RISC instruction set and only a few instructions are used. Later work [Nordin and Banzhaf, 1995] extended the system so that it was fully

Turing complete, however this full functionality need not be used [Francone et al., 1996; Nordin and Banzhaf, 1996].

A radically different program representation is used in Parallel Distributed Genetic Programming (PDGP) where program trees are replaced by directed graphs. However the (optionally weighted) links are constrained to connect nodes on a predefined grid of nodes. The nodes contain the program's functions and terminals and the links indicate how their outputs are passed to the inputs of other functions. As nodes within the graph have multiple outputs, the intermediate results calculated by a node can be readily used in many other parts of the program. It is this reuse which gives the technique its power. Crossover and mutation operators are defined with respect to the grid which ensure the syntatic correctness of the offspring. PDGP is a very flexible framework and has been demonstrated evolving solutions for symbolic regression, parity and artificial ant problems and evolving boolean logic networks, artificial neural networks, finite state automata, etc. [Poli, 1996c; Poli, 1996d; Poli, 1996a; Poli, 1997a]. Improved performance compared to standard GP and GP with ADFs (Section 2.3.2) has been shown on the Lawnmower and Max problems [Poli, 1997b].

In PADO [Teller, 1996] a new program representation is used to evolve programs that classify signals and images. In PADO programs are made up of several groups of programs each group being used to recognise a particular class of image. The group with the highest output means that its class is the overall output of PADO. The output of a group is a linear combination of the output of the programs included in the group. Programs are represented as directed graphs in which arcs represent possible flows of control and nodes perform actions and take decisions on which of the possible control flows should be followed. Each node includes an action, a branching condition and a stack. Programs have access to shared indexed memory (this is discussed in Section 7.4.9). In general loops may form in the directed graph so causing the programs to execute indefinitely. To allow for this, programs are executed for a fixed time after which they are aborted and their answer is extracted from a designated cell in the indexed memory. (The so called "anytime" approach, cf. Section 2.4.2).

Extended Closure.   In almost all genetic programming work the terminals and functions are chosen so that they can be used with each other without restriction. This is achieved by requiring that the system be closed so that all terminals are of one type and all functions can operate on this type and always yield a result also of this type. For example measures are taken to protect against divide by zero errors.

In Montana's Strongly Typed Genetic Programming (STGP) [Montana, 1994] a genetic program can contain multiple different types simultaneously. When manipulating the program (e.g. using crossover) care is taken that not only are there the correct number of arguments for each function but that they are of the expected type. This leads to an increase in the complexity of the rules that must be followed when selecting crossover points. However Montana shows that tight type checking can considerably reduce the size of the search space, which he says will reduce the effort to find the solution. Generic types are allowed in order to reduce the number of functions which must be explicitly specified.

Strong typing systems are increasingly being used in genetic programming, for example [Bruce, 1996; Haynes et al., 1995b; Haynes et al., 1996; Luke et al., 1997; Clack and Yu, 1997].

Other, more active, ways of using program syntax or run time behaviour will be discussed in Section 3.7.

Genetic Programming and State Information. Most computer programs make extensive use of storage, yet in almost all genetic programming examples, each genetic program is a function of its inputs and almost all storage requirements are dealt with by the framework used to support the genetic programs. This book, particularly Chapters 4, 5, 6 and 7, is primarily concerned with extending genetic programming's to cover this important topic. Section 7.4 provides an overview of other work using GP with evolvable memory.

2.4.2 Fitness Measure

In common with GAs, the vast proportion of machine resources consumed by GP are used running the fitness function to evaluate the population. Consequently there is great interest in evolvable hardware (EHW) which promises considerable speed up in fitness evaluation, either by parallel execution, by execution closer to the hardware or simply by providing faster hardware. There is also interest in parallel execution using networks of workstations (e.g. using PVM) and across the Internet using Java. However use of dedicated parallel processing machines has already been demonstrated [Turton et al., 1996; Stoffel and Spector, 1996; Juille and Pollack, 1996; Ikram, 1996; Andre and Koza, 1996; Oussaidene et al., 1996]. Often GP (and GAs) are parallelised by spliting the population so different parts of it are run on different CPUs. This also has the potential benefits associated with using a demic population (see Section 3.8). GP may also be parallelised by execution of different fitness cases on different computers.

Most genetic programming work uses a single fitness criterion namely the functionality of the program, ignoring issues such as size and run time. There has been some interest in using Pareto scoring [Goldberg, 1989; Fonseca and Fleming, 1995], which allows members of the population to be scored or compared using multiple criteria, such as functionality and run time. Scoring systems which combine several criteria (such as functionality and efficiency) to yield a single fitness score have been tried with some success. Section 3.9 describes Pareto scoring in more detail and it is used in Chapters 5 to 7.

Dynamic Fitness Functions Fixed test cases are widely used in GP, however advantages have been claimed for dynamic fitness tests. For example [Hillis, 1992; Angeline and Pollack, 1993; Jannink, 1994; Siegel, 1994]; [Koza, 1992, Chapter 16]; [Tettamanzi, 1996]; [Reynolds, 1994a] use co-evolution of the fitness function or competitive selection, [Beasley et al., 1993b] suggest a technique for derating the fitness function in regions "near" known solutions and [Fukunaga and Kahng, 1995] claims improved performance from pre-defined dynamic fitness functions. [Gathercole and Ross, 1994; Gathercole and Ross, 1997b] and [Longshaw, 1997] argue that changing which fitness cases are used as the population learns can be beneficial. While [Banzhaf et al., 1997b] shows GP can learn from a dynamic and noisy fitness function. (This seems reasonable since genetic algorithm selection techniques, such as roulette wheel selection, are inherently noisy [Blickle and Thiele, 1995]).

[Kinnear, Jr., 1993a] used a small number (15) fixed set of tests. However a second, more exhaustive, sequence of tests (556) is applied to the solutions produced by GP after the GP run has completed to test the generality of the evolved solutions.

While the Rational Allocation of Trials (RAT) method described by Teller and Andre [Teller and Andre, 1997] does not require the fitness function to change it proposes mechanisms for dynamically deciding how many of the fitness case to use. Since each fitness case is usually a major computational expense correctly choosing the number execcuted can considerably reduce run time with out affecting the quality of the solutions evolved.

Program Size as Part of Fitness In many modelling problems, solutions which not only fit the data but which are short (and therefore potentially easier to understand) are required. If unchecked, GP solutions tend to grow in length (cf. Sections 4.6.2 and 5.11 and [Tackett, 1995b, page 31]; [Langdon and Poli, 1997b]) and so it is common to include a "parsimony pressure" in the fitness function to encourage the evolution of shorter solutions. In some cases, such as classification, the size of the program is important in itself, rather than as an indicator of wasteful coding. In such cases the size of the program gives an indication of lack of generality or overfitting training data. Growth in program size is often delt with by simply placing either a limit on program size of maxiumum tree depth. The importance of these limits can be overlooked but constraining GP to small programs may increase its performance. Other methods of constraining program size include, editing trees to remove code which is not used or has no immediate effect, limiting size increase due to mutation or using mutation operators with a bias to produce smaller offspring and incorporating a parsimony bias in the fitness function.

[Kinnear, Jr., 1993b] claims advantages for adding a term inversely proportional to the program's length to its fitness. This yields shorter and more general programs. [Zhang and Mühlenbein, 1993b; Iba et al., 1994a] have used other techniques to include program size or complexity penalties into a single scalar fitness function. Interestingly [Koza, 1992, page 613] presents a counter example, "when parsimony (program size) is included in the fitness measure for this problem (6-Multiplexor), considerably more individuals must be processed in order to find a 100%-correct and parsimonious solution than when parsimony is not considered."

[Blickle, 1996] compares four means of exerting parsimony pressure on discrete and continuous symbolic regression problems. He concludes that all four are capable of evolving accurate and parsimonious regression formulae but that an adaptive parsimony (i.e. based on program length) component of fitness worked best overall.

[Gathercole and Ross, 1997a, page 112] argues that using program size to resolve ties when programs have equal fitness can be effective, while [Zhang and Mühlenbein, 1993a] uses Occam's razor to argue size should be an important component of fitness.

Minimum Description Length.   One of De Jong's arguments against the combination of traditional general purpose computer programming languages and genetic algorithms [De Jong, 1987] was that the behaviour of program statements written in such languages depend upon statements before it. [Iba et al., 1994a] have considered the problems of symbolic regression and classification using problem specific languages which are better behaved with respect to changes in the order of statements. In one case (GMDH) they show that earlier statements cannot reduce the value of latter ones. Such languages fit well with the schema theorem if we view good subtrees like good schema. These languages ensure that good overall individuals can be constructed of good schema, thus we should expect a genetic algorithm to perform well.

Iba etal use Quinlan's "decision trees", which are designed to classify sets of inputs. They allocate fitness based upon Quinlan's "Minimum Description Length" (MDL) which gives a natural means of basing fitness not just upon how well the program (or decision tree, in this case) performs but also on its size. Other investigators have used arbitrary combinations of program size and score to calculate a composite fitness. MDL is calculated by considering how many bits are needed to code the program and how many to code a description of its error, i.e. those cases where it returns the wrong answer.

Iba etal's STROGANOFF system is used to perform symbolic regression (i.e. to find formulae, or programs, that adequately match the output associated with a given set of inputs). STOGANOFF uses an MDL based fitness together with program trees composed of GMDH primitives. Good results have been obtained with both decision trees and STROGANOFF using small populations (e.g. 60).

Iteration and Recursion.   Genetic programming determines the fitness of an individual by running it. This makes it, compared to other genetic algorithms, particularly susceptible to badly behaving individuals. Badly behaved programs can be produced where there are recursive or iterative features, as these promote very long or even infinite loops. The presence of only one such program in the population effectively halts the whole genetic programming system. The fear of long or indefinite loops appears to have restricted the use of iteration in GP, with [Huelsbergen, 1996] reporting "for the most part . . . GP solutions are restricted to non-iterative (non-looping) programs". However there are a number of papers where programs containing loops have been successfully evolved.

They used a number of techniques to address the problem of indefinite loops; [Cramer, 1985] aborts any program that fails to stop within a specified time, [Teller, 1994b] proposes two solutions: "popcorn" which allows fitness testing to continue whilst it continues to do something interesting (which may increase its fitness) but imposes a maximum waiting time between interesting events, once this expires fitness testing stops. In contrast the "anytime" algorithm requires the program to have its best estimate available on demand. Once a fixed time limit has expired the program is stopped, even if it is in the middle of a loop, and its fitness is based upon this answer (which is extracted from an indexed memory cell). Teller's uses the anytime system in his PADO work [Teller and Veloso, 1995b, Section 2.1] (cf. Section 7.4.9).

The most popular approach (for example its use in this book, cf. Section 6.4.1) implements ad-hoc loop limits which time out badly behaving individuals and give them poor fitness scores. [Nordin and Banzhaf, 1995, page 324] enforces a limit on the total number of times loops within a program may be executed while [Koza, 1992, Chapter 18] applies both a limit on the total number of iterations (100) and a limit for each loop primitive (15 or 25). The same approach is used in [Kinnear, Jr., 1993a] but with larger limits (200 and 2000). In [Koza, 1994, Chapters 18 and 20] the indefinite loop problem is side stepped by predefining the loop and its limits so the loop contents are evolved but not its start or terminating conditions.

A more general mechanism to ensure programs which loop infinitely do not hang up the system has been suggested by [Maxwell III, 1994]. This applies an external time limit after which programs are interrupted if they are still running, thus allowing other members of the population to be run. The interrupted program is not aborted but is given a partial fitness. The partial fitness is used when selecting which programs to breed from and which are to be replaced by the new programs created. Programs which remain in the population are allowed to run for another time interval. Looping programs are given low partial fitness and so are eventually removed from the population, as new programs are bred. Maxwell claims his technique "effectively removes arbitrary limits on execution time (e.g. iteration limits) and yet still produces solutions in finite time" and often it will require "less effort" and produce solutions of "greater efficiency".

2.4.3   Control Parameters

Whilst there are many possible control parameters the one of most direct interest is the population size. Whilst [Goldberg et al., 1991] gives a population sizing rule for certain genetic algorithms, it would appear that most GP populations are smaller than their optimum being constrained by the available machine resources [Koza, 1994]. With the increasing use of large memory parallel machines we can expect population sizes to increase and so consideration of what is the optimum population size will be required.

2.4.4   Termination Criterion

The most common termination criterion is to stop the evolution of genetic program when either an exact or approximate solution is reached or 50 generations (or generation equivalents) is reached. This was used in most of Koza's original work [Koza, 1992] and has been adopted widely, exceptions include the work described in Section 2.4.2 on MDL and recent work [Gathercole and Ross, 1997a] where high mutation rates are used inconjection with many more generations. As with population size, the maximum number of generation allowed has a large effect upon the machine resources used. [Koza, 1992] argues that in many cases it is more effective to run a GP several times rather than increase the number of generations used by any one run.

2.4.5   Architecture

The problems on which genetic programming has been successfully demonstrated have, in the main been small. A common technique that people use when tackling any complex problem is to decompose it into smaller problems and to tackle each of these independently. In computer programming, the separate solutions or modules are combined to yield a large program which, all being well, solves the original problem. A high degree of skill is needed in choosing how to decompose the problem. Genetic programming has, of course, no such skill, however despite this there has been some success with incorporating a degree of modularity into genetic programming. Two distinct approaches have been tried to introduce modularity, Automatically Defined Functions (ADF) and Encapsulation, both with a measure of success.

Automatically Defined Functions.   ADFs are evolvable functions (subroutines) within an evolving genetic program, which the main routine of the program can call. Typically each ADF is a separate tree; consisting of its arguments (which are the terminals) and the same functions as the main program tree (possibly plus calls to other ADFs). If side effects are prohibited, ADFs act as functional building blocks. Crossover acting on the main program can then rearrange these building blocks within the program. ADFs can also be evolved, e.g. when crossover acts upon them. The overall format of the program is preserved by ensuring crossover and other genetic operations acts only within each ADF. That is code cannot be exchanged by crossover between ADFs and the main program. (Koza has demonstrated that it is possible to relax this restriction allowing crossover between program branches but the rules required to ensure the resulting offspring are still syntactically correct are much more complex [Koza, 1994]). The main program's function set is extended to allow (but not require) it to call the ADFs.

ADFs have been successfully used on problems that proved too difficult for genetic programming without ADFs.

Encapsulation.   The Genetic Library Builder (GLiB) [Angeline, 1994; Angeline, 1993] implements encapsulation by adding a complementary pair of genetic operators, compression (encapsulation) and decompression which are applied to any point in the genetic program chosen at random. Compression takes (part of) the subtree at the given point and converts it in to a function which is stored in a library. Those parts of the subtree not included in the function become its arguments. The original code is replaced by the function call. Decompression is the replacement of a function with its definition, i.e. it reverses the compression operator. Once code is encapsulated in a function it is protected from dissociation by crossover or other operators. The functions produced may be any mixture of functions, terminals and its own arguments. Thus they need not be modular in the software engineering sense. [Kinnear, Jr., 1994a, page 119] compares GP, GP+ADFs and GLiB and concludes "comparsion of the ADF approach with the MA [GLiB] approach shows that for the even-4-parity function the ADF approach yields a significant increase in performance, while the MA approach does not".

The Adaptive Representation through Learning (ARL) [Rosca and Ballard, 1996] has some similarities with Angeline's MA but uses information from the run time performance of individual programs, comparisons between parents and offspring and population statistics to guide which code to encapsulate or remove from the library and when to do so.

2.4.6   Search Operators

GP Mutation.   Mutation was used in early experiments with evolving programs, e.g. [Cramer, 1985; Fujiki and Dickinson, 1987; Bickel and Bickel, 1987], however it was not used in [Koza, 1992] and [Koza, 1994], as Koza wished to demonstrate mutation was not necessary and GP was not performing a simple random search. This has influenced the field so mutation is often omitted from GP runs. E.g. mutation is not used in this book, except in Appendix C. While mutation is not necessary for GP to solve many problems, [O'Reilly, 1995] argues that, in some cases, mutation (in combination with simulated annealing (see Section 2.8 page 16) or stochastic iterated hill climbing) can perform as well as GP using crossover. Mutation is increasingly used in GP, especially in modelling applications and Koza now advises use of a low level of mutation. For example mutation is used in [Koza et al., 1996b].

Recent comparisons of crossover and muatation have suggested mutation can be advantageous. [Chellapilla, 1997] found a combination of six mutation operators performed better than previously published GP work on four simple problems. [Harries and Smith, 1997] also found mutation based hill climbers out performed crossover on similar problems. They also suggest five new crossover operators. These are like standard crossover but with (probablistic) restrictions on the depth of crossover points within the parent trees. While [Luke and Spector, 1997] suggests the situation is more complex and the relative performance of crossover and mutation depends upon multiple factors as well as being problem dependent.

With linear bit string GAs, mutation usually consists of random changes in bit values. In contrast, in GP there are many mutation operators in use.

Subtree mutation replaces a randomly selected subtree with another randomly created subtree [Koza, 1992, page 106].

[Kinnear, Jr., 1993a] defines a similar mutation operator but with a restriction that prevents the offspring's depth being more then 15% larger than its parent.

[Langdon, 1998] proposes two mutation operators in which the new random subtree is on average the same size as the code it replaces. The size of the random code is given either by the size of another random subtree in the program or chosen at random in the range $l/2 \ldots 3l/2$ (where l is the size of the subtree being replaced). The first samples uniformly in the space of possible programs whereas the second samples uniformly in the space of program lengths. [Langdon, 1998] reports far more growth of useless code (bloat) with the first mutation operator (cf. Section 4.6.2).

Node replacement mutation (also known as point mutation) is similar to bit string mutation in that it randomly changes a point in the individual. In linear GAs the change would be a bit but in GP a node in the tree is randomly selected and randomly changed. To ensure the tree remains legal, the replacement tree has the same number of arguments as the node it is replacing, e.g. [McKay et al., 1995, page 488].

Hoist creates a new offspring individual which is copy of a randomly chosen subtree of the parent. Thus the offspring will be smaller than the parent and have a different root node [Kinnear, Jr., 1994b].

Shrink replaces a randomly chosen subtree with a randomly created terminal [Angeline, 1996a]. This is a special case of subtree mutation where the replacement tree is a terminal. As with hoist, it is motivated by the desire to reduce program size.

Permutation [Koza, 1992] does not used permutation [page 106], except for one experiment [page 600] which shows it having little effect. In contrast [Maxwell, 1996] has more success with a mutation operator *swap* (which is a special case of pemutation, in that it swaps the order of arguments of binary non-commutative functions, rather than acting on any function).

Mutating Constants at Random [Schoenauer et al., 1996] mutates constants by adding gaussianly distributed random noise to them. NB each change to a constant is a separate mutation.

Mutating Constants Systematically [McKay et al., 1995, page 489] uses a mutation operator that operates on terminals, replacing input variables by constants (and vice versa). However "Whenever a new constant is introduced" ... "a non-linear least squares optimisation is performed to obtain the 'best' value of the constant(s)".

[Schoenauer et al., 1995] also uses a mutation operator that effects all constants in an individual using "a numerical partial gradient ascent is achieved to reach the nearest local optimum".

While [Sharman et al., 1995] uses simulated annealing to update numerical values (which represent signal amplification gains) within individuals.

Compiling Genetic Programming System cf. Section 2.4.1. In CGPS the mutation operator acts on machine code instructions and is constrained to "ensure that only instructions in the function set are generated and that the register and constant values are within predefined ranges allowed in the experimental set up" [Banzhaf et al., 1996]. On some classification problems [Banzhaf et al., 1996] report best performance when using crossover and mutation in equal proportions. They suggest this due to the GP population creating "introns" (non fitness effecting code) in response to the crossover operator and that these are subsequently converted into useful genetic diversity by their mutation operator.

Multiple types of mutation are often used simultaneously e.g. [Kraft et al., 1994] and [Angeline, 1996a].

Context Preserving Crossover. [D'haeseleer, 1994] proposes two types of context preserving crossover, strong context preserving crossover (SCPC) and weak context preserving crossover (WCPC). By context preserving D'haeseleer means that the subtrees taken from one parent and inserted into the offspring is inserted in a position like the one it occupies in the parent. In other words, the context provided by the rest of the program is retained to some extent. [D'haeseleer, 1994] define's context in terms of the geometry of the trees. While being an interesting idea (which might lead to a homlogous crossover operator) results with SCPC and WCPC have been mixed.

One Point Crossover. Poli has recently proposed a new crossover operator [Poli and Langdon, 1997b; Poli and Langdon, 1997c; Poli and Langdon, 1997a]. Called one-point crossover (though multiple crossover points are possible) because the *same* crossover points are used in both parents. For this to be feasible the crossover location(s) are chosen at random from just those parts of both parents which have the same shape. A new schema theorem is derived for the new genetic operator. It is conjectured that GP with one-point crossover and node replacement mutation will behave more like a linear GA and the population will tend to converge. A potential advantage is separate locations within program trees may converge to provide distinct sub-solutions to the whole problem.

Probabilistic Incremental Program Evolution. Probabilistic Incremental Program Evolution (PIPE) [Salustowicz and Schmidhuber, 1997] is a very different approach to automatic program synthesis. Like GP it is a stochastic search technique which represents programs as trees. However it generates each tree anew using a master probablity tree which determines the probability of each function and terminal occurring at each point in the tree. The master tree initially contains no information (i.e. all trees are equally likely) but as trees are created the best of them are used to update the probabilties in the master tree so that PIPE becomes more likely to generate trees like to best programs found so far. Good results are reported on symbolic regression and 6-bit parity problems.

2.4.7   GA Techniques used in GP

Some genetic programming researchers have adopted a number of exotic techniques from the genetic algorithms world. Table 2.3 (based on [Goldberg, 1989]) lists exotic genetic algorithm techniques and indicates which have been considered or adopted by genetic programming researchers. As Table 2.3 shows, many of these have been tried but some have yet to be explored.

2.4.8   GP Development Tools

Almost all of the genetic programming experiments described in this chapter have used implementations either written or adapted by the experimenter. Table 2.4 lists the general purpose genetic programming implementations that have been placed in the public domain, Table 2.5 list others that have been described. [Deakin and Yates, 1996] briefly describes an evaluation of some of these tools, additionally [Tufts, 1996] may be useful.

2.5   GP APPLICATIONS

This section briefly lists real applications where genetic programming has been tried. Although these are real world applications the claims for genetic programming should not be over stated, i.e. the success of genetic programming should not be taken as implying there are no better techniques available for the particular application.

Table 2.3.   Exotic GA Techniques Applied to Genetic Programming

Genetic Algorithms Technique	Genetic Programming Reference	Here
Fitness Scaling	[Iba et al., 1994a]	
Rank and Tournament Selection	[Angeline, 1994] [Koza, 1994]	√
Coevolution	[Angeline and Pollack, 1993] [Siegel, 1994][Koza, 1992]	
Steady State Populations	[Reynolds, 1992] [Tackett and Carmi, 1994] [Koza, 1994]	√
Parallel processors	[Singleton, 1993] [Openshaw and Turton, 1994] [Andre and Koza, 1995] [Juille and Pollack, 1995]	
Inversion and Permutation	[Koza, 1992] [Maxwell, 1996]	
Diplodity, Dominance and Abeyance	[Angeline, 1994]	
Introns, Segregation, Translocation and Multiple Chromosomes	[Angeline, 1994] [Wineberg and Oppacher, 1994] [Nordin et al., 1995] [Andre and Teller, 1996]	
Duplication and Deletion	[Haynes, 1996]	
Sexual Determination and Differentiation		
Speciation, Restrictive Mating, Demes and Niches	[Tackett and Carmi, 1994] [D'haeseleer and Bluming, 1994] [Abbott, 1991] [Ryan, 1994]	√
Multiobjectives		√
Hybrids	[Zhang and Mühlenbein, 1993b] [Gruau, 1993]	
Knowledge-augmentation		
Approximate function evaluation	[Koza, 1992]	

Table 2.4.   Some Public Domain Genetic Programming Implementations

Name	Author	Language		Notes
		Implement	Evolved	
	Koza	Lisp	Lisp	Code from [Koza, 1992] & [Koza, 1994], widely copied
SGPC	Tackett & Carmi	C	own	Can import/export Lisp
GPSRegress	Nguyen	Mathematica		Package to do symbolic regression
cerebrum	Dudey	Lisp	ANN	Framework for genetic programming of neural networks
gpcplus3	Fraser	C++	own	
gepetto	Glowacki	C	own	Similar to SGPC but with enhancements
GP-QUICK	Singleton	C++	own	Described in [Singleton, 1994]
GPEIST	White	Smalltalk 80		
lilgp	Punch	C		Supports ADFs and multiple populations
gpsys	Qureshi	Java 1.1		Steady State, Strongly Typed, ADFs

Table 2.5.   Some other Genetic Programming Implementations

Name	Author	Language		Notes
		Implement	Evolved	
STGP	Montana	C++	Ada/Lisp	Section 2.4.1
STROGA-NOFF	Iba etal		Decision Trees GMDH	Section 2.4.2
GLiB	Angeline			Section 2.4.5
SSGP	Reynolds			Steady State GP
GP-GIM	Singleton	C++		486 distributed network desk top supercomputing
DGPC	Andre	C		Used in recent experiments by Koza and his students

2.5.1   Prediction and Classification

One application where GP is already making a contribution is that of generating models to automatically fit data. It can be particularly appropriate where the available data are noisy and the underlying processes are non-linear. Applications with both large and small data sets have been reported. Such models may help explain the process, be used for prediction, to optimise the process or control it.

Although developed before the term genetic programming was coined, BEAGLE [Forsyth, 1981] may be classified as a genetic programming system in that it evolves tree structured programs. BEAGLE is a rule-finder program that uses a database of case histories to guide the evolution of a set of decision rules (programs) for classifying those examples. Once found the rule base (knowledge base) can be used to classify new examples. PC/Beagle is commercially available and has been widely applied; e.g. in insurance, weather forecasting, finance and forensic science [Ribeiro Filho et al., 1994]. The BioX system [Bettenhausen et al., 1995] has been used to model chemical engineering processes and river flows. [Whigham and Crapper, 1997] model river flows based on rain fall measurements. On a very seasonal Austrialian river GP provided a better model than a conventional modelling tool, although their performance was similar on a Welsh river. [Willis et al., 1997] shows their GP system can accurately model complex chemical engineering processes using only observed data. While more accurate than a neural network they state "the main advantage ... is that it [GP] has automatically eliminated irrelevent model inputs ... [and] offers a degree of parsimony not attainable using a neural network."

[Handley, 1993] uses genetic programming to predict the shape of proteins. He was able to evolve programs which, using the protein's chemical composition, were able to predict whether each part of a protein would have a particular geometric shape (an α-helix) or not. Genetic programming was able to do this broadly as well as other techniques but all suffered from the fact that the structure depends upon more than local composition. [Koza, 1994] reports similar success on other protein geometry problems.

[Iba et al., 1993] use genetic programming to fit chaotic time series data, see Section 2.4.2. While [Longshaw, 1997] recasts the problem of detecting anomalies in streams of hundreds of thousands of events generated by computer simulations, as the problem of inducing a formal grammar which describes most events. The events it fails to match are then the interesting anomalies. [Longshaw, 1997, page 452] states "The algorithm itself has proved its worth to us in the areas of data-mining and the analysis of the results from simulation".

[Schoenauer et al., 1996] shows GP can evolve dynamic one dimensional models (rheological models) and static three diemensional hyperelastic models of novel engineering materials. Such materials (e.g. composites and polymers) may be complex and are potentially non-linear yet practical engineering models of their behaviour are required before they be safely used.

Andre has successfully used genetic programming in optical character recognition problems (OCR). In [Andre, 1994a] he combines genetic programming with a two dimensional genetic algorithm to produce an OCR program from scratch. In [Andre, 1994c] he shows genetic programming can be used to maintain existing hand coded programs. He shows genetic programming automatically extending an existing manually written OCR program so that it can be used with an additional font. It is perhaps on routine maintenance problems, such as this, that genetic programming will find most immediate commercial application.

2.5.2 Image and Signal Processing

[Tackett, 1993] describes the use of genetic programming to extract targets from low contrast noisy pictures. Various ($\approx$20) standard metrics are extracted from the image using standard techniques, which are then processed by a genetic program to yield target details. [Poli, 1996b] describes the use of GP to evolve filters to enhance or detect features within magnetic resonance and X-ray medical images.

[Oakley, 1994] describes obtaining blood flow rates within human toes using laser Doppler measurements. These measurements are both noisy and chaotic. He compares the effectiveness (at removing noise but preserving the underlying signal) of special filters evolved by genetic programming and various standard filters. He concludes that a combination of genetic programming and heuristics is the most effective.

[Johnson et al., 1994] was able to evolve 2D image processing programs to extract the location of peoples' hands from still silhouettes. They report these performed better than the best hand coded algorithms. [Poli and Cagnoni, 1997] evolves programs to improve the usefulness of 2D medical images while [Esparcia-Alcazar and Sharman, 1997] evolves digital signal filters which provide channel equalisation to restore the original signal after it has been distorted by noise and dispersion. [Nordin and Banzhaf, 1996] describes applications of GP to image and sound compression.

2.5.3 Design

[Koza et al., 1996a] shows the automatic design of electrical circuits to meet onerous design requirements.

[Nguyen and Huang, 1994] have used genetic programming to evolve 3-D jet aircraft models. The determination of which models are fitter is done manually. This work is similar to that in Section 2.5.7; however the aircraft models are more complex.

2.5.4 Trading

[Andrews and Prager, 1994] used genetic programming to create strategies which have traded in simulated commodity and futures markets (the double auction tournaments held by the Santa-Fe Institute, Arizona, USA). Their automatically evolved strategies have proved superior to many hand-coded strategies. [Chen and Yeh, 1996] also uses GP to model behaviour in economic simulations, while [Chen and Yeh, 1997] use GP to model volatility in Japanese and New York stock markets and [Oussaidene et al., 1996] model currency markets.

Other financial applications include direct marketing, credit card credit worthiness scoring, loan application evaluation, data mining and customer retention modelling [Eiben, 1997].

2.5.5 Robots

One the current active strands in robot research is the development of independent mobile robots which are programmed to react to their environment rather than to follow a global plan [Brooks, 1991]. Until recently robot controllers had been hand coded however Spencer has been able to use genetic programming to automatically generate a control program enabling a simulated six legged robot to walk [Spencer, 1994]. [Gruau and Quatramaran, 1996] and [Banzhaf et al., 1997b] have evolved control programs and run them on real robots using GP. While [Lee et al., 1997] evolve mobile robot controllers using GP and a simulator but demonstrate the controller running on the physical robot.

2.5.6 Artificial Life

Artificial Life is the study of natural life by using computer simulations of it. There is a ready connection to autonomous robots. For example, evolving a program to control a robot's leg may be considered either as an engineering problem or as a simulation of a real insect's leg.

One aspect of Artificial Life is the study of natural evolution using computer simulation. Early simulations [Ray, 1991] relied heavily upon mutation but genetic algorithms (e.g. [Sims, 1994] and genetic programming using crossover have also been used more recently. For example [Reynolds, 1992] describes a simulation of herding behaviour based upon genetic programming [Reynolds, 1994c; Reynolds, 1994b]. Reynolds' "boids" technique has been used as a basis for photorealistic imagery of bat swarms in the films "Batman Returns" and "Cliffhanger" [Reynolds, 1996].

[Handley, 1994b; Haynes et al., 1995b; Iba, 1996a; Qureshi, 1996; Raik and Durnota, 1994; Luke and Spector, 1996; Zhang et al., 1996] have also applied genetic programming to autonomous agents. However various multi agent pursuit "games" in distributed artificial intelligence (DAI) have already been considered using genetic algorithms with a linear chromosome [Manela, 1993]. (Some multi-tree multi-agent GP systems are described in Section 3.6).

2.5.7 Artistic

There have been a number of uses of genetic programming, perhaps inspired by Dawkins' biomorphs [Dawkins, 1986] or Karl Sims' panspermia [Sims, 1991], which generate patterns on a computer display. For example [Gritz and Hahn, 1997] describes GP being used to make a short single character video.

[Das et al., 1994] uses genetic programming to generate sounds and three dimensional shapes. Virtual reality techniques are used to present these to the user. As in Section 2.5.3, there is an interactive fitness function, with the user indicating a preference between the four objects presented to him. [Spector and Alpern, 1994] have used GP to automatically generate Jazz improvisations. While the music achieved high marks from an automatic critic, they report it was not pleasing to human ears! (Examples of genetic music are available from the Internet, e.g. via http://www.cs.bham.ac.uk/~wbl).

2.6 CONCLUSIONS

This chapter has briefly surveyed recent work on the technique of automatic program generation known as genetic programming. It has presented program generation as the task of searching the space of possible programs for a suitable one. This search space is vast and poorly behaved, which is the sort of search for which genetic algorithms are best suited. It is therefore reasonable to apply genetic algorithms to this search and, as this chapter shows, this has had a measure of success.

Genetic programming has been demonstrated in the arena of classification (Section 2.5.1), albeit not under the name genetic programming; with at least one commercial package available. It is as a general technique that genetic programming is a particularly new and emerging research area. It has solved a number of problems from a wide range of different areas. Genetic programming has also been successfully applied to real world applications, such as optical character recognition (OCR) and signal processing (Section 2.5.2).

It is expected that use of genetic programming in the production of commercial software will become more widespread, perhaps first in signal processing but perhaps also in automatic model generation (section 2.5.1).

3 ADVANCED GENETIC PROGRAMMING TECHNIQUES

In the first section (3.1) of this chapter we position this work. While Section 2.3.2 has explained in detail general GP concepts which are used in later chapters, Sections 3.2 onwards describe more specialist techniques, some of which are introduced into GP. In later chapters, where we first use one of these concepts, we will refer back to the appropriate subsection within Section 2.3.2 or 3.2–3.9. (There is also a glossary in Appendix B).

3.1 BACKGROUND

Almost all GP work concentrates upon the evolution of simple functions, e.g. for classification. While Koza [Koza, 1992] has performed small demonstration experiments on recursion, iteration and evolvable memory and others have investigated a fourth, evolving programs containing primitives of more than one type, these four areas are largely unexplored even today. Progress on memory and iteration or recursion (and probably on all four areas) is required if genetic programming is to be capable of evolving general (i.e. Turing complete) programs. However our book concentrates upon the issues surrounding the evolution of the use of memory within GP. (A survey of other work on Evolving memory in GP is given in Section 7.4).

Simple indexed memory read an write functions (if iteration or recursion are also included) extend GP so that the language used by evolving programs is Turing complete [Teller, 1994c]. While in theory, any computable function can be evolved using such a language, the lack of structure in the memory model makes it seem inherently difficult to produce solutions to complex problems in practice. We are motivated by the observation that even if considerable intelligence (in the form of people, either singularly or in teams) is available to guide the search for a program which solves a problem, then the search is easier and more likely to be successful if the program's use of memory is structured or controlled, rather than if random or unconstrained access to all memory is allowed. From this starting point we investigate if the same is true for genetic programming, where the unintelligent search is guided only by the fitness function. The thrust of the rest of the book is to show that this is indeed true.

3.2   TOURNAMENT SELECTION

In evolutionary algorithms there are many different techniques in use for deciding which individuals will reproduce, how many children they will have and which individuals will die (i.e. be removed from the population). The general characteristic is to reward better solutions with more offspring (and possibly also with longer life). However the question of how much to reward good individuals is important. If a single very good individual has many children then the genetic diversity of the population may fall too much. But if every individual has about the same number of children then there is little selection pressure on the population to evolve in the desired direction.

Various fitness re-scaling schemes have been used to rescale fitness values, so that the effective fitness of potential parents and so the number of children they are expected to have is within some prescribed "reasonable" range. For example, the rescaled fitness of the best member of the population might be twice that of the worst. Other schemes order potential parents by their fitness and use their position or "rank" within the population to determine how many children they will have. This can produce a prescribed reproduction pattern across the population, which is largely independent of the numerical fitness values returned by the fitness function (all that is important is whether fitness scores are bigger or smaller than others, not by how much). Arguably independence from numerical values makes the fitness function easier to produce.

The above schemes require information from the whole population. With small, centralised (i.e. not distributed), generational populations, this is not too bad a problem. However with large or distributed or dynamic (i.e. steady state, see next section) populations, maintaining global fitness data for selection becomes more onerous. Tournament selection has become increasingly popular as it performs (albeit noisy) rank selection based selection using only local information. As it does not use the whole population, tournament selection does not require global population statistics.

In tournament selection, a number of individuals (the tournament size) are chosen at random (with reselection) from the breeding population. These are compared with each other and the best of them is chosen. As the number of candidates in the tournament is small, the comparisons are not expensive. An element of noise is inherent in tournament selection due to the random selection of candidates. Many other selection schemes are also stochastic (i.e. contain an element of chance), in which case the level of "noise" they have on the selection process may be considered important. [Goldberg and Deb, 1991] and [Blickle and Thiele, 1995] compare features (including selection noise) of various commonly used selection schemes.

3.3 STEADY STATE POPULATIONS

In a traditional GA [Holland, 1992], evolution proceeds via a sequence of discrete generations. These do not overlap. An individual exists only in one generation, it can only influence later generations through its children. This is like many species of plants (and animals) which live only one year. In the spring they germinate from seeds, grow during the summer and produce their own seeds in the autumn. These survive the winter by lying dormant, but their parents die. These new individuals start growing again in the next spring. Thus the species as a whole continues through many years but no one individual lives longer than a year.

In contrast many plants and animals live many years and there is no distinct boundary between generations. In steady state GAs [Syswerda, 1989; Syswerda, 1991b] new children are continually added to the population and can immediately be selected as parents for new individuals. Usually as each new individual is added to the population an existing member of the population is removed from it. This ensures the population remains at a constant size.

To ease comparisons between steady state and generational GAs, the term *generation equivalent* is used. It means the time taken to create as many new individuals as there are in the population. Thus a generation equivalent represents the same computational effort (in terms of number of fitness evaluations) as a single generation in a traditional GA with the same sized population.

Steady state populations are increasingly popular. All the genetic programming experiments in this book use steady state populations.

3.4 INDEXED MEMORY

The indexed memory model used is based upon [Teller, 1994a]. The indexed memory consists of $2l + 1$ memory cells (numbered $-l \ldots + l$), each of which holds a single value. Attempts to access memory outside the legal range either cause the program to be aborted or the data being written to be discarded and a default value of zero returned. Details are given with each of the experiments. In contrast, Teller avoids the address range problem by reducing the address index modulo the size of the memory (which is addressed $0 \ldots m - 1$). In [Teller, 1994a] 20 memory cells addressed $0 \ldots 19$ are used.

Note, like other functions, write returns a value. We follow Teller's example and define it to return the *original* value held in the store it has just overwritten. Many of the evolved programs exploit this behaviour.

Some experiments also use a swap function. This takes two arguments which it treats as addresses within index memory of two data values. It swaps them, so they now occupy the other address in indexed memory. Table 6.4 (page 128) defines swap in detail.

3.5 SCALAR MEMORY

In addition to indexed memory the experiments make use of one or more scalar memory cells known as auxiliary variables. Depending upon the experiment there are primitives to set, read, increment and decrement them.

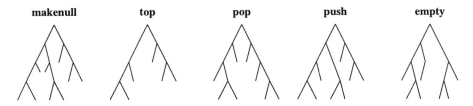

Figure 3.1.   One Individual – One Program: Five Operations – Five Trees

3.6   MULTI-TREE PROGRAMS

In Chapters 4 to 6 and Section 7.3 the evolved program must perform more than one action. This is represented by allocating an evolvable tree per action. When the program is used, e.g. during its fitness testing, then the tree corresponding to the desired action is called. For example, when evolving a stack in Chapter 4 there are five different operations that a stack data structure must support. Each of these is allocated its own evolvable tree. So each individual within the population is composed of five trees, see Figure 3.1.

This multiple tree architecture was chosen so that each tree contains code which has evolved for a single purpose. It was felt that this would ease the formation of "building blocks" of useful functionality and enable crossover, or other genetic operations, to assemble working implementations of the operations from them. Similarly complete programs could be formed whilst each of its trees improved.

The genetic operations, reproduction, crossover and mutation are redefined to cope with this multi-tree architecture. While there are many different ways of doing this [Raik and Durnota, 1994], we define the genetic operations to act upon only one tree at a time. The other trees are unchanged and are copied directly from the first parent to the offspring. Genetic operations are limited to a single tree at a time in the expectation that this will reduce the extent to which they disrupts "building blocks" of useful code. Crossing like trees with like trees is similar to the crossover operator with "branch typing" used by Koza in most of his experiments involving ADFs in [Koza, 1994].

In the case of reproduction, the only action on the chosen tree is also to copy it, in other words each new individual is created by copying all trees of the parent program.

When crossing over, one type of tree is selected (at random, with equal probability, e.g. 1/5). This tree in the offspring is created by crossover between the tree in each parent of the chosen type in the normal GP way [Koza, 1992]. The new tree has the same root as the first parent (see Figure 3.2). Each mating produces a single offspring, most of whose genetic material comes from only one of its parents.

In the first set of experiments in this book, all trees have identical primitives. In later experiments, each tree has its own set of primitives from which it may be composed, see Section 5.10.

Should the offspring program exceed the maximum allowed length, the roles of the two parents are swapped, keeping the same crossover points. Given that the parents are of legal length, this ensures the offspring will be legal.

This use of multiple trees and entry points appears to have been "invented" several times. The first use of multiple trees is probably [Koza, 1992, Sections 19.7 and 19.8]

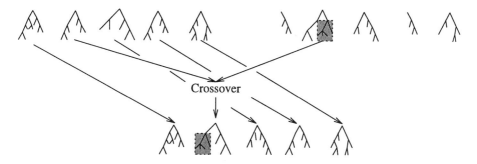

Figure 3.2.   Crossover in One Tree at a time

where there are two distinct branches in the same program with different terminal sets. Unlike the trees in Figure 3.2, the branches are not equal. One branch is subservient to the other, in that it is always called before the start of the main branch, and so there is only one entry point. However the two branches used in [Andre, 1994b] are more equal, with each having its own ADFs, while [Taylor, 1995] used three separate trees and also allowed each an ADF. Multi agent programs have also been evolved using this approach, with a tree per agent [Haynes et al., 1995a]. While [Reynolds, 1994a] has a single agent, the agent has two very different behaviours. In some experiments these are forced into separate code branches. Due to the high variation between runs and the use of mutation, it is unclear if syntactically separating the behaviours is beneficial on its own. Bruce's one tree per data method has been described above in Section 7.4.8.

The CoacH system [Raik and Durnota, 1994] allows the user to specify multiple trees within a single individual in the population. (Each individual represents a team and each tree corresponding to a team member within the team). This approach is slightly different in that it allows the user to specify how many trees participate in crossover and whether crossover must be between trees (team members) of the same type. While [Luke et al., 1997] evolves a team of 11 co-operating agents. The task is subdivided by splitting the eleven agents into four squads. Agents in the same squad share the same code. Each sqaud is composed of a main tree and (up to) two ADFs. Making a total of 12 trees, which are co-evolved together.

3.7   DIRECTED CROSSOVER

This section surveys approaches in which the standard random genetic operators have been modified to direct or bias the location within parent programs on which they act. However before we consider exotic techniques we shall explain the standard one.

[Koza, 1992, page 114] and most others (including this book) use a crude aspect of program syntax (based on differentiating between functions and terminals, i.e. internal nodes and leaf nodes) to stochastically guide the location of crossover points. Crossover is biased to increase the proportion of times it moves subtrees headed by functions, as these are larger than those headed by terminals (which contain a single leaf node). In [Koza, 1992] on average 90% of crossovers exchange functions. In this work the proportions are governed by the GP-QUICK parameter pUnRestrictWt. It determines the proportion of crossover points that can be either terminals or functions compared to those that must be functions. In large binary trees (where the number of terminals is approximately equal to the number of functions), the default value of pUnRestrictWt (70%) corresponds to $(100\% - 70\%) + 70\%/2 = 65\%$ of crossovers inserting trees larger than a single terminal. (Table 8.5 (page 197) shows the actual value can be quite close to 65% in practice).

[Angeline, 1996a, page 27] argues "that no one constant value for leaf frequency is optimal for every problem". While this seems likely to be true, we need to consider the part mutation and other non-standard techniques play in his experiments. Also determining optimal values for any problem is expensive, therefore we have retained the GP-QUICK default.

The remainder of this section describes more sophisticated techniques for guiding GP evolution. While such approaches could be used with mutation, work has concentrated upon the choice of crossover points. We start with the work in this book and then briefly consider work by others. Most experiments in this book use the standard choice of crossover points described above. However Chapters 5 and 6 contain techniques to probabilistically bias the choice of crossover points. Two methods are used; firstly ensuring offspring obey various semantic (described in Section 5.10.3) or syntactic (Section 6.4.2) restrictions. If these conditions are not met, the offspring is aborted and a replacement is generated by performing another crossover. The second approach (Section 6.6) actively drives the choice of crossover points using performance data gathered during fitness testing of the parents.

A number of papers show benefits in directing or biasing the operation of the crossover or other genetic operators. For example [Whigham, 1995a; Whigham, 1995b] uses a grammar to constrain the evolving trees but the grammar itself evolves based on the syntax of previously successful programs (in fact the best of each generation). The grammar does not become more constrictive but instead the rules within it are allocated a fitness which biases (rather than controls) the subsequent evolution of the population. [Whigham, 1996, page 231] says "recently there has been increasing interest in using formal grammars to represent bias in an evolutionary framework" and gives an overview of grammatically biased learning. LOGENPRO [Wong and Leung, 1995] and Generic Genetic Programming (GGP) [Wong and Leung, 1996] are also based upon formal grammars, while [Gruau, 1996b] argues strongly that GP workers should be forthright in using program syntax to guide the GP and shows improved GP performance by using an external grammar to define more tightly the syntax of the evolving programs.

[D'haeseleer, 1994] describes methods, based upon the syntax of the two parent programs, for biasing the choice of crossover locations so that code at similar physical locations within programs is more likely to be exchanged. The motivation is such code may be more likely to be similar than random code and so changes introduced may be smaller and so more likely to be beneficial. The assumption is that large changes are more random and so, in a complex problem, more likely to be harmful.

An approach to protect code from crossover is the use of genetic libraries ([Angeline, 1993] and [Rosca and Ballard, 1996], described in Section 2.4.5). The ETL group [Iba and de Garis, 1996] is also active in this area, work on their COAST system is reported in [Hondo et al., 1996b] and summarised in [Hondo et al., 1996a]. Also "introns" are suggested to protect code from crossover [Nordin et al., 1996] but [Andre

ADVANCED GENETIC PROGRAMMING TECHNIQUES   49

and Teller, 1996, page 20] concludes "that introns are probably damaging", while the EPI system [Wineberg and Oppacher, 1996] relies upon them. ([Blickle, 1996] reports explicit introns may sometimes caused performance degradation on a boolean problem). [Angeline, 1996b] advocates evolving the probability of crossover occurring at different points in the program along with the program itself. He also suggests multiple crossovers to produce an offspring. [Teller, 1995b] includes a library of callable code plus the co-evolution of "smart" crossover operators. The evolving "smart" crossover operators are free to select crossover points as they choose whilst they create offspring for parents in the main population.

[Blickle and Thiele, 1994, Section 4] claims improved performance by marking tree edges when they are evaluated and ensuring crossover avoids unevaluated trees, however the improvement is problem dependent. In [Blickle, 1996] a deleting crossover operator which removes unevaluated trees is shown to give more parsimonious solutions on a discrete problem.

The "soft brood" approach in [Tackett, 1995a] is different, in that the genetic operator itself is not biased, instead improved offspring are produced by producing multiple offspring per parent pairing and using a (possibly simple) fitness function to ensure only the best are released into the population and so able to breed. [Crepeau, 1995, Section 2.2.1] uses a similar technique. It could also be argued that fitness functions which reward parsimony (i.e. short code) are also biasing the genetic search process. The Minimum Description Length (MDL) and Occam's razor approaches have been described in Section 2.4.2.

There has been increasing interest in the use of "type" information to guide the creation of the initial population and its subsequent evolution via crossover since Strongly Typed Genetic Programming (STGP) was introduced by [Montana, 1993; Montana, 1994] (see Section 2.4.1). While [Montana, 1995] argues the reduction in search space is important, a more convincing explanation for the power of STGP is the use of type information to pick a better route through the search space by keeping to the narrow path of type correct programs.

3.8 DEMES

Various means to divide GA populations into subpopulations have been reported in conventional GAs [Stender, 1993; Collins, 1992] and genetic programming [Tackett, 1994; Ryan, 1994; D'haeseleer and Bluming, 1994; Koza and Andre, 1995b; Juille and Pollack, 1995]. Dividing the population limits the speed at which it converges and so may reduce the impact of premature convergence (i.e. when the population converges to a local optimum rather than the global optimum) and improve the quality of the solutions produced. (If the population is split, with very little genetic communication between its components, the population need never converge).

Demes are used in various experiments (notably in Chapters 5, 6 and 7). In this work, where direct comparisons were made, the use of a structured population, i.e. of demes, always proved to be beneficial in comparisons with simple non-demic, i.e. panmictic population. However in some cases better results were obtained by using fitness niches (see Section 3.6). Where demes are used, the model described in this section is used. In this model (which is based upon [Collins, 1992]) the whole population is treated as a rectangular grid of squares with two individuals in each square. Crossover can occur only between near neighbours, i.e. within (overlapping) demes. To avoid edge effects the grid is bent into a torus, so that each edge of the rectangle touches the opposite one.

In addition to crossover, reproduction is used. As usual two tournaments are conducted, the first chooses which individual (within the deme) to replace, and the second chooses which to copy.

Before a selection tournament occurs, the candidates for selection must be chosen. Without demes individuals are selected at random from the entire population. This leads to the population being well mixed, which is known as a panmictic population. When demes are used, all members of the selection tournament come from the same deme, i.e. a small part of the population. Figure 3.3 shows the sequence of selection events. This technique differs in detail from [Collins, 1992, Section 2.4.1] in that there are two individuals per grid square (rather than one), reverse tournament selection (rather than random) is used to select the individual to be replaced and tournament candidates are chosen with uniform probability from a square neighbourhood. [Collins, 1992] uses a random walk process to approximate a gaussian distribution centered about the individual to be replaced.

Demes have some similarities with cellular automata, in that (apart from its contents) each deme is the same as every other deme. Also the new population in a deme is related to its current population and the populations of its neighbours. This is similar to the way the next state of a cell within a cellular automata is determined by its current state and the states of its neighbours. However there are important differences: the contents of each deme is one or more programs, as the number of potential programs is huge (e.g. more than $1.4 \ 10^{262}$ for the stack problem in Chapter 4), the number of states a deme may be in is also enormous. In a cellular automata usually the number of states is small. New programs are created stochastically, so given the populations in a deme and its neighbours, the new population in the deme can be one of a huge number of different possibilities. Each possible new population has in general a different probability, being given by the fitnesses of the individuals in the deme and surrounding demes. Classically cellular automata operate in parallel, while demes are updated sequentially and stochastically.

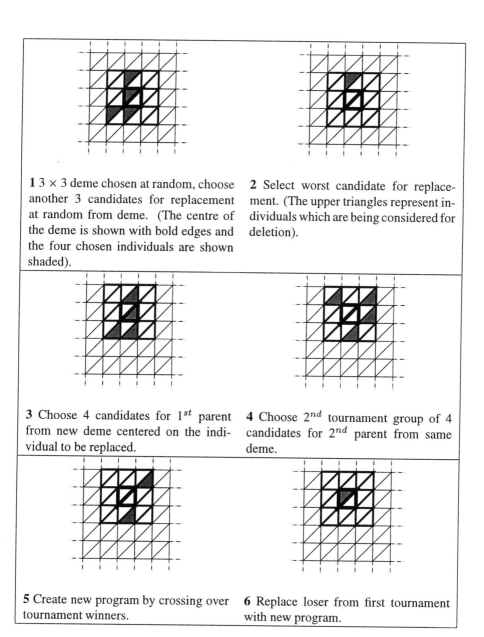

1 3 × 3 deme chosen at random, choose another 3 candidates for replacement at random from deme. (The centre of the deme is shown with bold edges and the four chosen individuals are shown shaded).

2 Select worst candidate for replacement. (The upper triangles represent individuals which are being considered for deletion).

3 Choose 4 candidates for 1st parent from new deme centered on the individual to be replaced.

4 Choose 2nd tournament group of 4 candidates for 2nd parent from same deme.

5 Create new program by crossing over tournament winners.

6 Replace loser from first tournament with new program.

Figure 3.3. Selecting Parents and Individual to be Replaced in a Demic Population

Limiting Convergence

Using this deme structure a fit individual's influence within the population is limited by how fast it can move through the population. The following analysis shows this depends upon how much better it is than its neighbours.

If a program is consistently better than its neighbours (and so too are its offspring), then its influence (i.e. its offspring) is expected to spread at a high rate across the population (NB this means its number grows quadratically, rather than exponentially). Each time it produces a new offspring, the new offspring will be about $1/2\sqrt{D/2}$ from its parent (where there are D grid points in the deme, see Figure 3.4). When considering how the individuals spread we need only consider those at the edge. When these reproduce only about 50% of their offspring will be outside the previously occupied area.

In a rectangular torrodial population of size M with each grid point containing P individuals, each deme is within $1/2\sqrt{\frac{MR}{P}}$ of every other (see Figure 3.5). (R denotes the ratio of the rectangle's sides). The influence of a program that is consistently of above average fitness can be expected to spread throughout the whole population in about $2\dfrac{1/2\sqrt{\frac{MR}{P}}}{1/2\sqrt{D/2}} = 2\sqrt{2MR/DP}$ time steps.

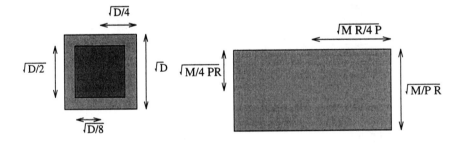

Figure 3.4. In a square deme containing D grid points, 50% points lie within $\frac{1}{2}\sqrt{\frac{D}{2}}$ of the center

Figure 3.5. In a rectangular population of M individuals, aspect ratio R and P individuals per grid point, each individual is within $\frac{1}{2}\sqrt{\frac{MR}{P}}$ of any other

The time taken to dominate the whole population is proportional to the program's reproduction rate, which in turn depends upon how much fitter it is than its neighbours. With tournament selection the fittest individual in a deme will win every tournament it is selected to be a candidate in. In demes on the edge of the program's influence, i.e. demes that don't yet contain many descendants of the individual, their chance of winning a selection tournament (of size t) is approximately t bigger than that of the average individual (see Section 8.4.2 page 188). With a crossover rate of p_c there are on average $1 + p_c$ tournaments per offspring created. Thus the maximum reproduction rate of an individual is about $t(1 + p_c)/M$. However in GP, crossover is asymmetric, with one parent usually contributing more genetic material than the other (see Figure 3.2). If we consider only those parents, the maximum reproduction rate is t/M. Thus the shortest time for a very fit individual to dominate the whole population is $\approx \frac{2}{t}\sqrt{2MR/DP}$ generation equivalents. (If $M = 10,000$, $D = 9$, $P = R = 2$, $t = 4$, this is approximately 24 generation equivalents).

If a program is only slightly better than its neighbours, it can be expected to have about one offspring per generation equivalent. This will be placed within the same deme as its parent, but in a random direction from it. Thus the original program's influence will diffuse through the population using a "random walk", with a step size of about $1/2\sqrt{D/2}$ (see Figure 3.4). The absolute distance travelled by a random walk is expected to be step size $\times \sqrt{\text{no. steps}}$. Thus the number of time steps required is (no. of steps required) squared. The number of generation equivalents it can be expected to take to spread through the whole population is $2\frac{MR}{DP}$ (If $M = 10,000$, $D = 9$, $P = R = 2$, then this is approximately 2200 generation equivalents).

Where selection is from the whole population, the chance of a program being selected to crossover with itself, is very small. However when each random selection is equally likely to be any member of a small (3×3) deme, the chance of any program being selected more than once is quite high. Possibly the increased chance of crossover between the same or similar programs may also be beneficial.

3.9   PARETO OPTIMALITY

Existing GPs (and indeed genetic algorithms in general and other search techniques) use a scalar fitness function where each individual is given a single measure of its usefulness. An alternative, explored later chapters of this book, is to use a multi-dimensional fitness measure where each fitness dimension refers to a different aspect of the trial solution.

In several experiments there is more than one task which the evolved program is to perform. For example when evolving a data structure there are multiple operations that the data structure must support. In the first experiments (Chapter 4) a single fitness measure is produced by combining the performance of the individual operations. Later work (particularly in Chapters 5, 6 and Section 7.3) separates the performance of each operation, each contributing a dimension to the overall multi-dimensional fitness measure. In some cases penalties for excessive CPU or memory usage also contribute a dimension to the fitness. (Since fitness testing often requires more than one operation to be active, e.g. when testing that operations work together, a total separation between fitness dimensions is not possible. Nevertheless a multi-objective fitness function does allow some measure of which parts of the program are working well to be recorded).

Pareto optimality [Goldberg, 1989, page 197] offers a way of comparing individuals within the population using multiple criteria without introducing an arbitrary means of combining them into a single fitness. Evidence for the effectiveness of Pareto Tournament selection is given in [Fonseca and Fleming, 1993] and [Louis and Rawlins, 1993]. [Fonseca and Fleming, 1995] contains a review of multi-objective optimisation techniques used inconjunction with various evolutionary computing algorithms. In a Pareto approach fitness values are compared dimension by dimension. If a fitness

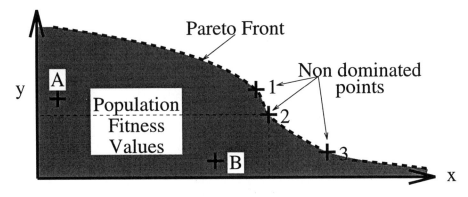

Figure 3.6.   Two Dimensional Example of Pareto Optimality and the Pareto Front

value is no worse than the other in every dimension and better in at least one dimension then it is said to dominate the other. For example in Figure 3.6, point 2 dominates B but does not dominate A.

Pareto scoring means individuals which make an improvement on any part of the problem tend to be preferred, whereas a scalar fitness will tend to require each improvement to match or exceed any deterioration in all other parts of the problem. Whether an improvement is more important than a deterioration is given by scaling parameters within the fitness function. Consequently setting them is complex and must be done with care. To some extent Pareto fitness avoids this problem.

With "fitness sharing" [Goldberg, 1989], the fitness of individuals which are "close" to each other is reduced in proportion to the number of individuals. This creates a dispersive pressure in the population, which counteracts the GAs tendency to converge on the best fitness value in the population. So the number of occupied niches remains high.

An alternative approach is to impose a fixed number of niches. [Yang and Flockton, 1995] describes dynamic niches, containing clusters of individuals which move across the representation space as the population evolves. Hill climbing, via mutation, provides effective local search within each niche. However keeping track of such niches is computationally expensive [page 196].

In the case of a multi-objective fitness measure there is also a tendency for the number of niches to fall however fitness sharing can again be used to create a dispersive pressure and keep the number of occupied niches high [Horn et al., 1993]. [Horn et al., 1993] suggests a method of fitness sharing based upon estimating an individual's Pareto rank by comparing it with a random sample of the whole population, known as the comparison set. (The implementation used in this work is described in the next subsection).

Figure 3.7 shows the evolution of the number of occupied points on the Pareto optimal surface in two runs starting from the same initial population. (The two runs were preliminary experiments on the list problem, cf. Chapter 6). We see the use of a comparison set leads to the retention of a large number of occupied niches, each of

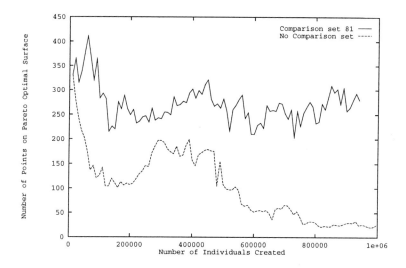

Figure 3.7. Number of different non dominated fitness values in a list population (Chapter 6) with and without a comparison set (no niche sharing, not elitist, pop=10,000, no demes)

which is the best on some combination of criteria. However without it, the number of niches falls.

[Oei et al., 1991] considered linear GAs with complete generational replacement and state the "naive" use of tournament selection to spread a GA population across equally fit niches will cause the population to behave chaotically. They predict [page 5] the number of niches, n, within a population of equally fit individuals will fall, being given by the formula:

$$n = \frac{1}{\frac{1}{n_0} + \frac{2G}{\pi^2 M}} \qquad (3.1)$$

where n_0 is the initial number of niches, G number of generations and M is the population size.

It can be seen that Equation 3.1 does not fit the lower curve in Figure 3.7 well. The derivation of Equation 3.1 made several assumptions that don't hold for Figure 3.7, perhaps the most important is that the fitness niches are static, whereas in Figure 3.7 each fitness value ceases to be a niche when a new solution which dominates is found. Nevertheless Figure 3.7 shows a general downward trend in the number of different non-dominated fitness values in the population (i.e. niches) after the initial high rate of fitness improvement slows and the population becomes more stable. The loss of variation with time in finite populations of equally fit individuals is also known as "genetic drift".

Both fitness sharing and demes encourage retention of genetic diversity. Demes promote breeding of nearby individuals (which are likely to be genetically similar) while fitness sharing retains a large fitness variation in the population. As the population has a large fitness diversity, it may also have a large genetic diversity, so fitness sharing promotes breeding between genetically diverse individuals.

Fitness Sharing Pareto Tournament Selection

Pareto optimality can be readily combined with tournament selection. In all the GP experiments described in this book a small number (4) of programs are compared and the best (or worst) is selected. With scalar fitness this is done by comparing each program in the tournament group with the current best. If it is better, then it becomes the new best. With Pareto selection, we need to consider the case where neither program is better than the other.

With Pareto ranking, instead of maintaining a unique "best so far" individual in the tournament, a list of "best so far" individuals is kept. Each member of the tournament group is compared with each member of the best so far list. If it is better than a "best so far" individual, that individual is removed from the list. If it is worse, then it is discarded. If after comparing with the whole list, it has not been discarded, it is added to the list. After comparing all candidates, the winner is taken from the "best so far" list. If there is more than one individual in the list and fitness sharing is not being used then the tournament winner is chosen at random from those in the list.

To reduce the size of the "best so far" list and so the number of comparisons, if a candidate has identical fitness to a member of the list, the candidate is discarded. This introduces a bias away from programs with identical scores, as it prevents them increasing their chances of selection by appearing multiple times in the "best so far" list.

Where a tournament group contains two, or more, non-dominated individuals (i.e. the "best so far" list contains more than one individual at the end of the tournament) the remainder of the population can be used to rank them. Thus an individual which is dominated by few others will be ranked higher than one dominated by many. NB this exerts a divergent selection pressure on the population as individuals are preferred if there are few others that dominate them. Following [Horn et al., 1993] the pareto rank is estimated by comparison with a sample of the population rather than all of it. Typically, in this work, a sample of up to 81 individuals is used.

Elitism. Using a conventional scalar fitness function and tournament selection a steady state population is *elitist*. That is the best individual in the population is very unlikely to be lost from the population. This is because it is very unlikely to be selected for deletion. This could only happen if the best individual was selected to be every member of a deletion tournament. The chance of this is M^{-k} (where M is the population size and k is the kill tournament size). If there is always a unique best individual then the chance of ever deleting it is $1 - (1 - M^{-k})^g$ where g is the number of individuals deleted. Assuming $M^k \gg g$ then we can approximate this with gM^{-k}. If G is the number of generation equivalents, then this becomes $GM^{-(k-1)}$. With $M = 10,000$, $k = 4$ and $G = 100$, the chance of deleting the unique best member of the population is $\leq 10^{-10}$. If there are multiple individuals with the highest fitness score then the chance of deleting any one of them is much higher, but then there will be at least one more individual in the population with the same high score.

Where the population is separated into demes the chance of deleting the unique best member of the population is much higher, however the best member will reproduce rapidly and so is unlikely to remain unique for long. The chance of selecting a deme containing the best individual is $1/M \times$ No. overlapping demes $= D/M$ (due to the implementation of overlapping demes, the number of individuals at each grid point need not be considered). The chance of selecting the best individual to be a candidate in a selection tournament is $1/D$ but for it to be deleted, it needs to be the only candidate, i.e. it needs to be selected k times. The chance of this is D^{-k}. Thus the chance the best individual will be deleted by any one kill tournament is $D/M \times D^{-k}$ $= D^{1-k}M^{-1}$. (If $M = 10{,}000$, $D = 9$, $k = 4$, this is approximately 0.14 10^{-6}). If there is always a unique best in the population (which need not always be the same individual) the chance of it ever being lost from the population is $1 - (1 - D^{1-k}M^{-1})^g$ $= 1 - \exp(g\log(1 - D^{1-k}M^{-1})) \approx 1 - \exp(-gD^{1-k}M^{-1}) = 1 - \exp(-G/D^{k-1})$. (If $G = 100$, $D = 9$, $k = 4$, this is approximately 0.13. I.e. in a steady state demic population in the worst case (where there is always only one copy of the best individual in the population) there is a small chance of deleting the best member of the population).

The combination of Pareto fitness and tournament selection is no longer elitist. This is because with the introduction of Pareto scoring there may be more than one, indeed many, individuals within the population which are the "best", in the sense that there is none better. The population will tend to converge to these "best" individuals, i.e. their numbers will grow. It is possible for the whole of the tournament group to consist entirely of "best" individuals in which case one of them must be selected for deletion. With Pareto scoring, these need not have identical scores, only scores that were not dominated by the deleted program. In this way programs which appear to have the best score so far can be lost from the population. Figure 5.26 (page 116) shows several cases where the program with the highest total score (i.e. the total number of tests passed) is lost from the population, resulting in a fall in the simple sum of five of the six fitness measures.

Figures 3.8 and 3.9 show the advance of the "best in the population" Pareto front to higher fitness as the population evolved (albeit projected onto just two dimensions). The two populations come from runs of the queue problem (Section 5.10). Note these graphs only plot scores on two of the criteria (dequeue and front), the other criteria account for some concavities in the front.

3.10   CONCLUSIONS

This chapter has described briefly described early work on evolving programs' use of memory and described in more detail the advanced GP techniques (tournament selection, overlapping generations, indexed and scalar memory, multi-tree programs, directed crossover, partitioning the population using demes and multi-objective fitness functions). These will be used in the experimental chapters, which follow immediately.

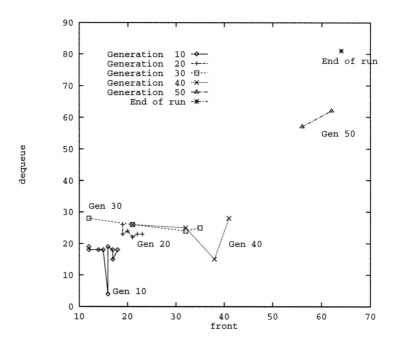

Figure 3.8. Evolution of the Pareto front (successful run of queue problem, cf. Section 5.10)

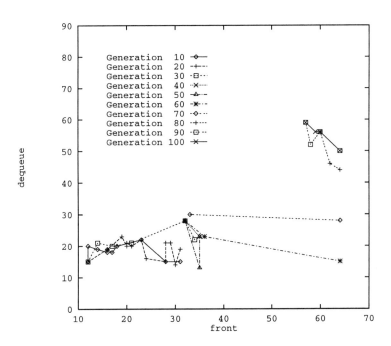

Figure 3.9. Evolution of the Pareto front (typical run of queue problem, cf. Section 5.10)

4 EVOLVING A STACK

The stack is one of the simplest and widest used abstract data types [Aho and Ullman, 1995, page 312]. Uses include, evaluating arithmetic expressions, parsing computer languages and, in most computer languages, storing function arguments and local data as programs are executed. Since they are so widely used many digital computers include explicit machine code support for one or more stacks. This chapter shows that genetic programming can automatically synthesise an integer stack from randomly addressable memory when guided by a fitness function that considers only the outputs of the stack and does not consider its implementation.

4.1 PROBLEM STATEMENT

The operation of a stack is shown in Figure 4.1 while a slightly more formal definition is given in Table 4.1. The stack can be thought of as like a pile of coins. We can add new coins to the top of the pile and remove coins from the top of the pile but we cannot access coins within the pile except by first removing those above it.

At first sight not being able to immediately access every part of the pile seems like a disadvantage, as indeed it would be if we need access to all previously stored data, however there are many problems where only data referring to the most recently encountered part of the problem is needed however when we finish processing that we need to return to a previous part of the problem and continue using data we have already saved for it. At this point we discard the current data, remove it from the top of the pile and so have access to the previous data. Such problems may be recursive.

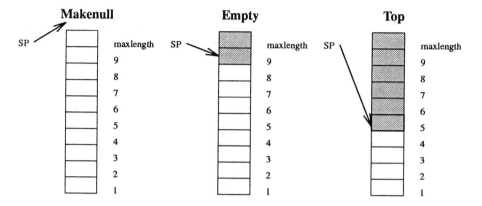

Makenull

Initialise stack to empty by setting the stack pointer SP to maxlength + 1.

Empty

If SP doesn't point to valid part of stack the stack is empty. In this example the stack contains two items, so Empty will return false.

Top

Read the top of the stack from the cell pointed to by SP.

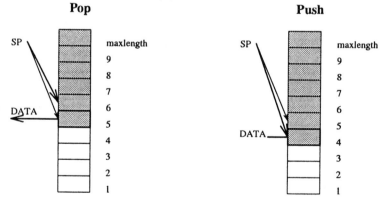

Pop

Read the top of the stack from the cell pointed to by SP then remove it by increasing SP by one.

Push

Put a new data value on the top of the stack by reducing SP by one and then writing the new value into the cell it now points to.

Figure 4.1.   Push-down Stack

Table 4.1.   Pseudo Code Definition of the Five Stack Operations

Operation	Code		Comment
makenull	sp	:= maxlength + 1;	initialise stack
empty	empty	:= (sp > maxlength);	is stack empty or not?
top	top	:= stack[sp];	top of the stack
pop	pop	:= stack[sp];	return top of stack
	sp	:= sp + 1;	and remove it
push(x)	sp	:= sp − 1;	place x on top of stack
	stack[sp]	:= x;	

4.1.1   Example Use of a Stack

A simple example where we need to store data but need access only to the most recent data item is passing through a maze (without loops). Figure 4.2 contains an example maze. To pass through the maze efficiently we need to remember which parts of the maze we have already searched for the exit. An efficient strategy is rather than record every point in the maze as we pass it, is to only record the points at which we had to make a decision whether to take the right or left branch. When we reach a dead end we return to the last decision point and take the unexplored branch. If we have explored both options we retrace our steps to the decision point before the one we have just reached and continue from there. The right hand side of Figure 4.2 shows this exploration strategy as an inverted tree. A simple strategy in which, when confronted with a new branch, we always take the left branch first is shown as a dotted line.

We need only record information about the branch points we have partially explored. Once both options have been taken we can discard the information we have gathered about that part of the maze and all the parts of the maze it leads to. We know they don't lead to the exit, so we are no longer interested in them. This means we need only keep information about the branch points between are current position and the start of the branching tree. Thus the maximum amount of data we need to keep is given by the height of the tree which could be very much less than the total size of the maze. However to take advantage of this saving in space we need a data structure which allows us to discard information on fully explored branches, including all the data we have accumulated about other branch points further down that branch.

A stack data structure does this naturally. As we reach a new branch point we push data about in onto the stack (all we need to know is which branch we are going to take next). Should this branch not lead to the exit, we return to the branch point, examine the top of the stack and explore the other branch, and record that we are doing so on the top of the stack. If this too leads to a dead end we return to the branch point. Now when we examine the top of the stack. It tells us we have fully explored this branch. We can discard all we have learnt about this branch by simply popping the top of the stack. We now return to the previous branch point. Note that as we have popped the stack, the top of the stack now contains data on the branch point we have just returned to. This is exactly the information we need to make our next decision! So not only is

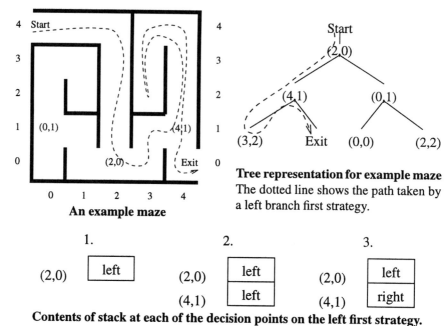

An example maze

Tree representation for example maze
The dotted line shows the path taken by
a left branch first strategy.

1.

(2,0) | left |

2.

(2,0) | left |
(4,1) | left |

3.

(2,0) | left |
(4,1) | right |

Contents of stack at each of the decision points on the left first strategy.

1. At (2,0) push left, to indicate we are exploring the left branch.

2. At (4,1) push left again.

3. On reaching the dead end at (3,2) we retrace our steps to (4,1). We now update the top of the stack to right. This indicates we are exploring the right branch and have already explored the left branch, thus if we reach a dead end in the right branch the top of the stack will indicate we have explored branch point (4,1) fully and we should return to (2,0).

Figure 4.2.   Solving a Maze Problem Using a Stack

a stack a compact way of storing the data we need but it automatically structures the data in a way which makes it easy to use.

4.1.2 Evolving a Stack

Having shown an example where a stack helps us to solve a problem, we return to the task of evolving a stack using genetic programming.

It is anticipated that the fitness test cases would have to cover each part of the functionality that is to be evolved. Thus reducing the functionality can be expected to reduce the complexity of the fitness testing. This in turn reduces the CPU time to complete fitness testing and makes it easier to devise the test cases. Therefore the definition of a stack given in [Aho et al., 1987] was simplified by removing the checks for stack underflow or overflow. These checks are not part of the essential operation of

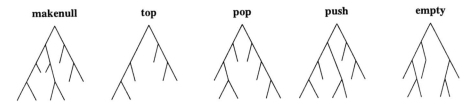

Figure 4.3. Each individual within the population is a trial implementation of the whole of stack and so implements each of the five operations that a stack supports (makenull, top, pop, push and empty). Each operation is programmed by its own tree. The complete individual is composed of one tree for each operation making a total of five trees.

a stack, instead they are included to make the system more robust by providing some "defensive programming" which traps and safely handles some user or coding errors.

The correctness of each trial solution is to be established using only the values returned by the stack operations, i.e. no account is taken as to how the memory is used. In [Aho et al., 1987] only two (top and empty) of the five operations return values. It was felt that not being able to directly check in any way the correctness of three of the operations was possibly too much and so the definition of pop used requires it to return the current top of the stack as well as removing it. This common alternative definition [Aho and Ullman, 1995, page 308] allows at least some level of correctness of pop to be directly assessed.

Note that the stack problem requires the GP to evolve five operations so together they implement a stack. That is, we are requiring the GP to simultaneously co-evolve five operations.

As with most programming problems, there are many possible implementations but as the evolution proceeds we do not measure each trial solution's conformance to an imposed "correct" implementation. We don't impose a specific implementation. Instead evolution, guided only by how well the operations work together, must find an implementation which each operation is compatible with.

In any implementation of a stack there must be a limit on its size [Aho and Ullman, 1995, page 307]. This is represented by maxlength in Figure 4.1 and Table 4.1. A limit of ten integers is sufficient to demonstrate the idea. In fact the programs evolved scale up to stacks of any required depth.

4.2 ARCHITECTURE

The multi-tree architecture and multi-tree crossover described in Section 3.6 was chosen as this allows each individual within the population to simultaneously implement trial solutions to each of the five operations that form the complete stack program; see Figure 4.3.

4.3 CHOICE OF PRIMITIVES

Primitives like those a human programmer might use, were chosen. Firstly this ensures a solution is possible, i.e. a program which solves the problem can be written using

Table 4.2.   Tableau for Evolving a Stack

Objective	To evolve a pushdown stack	
Architecture	Five separate trees	
Primitives	+, −, 0, 1, max, arg1, aux, inc_aux, dec_aux, read, write, write_Aux	
Fitness Case	4 test sequences, each of 40 tests (see Tables 4.3 to 4.5)	
Fitness Scaling	1.0 for each test passed	
Selection	Scalar tournament of 4	
Hits	n/a	
Wrapper (page 68)	makenull	result ignored
	top	no wrapper
	pop	no wrapper
	push	result ignored
	empty	result > 0 ⇒ TRUE, otherwise FALSE
Parameters	Population = 1000, G=101, program size <= 250	
Success Predicate	Fitness >= 160.0	

only these primitives. (The need for the available primitives to be powerful enough so that a solution to the problem can be express using them is called the *sufficiency* requirement [Koza, 1992, page 86]). Secondly as some constructs are useful to human programmers it was expected that corresponding primitives might be useful to the GP. For example primitives were included that aid maintenance of a stack pointer, although their functionality could in principle be evolved using combinations of the other primitives.

The following primitives were available to the GP:

■ arg1, the value to be pushed on to the stack. When arg1 is used by any of the operations except push it has the value zero. Evolving programs can read arg1 but they can not change it.

■ arithmetic operators + and −.

■ constants 0, 1 and the maximum depth of the stack, max (which has the value 10).

■ indexed memory functions read and write.

■ primitives to help maintain a stack pointer; aux, inc_aux, dec_aux and write_Aux (cf. Section 4.3.2).

(We use the name "write_Aux" even though it has slightly odd capitalisation as it is the actual name of the primitive used in the GP system. Similarly we use the actual names of all the other primitives. All these names are case sensitive. However similar primitives are grouped together in the index, so names in the index need not be identical to those in the main text).

It was decided to evolve a stack of integer values as integers are naturally compatible with addressing operations required with indexed memory and the arithmetic required with a stack and so all primitives can be of the same type (i.e. 32-bit signed integers). This naturally meets the closure requirement (Section 2.3.2).

No restrictions were placed upon which primitives could be used by which operation. That is the terminal and function sets were identical for each of the five trees. Apart from differences caused by primitives having different numbers of arguments, each primitive was equally likely to be used in the initial random population.

4.3.1 Indexed Memory

63 integer memory cells (numbered $-31 \ldots 31$) were available (see Section 3.4 for a discussion of indexed memory). This is more than sufficient for a stack of no more than ten integers. The symmetric addressing range allows evolving stacks to implement either a push-up or a push-down strategy and avoids some bias towards one or other. (As Figures 4.4 to 4.11 show solutions using both implementations were evolved).

read's and write's first argument specifies which of the 63 cells to use. If it yields an illegal value (i.e. outside the legal range $-31 \ldots 31$) fitness testing of the trial program is aborted. There are several other strategies that may be adopted:

1. Reduce the range of integer values to just those that are legal memory addresses. This means changing the closure so that every function returns reduced integer values. In particular the arithmetic operators would have to ensure their output remained within the reduced range. This approach has been adopted by both Teller [Teller, 1994a, page 202] and Andre [Andre, 1995b].

2. Define behaviour for read and write following an address error. This could be to coerce the address to be legal, e.g. using modulus, or to discard the data to be stored and provide a default value when reading.

3. Increase the range of legal memory addresses to the range of legal integers.

4. Allow more than one type in the evolving programs; 32-bit integers for data values and contents of memory cells and a restricted integer for memory addressing.

One of the motivations for studying the evolution of data structures is to investigate how GP can handle software engineering problems. A frequent problem is range checking or more particularly what happens when an index is used outside its valid range. Therefore options 1. and 3. were rejected (even with virtual memory 3. would not be feasible with 32-bit integers, but might be feasible with 16-bit integers). In this chapter the unsophisticated option of stopping the program was used, however in later chapters option 2. is investigated.

Strongly typed GP [Montana, 1995] is a relatively immature field so option 4. was rejected as it might have distracted from the primary interest – the evolution of data structures.

4.3.2 Register

In addition to the addressable memory a single auxiliary variable "aux" was provided which, like each indexed memory cell, is capable of storing a single 32-bit signed integer. The motivation for including it and the primitives that manipulate it was that it could be used as a stack pointer, holding addresses to be used with the index memory. However, as with all the other primitives, the GP is not forced to use it in any particular way or even use it at all.

There are four associated primitives:

1. aux, which evaluates to its current value.

2. inc_aux, which increases the current value by one and returns the new value.

3. dec_aux, which decreases the current value by one and returns the new value.

4. write_Aux, which evaluates its argument and sets aux to this value. It behaves like write in that it returns the original value of aux rather than the new one, cf. Section 3.4. Later chapters use the simpler Set_Aux functions, which return the new value.

4.4   FITNESS FUNCTION

The fitness of each individual program is evaluated by calling its constituent operations (i.e. the trees: makenull, top, pop, push and empty) in a series of test sequences and comparing the result they return with the anticipated result. If they are the same the individual's fitness score is incremented. Calling the operation and the subsequent comparison is known as a fitness test. NB all testing is **black box**, no information about the program's internal behaviour such as use of memory is used. However programs which read or write outside the available memory are heavily penalised because their testing stops immediately. They retain their current fitness score but are not tested further and so can't increase their fitness.

The two operations makenull and push do not return an answer. Since we don't have a "correct" implementation to measure them against, they can only be tested indirectly by seeing if the other operations work correctly when called after them. They are both scored as if they had returned the correct result, which means each makenull or push operation successfully completed (i.e. without memory bound error) increments the program's score. This is useful because it means in general makenull and push operations which don't violate the memory bounds have better scores than those that do.

The empty operation returns either true or false (cf. Table 4.1) however, like the other four operations, it is composed of signed integer functions and terminals and the evolved code returns a signed integer. Therefore their answer is converted to a boolean value before fitness checks are performed ([Koza, 1992, page 134] calls the output interface code a *wrapper*). The wrapper chosen splits the space of signed integers approximately in half, with positive numbers being taken to mean true and the rest as false (see Table 4.2. We follow [Koza, 1992, page 137] and summarise the key features of each GP problem in a table with a format similar to Table 4.2. These are referred to as the *tableau* for the problem). Although intended to be unbiased, because of the strong relationship between a stack pointer and whether the stack is empty or not, it is possible this choice lead to a bias in favour of stacks adopting a push-down strategy. If a simple push-down stack starts at zero then a non-empty stack will have a negative stack pointer. Although more push-down stacks than push-up stacks were

Table 4.3. Number of each the five stack operations in the four test sequences which form the fitness test case for the stack problem.

Test Sequence	makenull	top	pop	push	empty	Totals
1	2	2	14	14	8	40
2	14	3	2	13	8	40
3	6	2	7	12	13	40
4	3	18	5	8	6	40
Totals	25	25	28	47	35	160

evolved, the difference can be explained by random fluctuation, i.e. the difference is not statistically significant.

As was explained in Section 4.1, the stack is defined to exclude error checks and so the fitness test case was designed to avoid causing the logical errors that these checks would trap. I.e. it never caused stack over flow or under flow, top is never called when the stack should be empty and the stack is always initialised by makenull before any other operation is used.

All storage, i.e. the indexed memory and aux, is initialized to zero before each test sequence is started. This ensures all potential inputs are in a known state before testing begins, this means the test case may be re-run and the same result reached and also prevents "leakage" of information from one member of the population to any other. It was felt initializing at the start of each test sequence, i.e. a total of four times per program tested, might help discriminate between programs early in the evolutionary process as this gives imperfect programs three more tries to pass some of the tests from a clean background state. ([Spector and Luke, 1996] avoids re-initialising memory between fitness testing of individuals and so information may pass between them apart from by inheritance. [Spector and Luke, 1996] call this "cultural" transmission of information. They present examples where it is beneficial, but on [page 213] they note that on some variations of their problems cultural transmission is not beneficial).

4.4.1 Test Case

The fitness of each trial stack program was determined using the same fixed test case for all trial programs, cf. Section 2.3.2. The test case comprised four fixed test sequences each of which called 40 operations and checked the value returned. The four test sequences contain different proportions of each of the five operations. For example, the second test sequence was designed to test makenull by containing a large number of makenull and push calls (see Table 4.3).

Although the stack was defined to operate with stacks of up to ten integers, as Table 4.4 shows, it was not necessary for the fitness test case to cover the deeper stacks. In fact the fitness function tested only as far as depths of four items.

The integer data values pushed onto the stack (i.e. the values of arg1) were generated at random uniformly in the range $-1000 \ldots 999$. The 47 actual values used are given in Table 4.5.

Table 4.4. Number of each the five stack operations used in the fitness test case at each depth in the stack.

Stack length	makenull	top	pop	push	empty	Totals
undefined	4					4
0	11			27	15	53
1	5	6	14	15	9	49
2	5	7	9	3	5	29
3		6	3	2	2	13
4		6	2		4	12
5–10						0
Totals	25	25	28	47	35	160

Table 4.5. Data values pushed onto the stack in each of the four test sequences which form the fitness test case for the stack problem.

Seq	Values pushed	No.
1	658 544 923 -508 709 560 816 810 149 -179 -328 1 490 -451	14
2	-23 -365 814 -464 -885 -702 123 -248 -284 828 177 635 -588	13
3	557 113 942 -918 -233 616 223 -95 238 -634 -262 590	12
4	217 539 496 -377 -848 -239 -233 331	8

4.5 PARAMETERS

The default values for parameters given in Section D.3 were used except for, the population size, the maximum program length and the length of each run (101 generation equivalents, cf. Table 4.2). In these experiments a homogeneous population of 1,000 trial solutions was chosen, which proved to be adequate.

Each genetic program is stored in a fixed length prefix/jump-table (cf. Section D.1). The five program trees (one for each operation) are stored sequentially within the table. There are no restrictions on each tree's size, however their combined lengths must sum to no more than the size of the jump-table. The jump-table (and so the maximum program size) was chosen to be 250. This is five times the GP-QUICK (cf. Section D.3) default of 50, which itself is several times more than sufficient to code each of the five operations. Figures 4.15 and 4.16 show individual programs within the population were typically much shorter than this and so its effects, in these experiments, can be neglected. In 50 of the 60 runs conducted, including all successful runs, this limit had no effect at all. Of the remaining ten runs, typically there was no effect until after generation 90. Even in the run with largest number of effected crossovers, there was no effect before generation 44, when a few crossovers per generation reached the limit. This rose to a maximum of 2% of crossovers in generation 96.

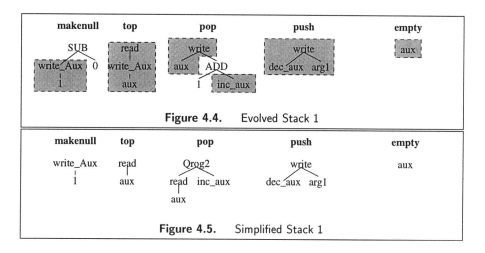

Figure 4.4.   Evolved Stack 1

makenull	top	pop	push	empty
write_Aux	read	Qrog2	write	aux
1	aux	read inc_aux	dec_aux arg1	
		aux		

Figure 4.5.   Simplified Stack 1

4.6   RESULTS

With the above parameters four runs, in a group of 60, produced successful individuals. The first program, from each successful run, that passed all 160 fitness test cases are shown in Figures 4.4 to 4.11. As was expected each successful program is a different solution to the problem of passing the test cases. Although coded differently, the first three adopted the same strategy of using aux as a stack pointer for a push-down stack with makenull initialising aux to one. The fourth also uses aux as a stack pointer but initialises it to minus one and adopts a push-up strategy.

In two respects the evolved solutions are better than might have been anticipated. Firstly, in all cases they not only pass all the fitness test cases but analysis of their code shows they are general solutions to the problem defined in Section 4.1. That is they would pass any set of tests that are consistent with the problem.

Secondly, the definition in Section 4.1 specifically limited the operation of the stack to a depth of ten, however all the solutions correctly implement a general stack (within the limits of the available memory). That is, given sufficient memory, each implements an integer stack of any size. So not only has genetic programming found solutions but it has been able to generalise from the limited information in the fitness tests.

Each program contains redundant code, i.e. code that can be removed yielding a shorter program but with the same functionality. The essential code is shown within the shaded boxes in Figures 4.4, 4.6, 4.8 and 4.10. The equivalent simplified code is given in Figures 4.5, 4.7, 4.9 and 4.11 (QROG2 is defined on page 85).

As has already been mentioned only four of the 60 runs yielded solutions. The fitness of the best solution found by each run is plotted by the frequency histogram in Figure 4.12. This shows that most runs produced partial solutions which pass about 130 of the 160 fitness tests. Figures 4.13 and 4.14 show that typically the highest fitness score was found by generation 6 and no further improvement in the best score was made before the end of the run, 94 generations later. They also show the population as a whole rapidly converges to the best value with a few individuals having very low fitness values.

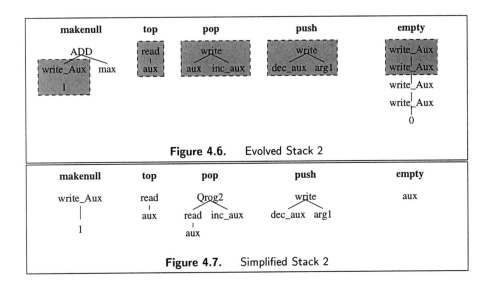

Figure 4.6.   Evolved Stack 2

Figure 4.7.   Simplified Stack 2

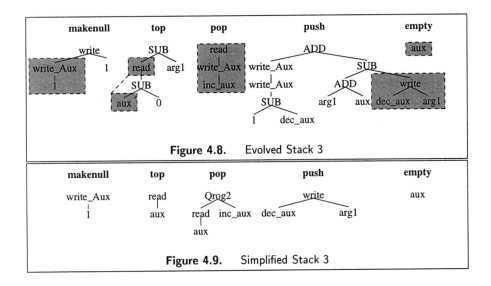

Figure 4.8.   Evolved Stack 3

Figure 4.9.   Simplified Stack 3

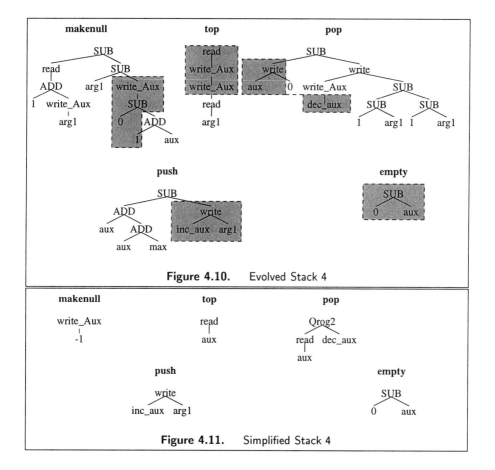

Figure 4.10.   Evolved Stack 4

Figure 4.11.   Simplified Stack 4

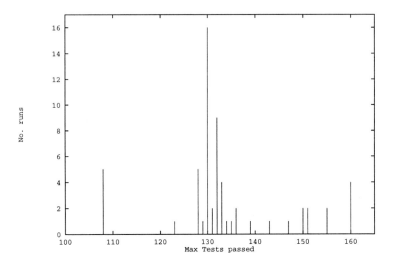

Figure 4.12.   Distribution of maximum fitness found by 60 runs of the stack problem

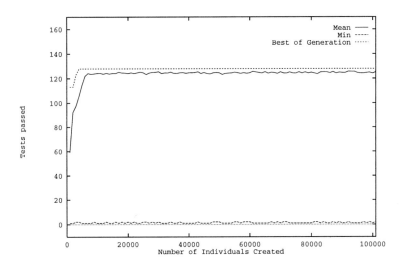

Figure 4.13.   Evolution of fitness in a typical stack run.

A typical imperfect evolved strategy is to store only one item at a fixed location. Further improvement from this partial solution appears to be difficult, perhaps due to loss of genetic diversity (i.e. functions, terminals or key blocks of functions and terminals) exacerbated by the relatively small population size or the effects of "neutral crossover", i.e. crossovers whose offspring has identical fitness to its parents (cf. Chapter 8).

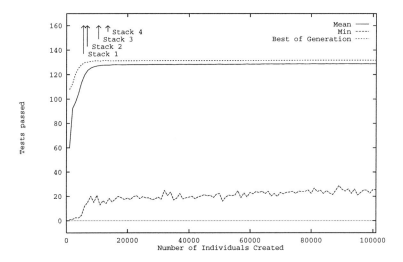

Figure 4.14.   Evolution of fitness, means of 60 stack runs. The four solutions to the stack problem are also shown.

4.6.1   *Effort Required to Find a General Stack*

Following [Koza, 1992, page 194] $P(M, i)$ denotes the probability of a solution being found at generation i when using a population of size M. Therefore the probability of not finding a solution is $1 - P(M, i)$. In R independent runs, the chance of finding no solutions is $\left[1 - P(M, i)\right]^R$. Therefore the chance of finding one or more solutions is $1 - \left[1 - P(M, i)\right]^R$. Requiring to be assured (to within probability ϵ) of obtaining at least one solution and rearranging yields the number of GP runs required:

$$1 - \left[1 - P(M, i)\right]^R \geq 1 - \epsilon$$
$$\left[1 - P(M, i)\right]^R \leq \epsilon$$
$$R \log\left(\left[1 - P(M, i)\right]\right) \leq \log \epsilon$$
$$R = \left\lceil \frac{\log \epsilon}{\log(1 - P(M, i))} \right\rceil \tag{4.1}$$

Given that 4 out of 60 runs succeeded by generation 14, the maximum likelihood estimate of $P(1000, 14)$ is 4/60, i.e. 1/15. Substituting $\epsilon = 0.01$ and $P(1000, 14) = 1/15$ yields 67. I.e. 67 independent runs, with each generating up to 14,000 trial solutions, will (assuming our estimate of the probability of solution is correct) ensure that the chance of producing at least one solution is better than 99%. This would require a total of up to $14,000 \times 67 = 938,000$ trial programs to be tested.

For the sake of comparison, a large number of random programs were generated, using the same mechanisms as the GP, and tested against the same fitness tests. A total of 49,000,000 randomly produced programs were tested, none passed all of the tests.

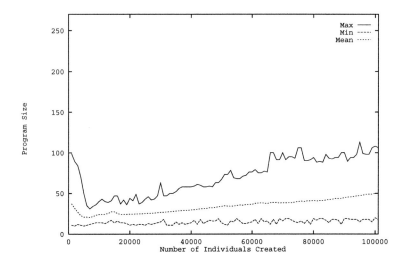

Figure 4.15.   Evolution of program size in a typical stack run.

4.6.2   Evolution of Program Size

Figures 4.15 and 4.16 show a marked and rapid fall in program size initially coincident with finding improved solutions. (A program's size is the number of nodes within it, i.e. the number of functions plus the number of terminals). However once the GP stops finding improved solutions the programs within the population become longer and this growth continues as the population evolves.

The long term growth in program size was expected as similar effects (variously called "fluff", "bloat" and "introns") have been widely reported in other GP work [Angeline, 1994, page 84], [Nordin et al., 1996]. (Ways of using the fitness function to control bloat are described in Section 2.4.2). However in one extended run of the Boolean 6-multiplexor problem [Koza, 1992, page 617] also reports such growth but says the program size stabilizes after generation 50. The following section analyses the reasons for this.

Evolution of Size in the Boolean 6-Multiplexor Problem.   The anomalous behaviour of program size of the Boolean 6-multiplexor may be explained by the fact that a limit on the tree height of 17 was enforced. At first sight this would not appear to be unduly restrictive but if we consider the sizes of various random trees for this problem we see a tree height limit can have a significant impact on program size.

Two of the functions used in the 6-multiplexor problem take two arguments, one takes three and the fourth takes one. Thus the size of a tree of the maximum height will be between the size of a program containing functions with only one argument and that of a tree where every function has three arguments, i.e. between 17 and $\frac{1}{2}(3^{17} - 1) = 64,570,081$. In addition to the four functions there are six terminals, thus a tree composed of randomly selected primitives will have on average $0 \times 6/10 +$

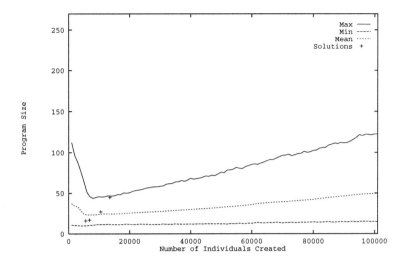

Figure 4.16. Evolution of program size, means of 60 stack runs. The lengths of the four solutions to the stack problem are also shown.

$1/10 + 2 \times 2/10 + 3 \times 1/10 = 0.7$ nodes above each node in the lower level. As this is less than one a random tree will be short (so as an approximation the maximum tree height can be neglected) and will contain about $\frac{1}{1-0.7} = 3\frac{1}{3}$ nodes. If we consider a tree of maximum height then it must contain at least one chain of 16 functions. If this is composed of randomly selected functions then each node within it will have on average $1/4 + 2 \times 2/4 + 3 \times 1/4 = 2$ nodes above it. One of these will continue the chain and the remainder will start new trees. If the new trees are composed of randomly selected primitives they will on average also contain about $3\frac{1}{3}$ nodes. Thus such a tree will on average contain about $16 \times ((2-1) \times 3\frac{1}{3} + 1) + 1 = 70\frac{1}{3}$ nodes. That is on average a tree of maximum height composed of randomly selected primitives will contain about 70 nodes.

While the above analysis assumes random trees which is highly unrealistic, it does highlight the importance of low numbers of branches per function node and the way this may cause even small trees to be unexpectedly tall. Returning to [Koza, 1992, pages 617–618] we see that Figure 25.23 and the example program presented also give some weight to the argument that the tree height limit is constraining growth of program size. Figure 25.23 shows the population mean of the program size in one run of the 6-multiplexor problem lying near 110 from generation 50 to 200. This is close to the value of 70 we would expect if the population was composed of random trees whose growth was only restricted by the tree height limit. Secondly the height of the example large program (242 nodes) is 14, i.e. only three short of the maximum tree height.

Bloat in Variable Length Representations.   Once the GP has stopped finding improved solutions, the best an individual can do is to produce offspring with the same fitness as itself. [Angeline, 1994], [Nordin et al., 1996] etc. suggest that this explains why programs tend to get bigger; programs are bigger than others with the same fitness because they contain more "junk code" or "introns", i.e. code which, although it may be executed, has no impact on the program's fitness. Crossover points are chosen at random, so the larger a portion of code is the more likely it is to be chosen as a crossover point. [Nordin et al., 1996] suggests this leads to an "implicit parsimony pressure" for fitness affecting parts of programs to be as small as possible (and so less likely to be the target for crossover and so be disrupted by it, i.e. the offspring not being as fit as its parents) and for introns to occupy as much space in the program as possible. This explanation assumes that on average non-fitness affecting code will continue to have no impact on fitness after it has been changed by crossover.

A slightly more general way of looking at bloat is in general there are many more ways to code long programs which have a particular fitness than short programs. Since they have the same fitness, fitness selection does not guide the search and the search is random. In a random search we expect to find solutions which occur often in preference to those that are rare. Thus growth of program size, once discovery of higher fitness individuals has slowed or stopped, can be explained as due to GP preferentially discovering short and therefore rare solutions initially followed by random discovery of longer and more common ways of expressing the same solution with consequent growth of program size in the population. In general, unless there is some factor which prefers shorter solutions, we would expect bloat to occur in all stochastic search techniques which use a variable length representation.

Initial Fall in Program Size.   While growth in program size is a common, the initial reduction was unexpected (cf. Figures 4.15 and 4.16). A possible explanation for the fall is that initially shorter programs are fitter but, as Figures 4.17 and 4.18 show there is little correlation between an initial program's fitness and its size. Instead program size falls because initially crossover produces fitter programs which are shorter than average. This may be because it is easier for shorter programs to be more general (and so fitter) or because they are closer to the length of actual solutions found. Indeed it is possible that better performance might be achieved by starting with an initial population composed of shorter programs.

4.7 SUMMARY

This chapter (which was published, in part, in [Langdon, 1995b]) shows that genetic programming can automatically synthesise general implementations of an integer stack from randomly addressable memory when guided only by a small number of fixed test cases which examine the external behaviour of trial solutions, i.e. without consideration of how they try to implement a stack. Whilst [Andre, 1995b] has demonstrated two communicating programs co-evolving, the stack problem (excluding work described in later chapters) was unique in requiring the co-evolution of five independent operations to solve it ([Bruce, 1996] also uses five independent operations). As with Andre's approach, the GP architecture used treats each separate individual within the population as a multi-part program, each part operating and evolving independently but

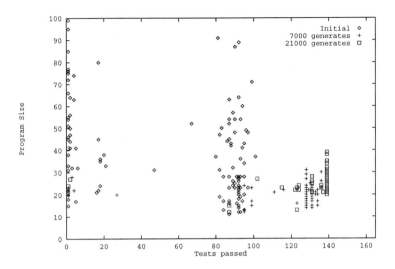

Figure 4.17. Fitness v. Program Size, Typical stack run. (To improve presentation only extrema and 10% of the data are plotted).

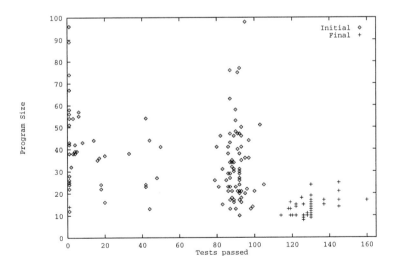

Figure 4.18. Fitness v. Program Size, Stack 2. (To improve presentation only extrema and 10% of the data are plotted).

communicating via shared memory and co-evolving to solve the problem by working together.

The relative ease with which GP solved the stack problem may be due to the decision to provide stack pointer manipulation primitives. Certainly experience with more complex data structures indicates the importance of higher level index operations, even though these can in theory be fabricated from lower level primitives (cf. Section 5.10).

There are many ways to implement a program which will pass the test cases. If we regard automatic programming as a search process, then the existence of multiple implementations means there are multiple solutions (or optima) in the search space. In a random search this would make the search easier. However the requirement for co-operation means multiple implementation might make the search harder.

1. The five operations are initially created independently of each other, so multiple possible implementations reduce the chance of the operations in a single individual being compatible with each other.

2. It is reasonable to speculate that crossover between individuals which use incompatible implementations will be less likely to lead to superior offspring.

These may be contributory factors to the tendency for GP population to become trapped at suboptimal solutions. The bulk of the population converging to a partial solution found early in the run and little or no improvement in fitness occurring subsequently.

On this problem, genetic programming has been shown to be more successful than random search, which has never produced a program that passed all the fitness test cases, let alone a general one.

From an information theory perspective, genetic programming has converted the information held in the test cases (the specification) into the information held in a program (the solution). The information content of test cases is about 886.9 bits, whereas that of the solutions (including redundant code) is much less, e.g. 57.4 bits for stack 1. That is the GP has lost information, however this is exactly what we want it to do! We want the solutions to be more general than the test cases. Not only has GP produced less specific (i.e. containing less information) programs it has chosen the correct information to retain from which it has produced correct general solutions. Since this has been done without explicit guidance, we can conclude that, in this case, GP has some correct implicit bias (possibly via the function and terminal sets). However it seems reasonable to speculate that similar implicit biases will apply to other programming problems and so we may hope GP will evolve other general solutions to specific test cases.

5 EVOLVING A QUEUE

Like the stack, the queue is an important data structure based upon the list data model. A common use of queues is to hold data requiring processing until a service provider is able to process it. Data for each new request enters the queue at its rear and waits until data in front of it has been processed and removed from the front of the queue. When it reaches the front of the queue, it too is processed and removed from the front queue. Queues are also known as "FIFO" (First-In First-Out) lists [Aho and Ullman, 1995, page 318].

This chapter shows that genetic programming can automatically synthesise a queue of integer values from randomly addressable memory. In contrast to the stack, when GP was guided by a fitness function that considers only the behaviour of the queue and did not consider its implementation at all, resource hungry solutions were evolved. Whilst these may be considered "correct" they are not practical. However GP can evolve practical implementations when the fitness function includes consideration of the resources used. As with the stack, apart from resources consumed, evolution was not guided by considering the implementation used.

5.1 PROBLEM STATEMENT

The definition of a queue is given in Table 5.1. Note the use of the function "addone". Table 5.1 is analogous to the definition of a stack given in Table 4.1 on page 63. A circular buffer implementation of a queue is shown in Figure 5.1. As with the stack (Section 4.1), the definition given in [Aho et al., 1987] was simplified to reduce the complexity of the fitness testing by removing the checks for underflow and overflow.

Table 5.1.   Pseudo Code Definition of the Five Queue Operations

Operation	Code		Comment
addone (i)	addone	:= (i + 1) % maxlength;	cyclic increment function
makenull	head	:= 0;	initialise queue
	tail	:= maxlength − 1;	
empty	empty	:= (addone (tail) = head);	is queue empty?
front	front	:= queue[head];	front of queue
enqueue(x)	tail	:= addone (tail);	add x to queue
	queue[tail] := x;		
dequeue	dequeue	:= queue[head];	return front
	head	:= addone (head);	and remove it

Such checks are sometimes included to safely handle coding or user errors however they are not part of the essential operation of a queue [Aho and Ullman, 1995, page 318].

As in Chapter 4, the correctness of each trial solution is established using the values returned by the operations and in the definition given in [Aho et al., 1987] only two of the five operations return values. As in Section 4.1, it was felt that not being able to directly check in any way the correctness of three of the operations was possibly too much and so the definition of dequeue (cf. pop) requires it to return the current front of the queue as well as removing it. This alternative definition [Aho and Ullman, 1995, page 318] allows at least some level of correctness of dequeue to be directly assessed.

Note that the queue problem, like the stack, requires the GP to evolve five operations so together they implement an abstract data type. That is, again we are requiring the GP to simultaneously co-evolve five operations.

A queue can be implemented in at least three fundamentally different ways, packed array (where the data is moved from the rear to the front of the array), linked list and circular buffer (see Figure 5.1). There are many possible implementations of each of these. As with the stack, a trial solution's fitness is not assessed by how well its implementation conforms to any specific implementation. Instead evolution, guided by how well the operations work together, must find an implementation which each operation is compatible with. Whilst the GP is free to choose to use any implementation of any of the three different types, the index primitives (Section 5.9) were included specifically for circular queue implementations.

From a practical point of view any implementation of a queue data type will have some restriction on the amount of data it can contain. maxlength (cf. Table 5.1) was chosen to have the same value as in the stack experiments, i.e. ten. However in order to allow the evolution of circular implementations of a queues (like that given in [Aho et al., 1987]) which require a gap between the head and tail of the queue, the number of items in the queue is limited to nine, i.e. ten less one for the gap. The presence of this gap shows there is something in the queue, whilst its absence indicates the queue is empty (rather than all available slots are used).

Makenull

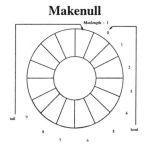

Empty

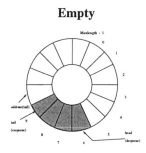

Front

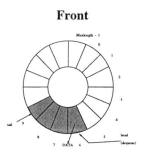

Initialise queue to empty by setting tail to one slot before head.

If tail is one slot before head then the queue is empty. In this example the queue contains four items, so Empty will return false.

Read the data item at the front of the queue from the cell pointed to by head.

Enqueue

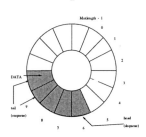

Dequeue

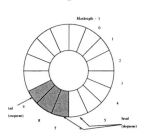

Put a new data value onto rear of the queue by increasing tail by one (and wrapping round if needbe) and then writing the new value into the cell tail now points to.

Read the front of the queue from the cell pointed to by head and then remove it by increasing head by one (and wrapping round if needbe).

Figure 5.1. Circular Implementation of queues. (Cells containing data are shaded)

5.2   ARCHITECTURE

The multi-tree architecture and multi-tree crossover described in Section 3.6 was chosen as this allows each individual within the population to simultaneously implement trial solutions to each of the five operations that form the complete queue program. All the experiments reported in this chapter use Automatically Defined Functions (ADFs, see Section 2.3.2). Each ADF is represented by an additional tree following the five operation trees.

5.3   CHOICE OF PRIMITIVES

The experiments described in this chapter used different combinations of primitives. The details are given in Tables 5.4, 5.5, 5.7 and 5.10. The reasons for the differences between each experiment are discussed later with each experiment, however all the primitives used in this chapter are described in this section.

The choice of which primitives are available to the GP follows the reasoning of the stack problem (Section 4.3) i.e. primitives like those a human programmer might use to implement a queue were chosen. This ensures a solution can be coded using the available primitives and, as some constructs are useful to human programmers, it was expected that corresponding primitives might be useful to the GP. For example primitives were included that aid maintenance of pointers to the front and rear of the queue, although their functionality could in principle be evolved using combinations of the other primitives.

The following primitives were used in the experiments in this chapter:

- arg1, the value to be added to the end of the queue or the argument of the ADF. When arg1 is used by any of the operations except enqueue it has the value zero. Evolving programs can read arg1 but they can not change it.

- arithmetic operators + and − and the "protected" modulus operator, mod. mod is included to support the manipulation of pointers required by a circular buffer (cf. function addone in Table 5.1).

  In mathematical terms the modulus of a number modulo zero is not defined and often computer implementations of the modulus operator have ill defined behaviour or create run time exceptions if the divisor is zero. To avoid this we follow common GP practice and insist that the modulus function be able to accept any value (i.e. including zero, this is known as "closure", see Section 2.3.2) and use a "protected" modulus function which returns a well defined legal value for every legal input.

  The protected modulus function, mod, returns the first argument modulo the second unless the second is zero, in which case it returns value of first argument.

  In the C programming language, which was used to implement these experiments, the behaviour of the modulus operator (%) with negative arguments is implementation dependent [Kernighan and Ritchie, 1988, page 205]. It is important that the results of these experiments should be reproducible which requires the behaviour of all primitives to be known, therefore the behaviour of mod is defined for negative inputs. Unless the divisor is zero, mod is defined to yield a non-negative result no

Table 5.2.   Implementation of "Protected" Modulus Function

a = *first argument*; b = **abs** (*second argument*); **if** (b = 0)   **return** a; **else**   **return** (a % b + b) % b;

matter what sign its arguments have. This is implemented by using the absolute value of the divisor (see Table 5.2). Other protected modulus function have been used [Koza, 1992, page 400] and [Jannink, 1994].

- constants 0, 1 and max (which has the value ten).

- indexed memory functions read and write.

- primitives to help maintain pointers; aux1, aux2, aux3, Inc_Aux1, Inc_Aux2, Inc_Aux3, Dec_Aux1, Dec_Aux2, Dec_Aux3, Set_Aux1, Set_Aux2, Set_Aux3, MInc1, MInc2, and MInc3 (Implementation of MInc$n$ given in Table 5.3).

- Functions that simply link subtrees together; PROG2 evaluates both its arguments and returns the value of the second, whilst QROG2 evaluates its two arguments but returns the value of the first.

- The Adf1 primitive provides the mechanism for calling the Automatically Defined Function (see Sections 2.3.2 and 5.6).

In some experiments it is possible for one operation to call another as a function. When the called operation is finished, execution control returns to the calling operation rather than terminating the evolved program as it would normally do. The mechanism used to implement this is the same as that used to implement ADFs. The corresponding primitives have the same name as the operation (except the first letter is capitalised). Thus the Front terminal (front takes no arguments) provides the means for other operations to use the front operation. (We have adopted the convention of using the actual names of the primitives and trees used in the code, including the case of the letters. The code uses the convention that the names of primitives which invoke other operations contain only lowercase letters, while the names of the corresponding program tree are capitalised).

Once again all of the above function accept 32-bit signed integers and the both the functions and terminals yield 32-bit signed integers.

In the first experiments all primitives were used in all trees but in later ones the syntax was made more sophisticated allowing each tree (i.e. operation or ADF) to have its own set of primitives. As in all the experiments in this book, apart from differences caused by primitives having different numbers of arguments, if a primitive is included in the syntax for a particular tree, it is as likely as any other legal primitive to be used in that tree in the initial random population.

5.3.1   Indexed Memory

The memory structure used for the stack was retained (cf. Sections 3.4 and 4.3.1) which provides 63 32-bit signed integer memory cells (numbered $-31\ldots31$). The symmetric addressing range allows the GP additional implementation freedom. Array and circular buffer implementations for such a queue are relatively memory efficient (requiring n and $n+1$ memory cells respectively) and so easily fit into the 63 cells available. A linked list implementation requires $2n$ or $3n$ (if a double link chain is used). Thus 63 cells is more than sufficient for all of the common implementations of a queue of up to nine integers.

As Section 5.7 will describe, memory hungry partial solutions can arise. One of the ways used to discourage these was to reduce the memory available so that such partial solutions reach the limit of the available memory earlier. This allows evolution to explore other solutions when it might otherwise have been trapped by the population converging to a memory hungry partial solution. In the final experiments in this chapter (Section 5.10) the memory was reduced to $-15\ldots15$. Although there is still sufficient memory for linked list implementations, they were not observed in any of these experiments.

In the first experiments presented in this chapter, attempts to access, via read or write, memory cells outside the legal range cause fitness testing to stop, as described in Section 4.4. In later experiments, fitness testing was allowed to continue on addressing errors by write discarding the data to be stored (in which case it returns zero) and providing a default value of zero when reading from an illegal address.

In the initial population the first argument of read and write (like all functions' arguments) is random code and so will yield a random value. In practice this is likely to be near zero but could be anything. If it is outside the range $-31\ldots31$ then fitness testing will stop and the program containing the read or write will probably have a low fitness. If a function consistently causes programs containing it to have below average fitness the number of times the function appears in the population will fall, eventually being removed entirely (see Section 8.1 for a discussion of Price's theorem). It was felt that this might be happening and so be the cause of poor GP performance. However if read and write are allowed to continue following a memory addressing error (i.e. first argument > 31 or < -31) the current test may fail but the program will get the opportunity of running other tests which it may pass. Thus the negative impact of random code on read and write may be reduced allowing the population to retain them for longer, which may enable evolution to provide useful arguments for them. As was expected, programs evolved which rely on how memory addressing errors are dealt with (e.g. Figure 5.9).

5.3.2   Registers

In addition to the addressable memory two or three auxiliary variables, "auxn", were provided. The motivation for including them and the primitives that manipulate them was that they could be used as pointers, holding addresses to be used with the index memory. However, as with all the other primitives, the GP is not forced to use them in any particular way or even use them at all.

Table 5.3.   Implementation of Modulo Increment Terminals

aux$n$++;
aux$n$ = mod(aux$n$, 10);   (NB max = 10)
return aux$n$;

There are five primitives associated with each variable (however not all five are used in all experiments):

1. aux$n$, which evaluates to the current value of register n.

2. Inc_Aux$n$, which increases the current value of register n by one and returns its new value.

3. Dec_Aux$n$, which decreases the current value by one and returns the new value.

4. Set_Aux$n$, which evaluates its argument and sets register n to this value. Unlike write_Aux (cf. Section 4.3.2) it returns the new value.

   This change was made after it was noted that the GP could exploit the implicit storage in the write_Aux$n$ primitives, to ease the formation of "shuffler" type solutions (Section 5.8).

5. MInc$n$, Modulus Increment, sets register n to one plus its current value reduced modulo max and returns its new value (see Table 5.3).

   A key ingredient to successfully evolving circular buffer implementations of queue data structures seems to be the manipulation of pointers to the two access points for the data structure, i.e. the front and back. Experiments in Section 5.9 included the MInc$n$ terminals to provide this functionality. In other experiments the GP was required to evolve this functionality from the other primitives.

5.4 FITNESS FUNCTIONS

The fitness of each individual program is evaluated by calling its constituent operations (i.e. the trees: makenull, front, dequeue, enqueue and empty) in a series of test sequences and comparing the result they return with the anticipated result. Only if they are the same is the individual's fitness increased. NB whilst all testing is **black box** with no information about the program's internal implementation being used, following the discovery of memory hungry solutions (Section 5.7) the fitness function was modified to include penalties for excessive resource (i.e. memory) usage and we show that memory efficient implementations can be evolved (see Sections 5.8, 5.9 and 5.10.5).

The two operations makenull and enqueue do not return an answer. As with the stack makenull and push operations, they can only be tested indirectly by seeing if the other operations work correctly when called after them. They are both scored as if they had returned the correct result.

As with the empty operation in the stack data structure, the empty operation returns either true or false (cf. Table 5.1) however, like the other four operations, it is composed of signed integer functions and terminals and the evolved code returns a signed integer. Therefore a wrapper is used to convert the signed integer to a boolean value before fitness checks are performed.   The wrapper converts a zero value to true and all other values to false. The evolved code can compare two values using subtraction (no explicit comparison operators are provided). If they are equal, subtracting them yields zero which the wrapper converts to true. This wrapper also avoids the potential bias in the wrapper used with the empty stack operation (Section 4.4).

As was explained in Section 5.1, the queue is defined to exclude error checks and so the fitness test case is designed to avoid causing the logical errors that these checks would trap. I.e. they never try to enqueue more than nine integers, never uses dequeue or front when the queue should be empty and the data structure is always initialised by makenull before any other operation is called. All storage (i.e. the indexed memory and the auxiliary registers) is initialized to zero before each test sequence is started.

Initially the fitness function was identical to that used for the stack, with the supposition of enqueue for push etc. (cf. Section 4.4). However unlike the stack, various programs were evolved which passed the whole test case but did not correctly implement a FIFO (First-In First-Out) list. As these were produced the fitness test case was changed, to include more tests, different test orders and to enqueue different numbers.

Initially the fitness function, like the stack, was simply the sum of the number of tests passed. Different fitness scalings were tried, which gave less weight to "easy" tests. In the experiments in Sections 5.7 and 5.8, makenull and enqueue tests are equivalent to only 5% of dequeue, front and empty tests. In later experiments a single fitness value for each program was replaced by "Pareto" scoring (See Sections 3.9 and 5.10.1). The details of each fitness function used are described with each experiment.

5.4.1   Test Case

Initially the fitness test case, like the rest of the fitness function, was identical to that used for the stack, with the supposition of enqueue for push etc. and so the argument of enqueue was identical to that used with push (Table 4.5, page 70), i.e. an integer between -1000 and 999. As memory was initialised to zero and all enqueued data is non-zero (cf. Table 4.5) an effective test of whether a memory cell has been used or not is to see if it contains a non-zero value. In the case of the queue, partial solutions were produced which exploited this and used it to estimate whether the queue was empty or not. Such solutions could fail if tested on a queue containing the value zero. The GP found and exploited this and a few similar "holes" in the test sequences to produce high scoring individuals which solve the test case rather than the queue problem. Therefore (from Section 5.8 onwards) the test data values were changed to increase the proportion of small integers and a fifth long test sequence was added to test for memory hungry solutions.

A possible explanation for why additional measures were needed in the fitness testing of the queue that were not required with the stack is that without appropriate cursor primitives (such as MIncn), the queue is a harder problem and the absence of a solution allows the GP to explore the fitness function more fully and then exploit "holes" in it.

5.5 PARAMETERS

The default values for parameters given in Section D.3 were used except: the population size, the maximum program length, the length of each run and the use of a fine grained demic population (see Section 3.8). The values of these parameters were changed between the various experiments described in this chapter, details are given in Tables 5.4, 5.5, 5.7 and 5.10.

5.5.1 Population size

Initial runs with a population of 1,000 were very disappointing. Whilst the initial fitness function, the initial primitives used or loss of genetic diversity caused by premature convergence (i.e. when the population converges to a local optimum rather than the global optimum) may have contributed to this, it was decided to follow advice in [Kinnear, Jr., 1994c] and [Koza, 1994, page 617] and make the population as big as possible. All the queue experiments described in this chapter have a population size of 10,000.

5.5.2 Maximum Program Size

As was discussed with the stack problem (see Section 4.5) each genetic program is composed of six trees (cf. Section 5.2) which must fit into a fixed length table (cf. Section D.1). There are no restrictions on each tree's size, however their combined lengths must sum to no more than the size of the table. The table size was the same as in Chapter 4, despite having an additional tree (adf1). This is reasonable as [Koza, 1994, page 644] suggests using an ADF generally reduces the total size of the program.

As Figures 5.28 and 5.29 show individual programs within the population typically grew towards the maximum available space and so its effects can not be neglected. Section 3.1 described how the crossover operator ensures this limit is not violated.

Random queue programs are bigger on average than random stack ones (compare Figures 5.28 and 5.29 with Figures 4.15 and 4.16 (pages 76 and 77)) principally because of the higher proportion of functions with two arguments amongst the primitives (45% versus 25%, cf. Table 5.10 and Table 4.2 (page 66)). Random trees are created from the root (using the "ramped-half-and-half" method [Koza, 1992, page 93]) so the higher the number of branches (i.e. function arguments) at each level the bigger the tree will be and (when using the grow mechanism) the greater the chance of growing to another level. Thus the limit on total tree size (i.e. program length) is more of a constraint in this chapter than it was in Chapter 4. (Alternative means of creating random trees for the initial population are proposed in [Bohm and Geyer-Schulz, 1996] and [Iba, 1996b]).

[Gathercole and Ross, 1996; Langdon and Poli, 1997a] consider the impact of restrictions on program size in the case of programs consisting of a single tree and shows the standard GP crossover operator can lead to loss of diversity at the root of the tree. Whilst the analysis does not include multi-tree programs or treat in details restrictions on total program size rather than tree height, it may be the case that the restriction on total program size does cause problems in these experiments. There is some evidence that roots of trees in this chapter may converge to inappropriate primitives which the GP then has to work around to evolve operational code.

When the initial random population is created, the trees within the individual are created sequentially. As each primitive is added to the current tree the code ensures that the individual remains within the total restriction on program size. Thus the total size limit has little impact on the first trees created but as each new tree makes the total program longer, the size limit has a disproportionate effect on the last tree to be created (i.e. adf1). If as a random program is being created, its length nears the length limit, the chance of adding a terminal (rather than a function) to the program is increased to restrict the addition of new branches to the tree and thus constrain its growth. This leads to asymmetric trees. (Section 6.7 introduces a per tree restriction on program size which ensures the effects do not fall disproportionately on the last tree). The crossover operator used (Section 3.1) ensures the offspring will never exceed the total size limit and so the effect of the size limit does not fall unduly on the last tree after the creation of the initial population.

5.6 AUTOMATICALLY DEFINED FUNCTIONS

The failure of early trials without Automatically Defined Functions (ADFs) and Koza's strong advocacy of them [Koza, 1994, page 646] lead to the decision to implement ADFs within the GP-QUICK frame work (cf. Section 2.3.2).

The initial implementation was very much like that used by Koza but contained no restrictions upon the primitives that could be used within the ADF tree. I.e. each primitive could occur in each of the operations and the ADF. In Koza's ADFs the function and terminal set are usually different from those in the main tree (in his terminology, "the result producing branch"). Typically his ADFs do not have primitives that enable them to access the actual variables of the problem, instead access is indirect via the ADFs' arguments [Koza, 1994, page 75].

Subsequently the implementation was extended to allow each tree to have unique terminal and function sets. NB each operation ("result producing branch") can also have a unique set of primitives (Section 5.10).

In later experiments described in this chapter the ADF concept was extended in three ways:

1. The five operations may themselves be treated as evolving functions and be called by other operations. When they finish processing instead of causing the program to halt, control returns to the caller, which continues execution.

   This new ability was introduced because sometimes the requirements of one operation can be a subset on another's. For example front's functionality is a subset of that required of dequeue (cf. Table 5.1) and so in later experiments (Sections 5.9 and 5.10) dequeue is allowed to treat front as an ADF. Whilst this would seem intuitively reasonable, in principle it means more analysis must be performed before the problem is given to the GP. An alternative could be to use an ADF which the two operations could share. This would be more general in that it allows the operations to have common functionality, rather than one being a subset of the other but this would require the co-evolution of three program trees rather than two.

2. As the name implies, automatically defined functions are normally viewed as computing a function of their inputs which they return to their caller. However their purpose in GP is to ease the evolution of functionality, especially where it is repeatedly required. If the ADF is restricted to returning its answer but the functionality requires some variable to be updated, then code to transfer the ADF's answer to the variable must be used whenever the ADF is called.

   For example if, as part of a bigger program, we wish to evolve code that increments one of a number of variables. We would expect a parameterised ADF to be helpful. The ADF can simply increment its argument and then the ADF can be called with each variable as its argument. But if the ADF can only read its arguments, it must return the value of the variable plus one and rely on code at each point where it was called to update the correct variable with the new value.

   It is expected that generally it will be harder to evolve such multiple instance of code (which may deal with different variables and could be in different trees, and thus cannot share genetic material at crossover, Section 3.1) than if a single instance of code to update the ADF's argument, which automatically ensures the correct variable is modified, could be evolved once within the ADF.

   In traditional programming languages, this is done by passing the variable to the function by reference so the function can manipulate the variable directly. When the function is called a check is often made that the function's argument is indeed a variable and a reference for it exists. Whilst it would be possible to build such a check into GP crossover (and other genetic operators), thus ensuring only legal programs are generated, this means making a distinction between variables and constants. In normal GP there is no such distinction, all genetic material has the same type. Whilst such distinctions can be made, as discussed in Section 4.3.1, this is a field of research in its own right and would been too much of a distraction to consider as part of this work. Therefore the genome interpreter was made sufficiently robust to cope with arbitrary code as the argument of ADFs that use pass-by-reference. Should more than one variable occur in the the ADF's argument, the reference of the last is used. If there are only constants, the ADF does not try and update them.

   Instead of introducing primitives to explicitly update ADF arguments, it was decided that such ADFs should implicitly update their argument by setting it to the final value calculated by the ADF as it returns to its caller. The ADF also returns the calculated value. Whilst this is straightforward and reduces the volume of code in the ADF it means it is impossible for an ADF with more than one argument to update them independently. For our purposes this was not necessary and the implementation only allows an ADF's first argument to be passed by reference.

   Section 5.10.4 describes one case where this feature was used.

3. Syntactic and semantic restrictions on the ADF were also introduced. These are described in Section 5.10.3.

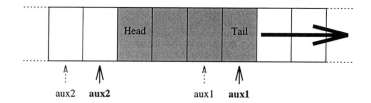

Figure 5.2. Execution of "caterpillar" program. Labels in bold indicate current values, dotted show previous values. Shaded cells hold queue. The heavy arrow indicates the general movement of the caterpillar as data items are added to the queue. As items are removed from the head of the queue it moves to the right, i.e. it acts like the tail of a caterpillar.

There has been only a limited amount of work on allowing recursion within genetic programming; [Koza, 1992, page 473], [Brave, 1996c], [Sharman and Esparcia-Alcazar, 1993], [Whigham and McKay, 1995, page 19], [Nordin and Banzhaf, 1995] and [Wong and Leung, 1996]. Recursion and GP is a big and important research topic which would be too much of a distraction from the central theme of data structures. Therefore, whilst recursive calls are implemented, recursion is not allowed in any of the experiments in this book. In Sections 5.7 and 5.8 recursion is prevented by a run time check which aborts fitness testing (in the same way as memory address errors in Section 4.3.1). In all other experiments the syntax of the evolving programs is designed to prevent recursion occurring.

5.7   EVOLVED SOLUTIONS – CATERPILLAR

In a group of 66 runs (ignoring those that aborted due to time constraints) four partial solutions were found. All four passed all 160 tests, but subsequent analysis showed that two were not general and had exploited the fact that the test case did not simultaneously enqueue more than four integers (cf. Table 4.4 page 70). I.e. they were able to pass all the tests whilst only implementing a queue of four items and so could fail if five or more items were simultaneously in the queue. However two programs (e.g. Figure 5.3) evolved which, given sufficient memory, correctly implement a queue.

These are known as "caterpillar" solutions (see Figure 5.2) because they enqueue new items in front of the last item in the queue (the caterpillar's head) thus causing the caterpillar to grow one cell. Data is dequeued from the other end of the queue (the caterpillar's tail) causing the caterpillar to shrink as its tail moves one cell, in the same direction as the head moves. The distance between the head and the tail grows as items are enqueued and decreases as they are dequeued but the caterpillar as a whole moves forward. Unfortunately to be general such a solution requires infinite memory as it always crawls forward and never wraps round as a circular implementation of a queue would. Note although adf1 is available it is not used.

See Table 5.4 for details of the primitives and parameters used in these runs. The fitness case was identical to that used with the stack, except front replaced top, dequeue pop and enqueue replaced push (cf. Tables 4.3, 4.4 and 4.5, pages 69 and 70).

Table 5.4.   Tableau for Evolving a Queue: Caterpillar solution found

Objective	To evolve a first-in first-out queue	
Architecture	Five separate trees, plus a single ADF	
Primitives	+, −, 0, 1, max, mod, arg1, aux1, Inc_Aux1, Dec_Aux1, aux2, Inc_Aux2, Dec_Aux2, read, write, Set_Aux1, Set_Aux2, Adf1	
Fitness Case	Test case as for the stack; replacing push by enqueue etc. I.e. 4 test sequences, each of 40 tests (see Tables 4.3 to 4.5)	
	Memory errors or recursive adf1 calls abort program	
Fitness Scaling	1.0 for each front, dequeue and empty test passed plus 0.05 for each makenull and enqueue test passed.	
Selection	Scalar tournament of 4	
Hits	n/a	
Wrapper	makenull	result ignored
	front	no wrapper
	dequeue	no wrapper
	enqueue	result ignored
	empty	result = 0 ⇒ TRUE, otherwise FALSE
	adf1	n/a
Parameters	Population = 10,000, G=50, program size ≤ 250	
Success Predicate	fitness ≥ 91.5999, i.e. all 160 tests passed	

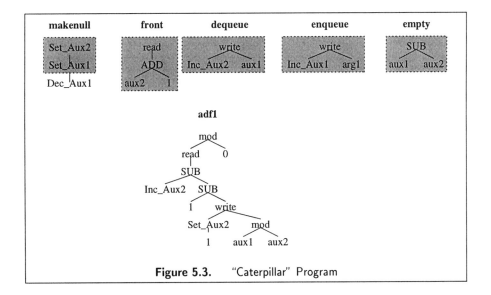

Figure 5.3.   "Caterpillar" Program

5.8 EVOLVED PROGRAMS – SHUFFLER

After the "caterpillar" runs described above, a number of changes were made with a view to discouraging caterpillar like programs and encouraging circular queue implementations (see also Table 5.5):

- The number of tests run was doubled from 160 to 320 by adding a 5th test sequence of 160 tests. This prevents caterpillar like solutions by adding sufficient enqueue operations to ensure a caterpillar will run into the end of the indexed memory.

- However after the addition of the 5th test sequence, it was noted that in some cases the population still converged to caterpillar like partial solutions. Until they ran out of memory these were fitter than the rest of the population and so dominated it but the 5th test sequence prevents them from passing all the tests.

  To discourage memory hungry partial solutions early in the population's evolution, a memory penalty was introduced. This reduced an individual's fitness by 2.0 per word of indexed memory used, above 15 words. 15 was chosen to allow for a circular queue implementation (10) and to allow the two pointers to be stored in indexed memory (2) plus a few spare.

  The penalty is calculated from the maximum memory used across the five test sequences. Memory usage need not be symmetric but it is assumed to be contiguous, i.e. the penalty is based upon the index number of the highest memory cell used minus that of the lowest cell used plus 1.

  Whilst penalising caterpillar like solutions it may also have penalised memory intensive solutions such as linked lists but (as the next section will show) it does not prevent other implementations such as packed arrays which make efficient use of memory.

- It was noted that various partial solutions exploited holes in the test sequences, such as the lack of small values (particularly zero) in the queue. Therefore the distribution of values in the queue was changed from uniform to a "tangent" distribution. A tangent distribution is produced by generating random numbers uniformly between 0 and π and taking their tangent. The answer is multiplied by a scaling factor, F. 50% of the numbers generated are expected to be in the range $-F \cdots + F$ (ignoring rounding to integers). The other 50% can be very large or very negative, see Figure 5.4. In this section F was set to 31.4, so approximately half the values enqueued correspond to legal memory indices.

In a group of 379 runs, one run found a solution which passes all 320 tests (see Figures 5.5 and 5.6. Many partial solutions (i.e. which passed many of the tests) of this type were also found and a few solutions which pass the whole test case were found by runs with slightly different parameters or primitives).

As Figure 5.5 shows, this solution correctly implements a first in first out queue of up to nine items. Unexpectedly it does this by physically moving the contents of the memory cells. I.e. as each item is removed from the queue, all the remaining items are moved (or shuffled) one place down. Thus the front of the queue is always stored in a particular location. One of the auxiliary variables is used to denote the newest item in

Table 5.5.   Tableau for Evolving a Queue: Shuffler solution found

Objective	To evolve a first-in first-out queue
Architecture	Five separate trees, plus single ADF
Primitives	+, −, 0, 1, max, mod, arg1, aux1, Inc_Aux1, Dec_Aux1, aux2, Inc_Aux2, Dec_Aux2, read, write, Set_Aux1, Set_Aux2, Adf1
Fitness Case	4 test sequences like those for the stack (see Tables 4.3 and 4.4) plus 5th test sequence of 160 tests, use of tan argument distribution (F = 31.4)
	Memory errors or recursive adf1 calls abort program
Fitness Scaling	1.0 for each front, dequeue and empty test passed, plus 0.05 for each makenull and enqueue test passed, less 2.0 for each word of indexed memory used above 15.
Selection	Scalar tournament of 4
Hits	n/a
Wrapper	makenull	result ignored
	front	no wrapper
	dequeue	no wrapper
	enqueue	result ignored
	empty	result = 0 ⇒ TRUE, otherwise FALSE
	adf1	n/a
Parameters	Population = 10,000, G=50, program size ≤ 250
Success Predicate	fitness ≥ 187, i.e. all 320 tests passed

the queue. This is also the number of items in the queue and so can be used directly by empty to decide if the queue is empty or not. The other variable is used by dequeue as scratch storage. It is always zero when not being used by dequeue. adf1 has the "trivial" use of clearing the second auxiliary variable when called by makenull.

Figure 5.6 gives the clear impression of being built up in stages. As each stage is added to dequeue it can process longer queues and so pass more tests, i.e. it has a higher fitness.

5.9   CIRCULAR BUFFER – GIVEN MODULUS INCREMENT

Whilst the "shuffler" solution is an entirely correct solution to the queue problem, it is a very rare one (in that it was found only once in 379 runs). The experiments in this section are designed to test the feasibility of evolving circular queue implementations with the fitness function when given primitives which perform the appropriate increment operations. The "modulus increment" (MInc$n$) terminals correspond to inc_aux and dec_aux used in the stack experiments (cf. Section 4.3.2). They take the value of the corresponding auxiliary variable, increase it by one, reduce it modulo max (i.e. 10) and store the new value back into the auxiliary variable (cf. Table 5.3). The complete parameters are given in Table 5.7, and Table 5.8 contains all the changes between these experiments and those that produced the Shuffler solution.

In one set of runs of the 11 runs that completed, 5 produced solutions which passed the whole test case (another 7 aborted due to run time constraints). Figure 5.9 shows

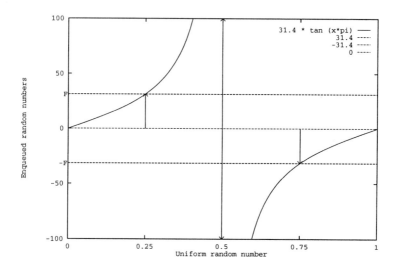

Figure 5.4. Tangent function used to generate distribution of test data values from $F\tan(\pi x)$. Where x is a uniform random number and F is a scaling coefficient.

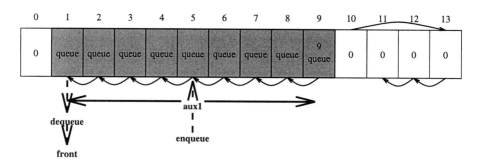

Figure 5.5. Execution of "Shuffler" program. Note data are always dequeued from cell 1 but may be enqueued into any cell $1 \ldots 9$.

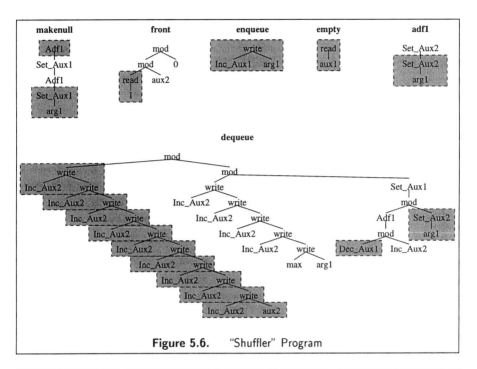

Figure 5.6.   "Shuffler" Program

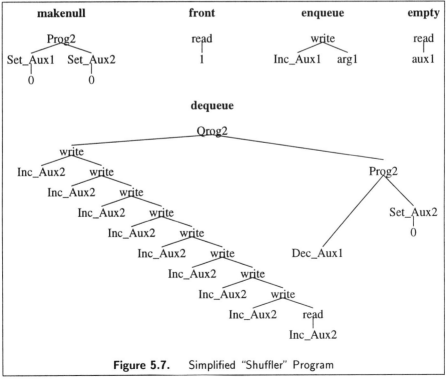

Figure 5.7.   Simplified "Shuffler" Program

Table 5.6. Number of each the five queue operations used in the fitness test case for each length of queue. (Test case used in experiments where "Modulus Increment" was provided and where it was evolved).

Queue length	makenull	front	dequeue	enqueue	empty	Totals
undefined	5					5
0	10			27	16	53
1	4	9	14	18	7	52
2	4	12	11	8	7	42
3		9	6	7	5	27
4		4	6	11		21
5		4	11	9	3	27
6		8	9	11	5	33
7		10	11	9	3	33
8		3	9	4		16
9		5	4		2	11
Totals	23	64	81	104	48	320

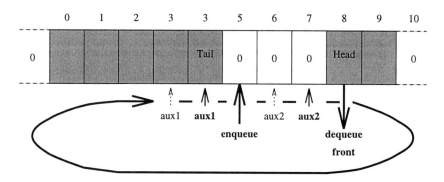

Figure 5.8. Execution of "Modulus Increment" program. Data are enqueued in front of cell indicated by aux1 and dequeued from cell in front of that indicated by aux2. Labels in bold indicate current values, dotted show previous values.

the simplest. This program can be simplified to Figure 5.10 using the facts that in this program aux3 is always 1 and noting that for *these test sequences* twice the next item to be dequeued (i.e. the front of the queue) is always an address outside the used part of the index memory and so is always zero. (In the runs described in this section, reading outside the indexed memory returns zero rather than aborting the program).

The probability of a successful run $P(10^4, 42)$ is estimated as $5/11$, i.e. 5 successes in 11 trials. (A pessimistic estimate includes all the runs and assumes the runs which ran out of time would have failed, i.e. $P(10^4, 42) = 5/18$). Using Equation 4.1 (Section 4.6.1) the number of runs required to be assured (to within probability 1%) of obtaining at least one solution is 8 (pessimistically 15). This requires $8 \times 10,000 \times 42 = 3,360,000$ (pessimistically 6,300,000) individuals to be processed.

Table 5.7. Tableau for Evolving a Queue: Given Modulus Increment Primitives

Objective	To evolve a first-in first-out queue	
Architecture	Five separate trees, plus single ADF	
Primitives	makenull	+, −, 0, 1, max, mod, PROG2, QROG2, aux1, aux2, aux3, Set_Aux1, Set_Aux2, Set_Aux3, Inc_Aux1, MInc1, Inc_Aux2, MInc2, Inc_Aux3, MInc3, Dec_Aux3, read, write, Adf1
	front	+, −, 0, 1, max, mod, PROG2, QROG2, aux1, aux2, aux3, read, Adf1
	dequeue	+, −, 0, 1, max, mod, PROG2, QROG2, aux1, aux2, aux3, Inc_Aux1, MInc1, Inc_Aux2, MInc2, Inc_Aux3, MInc3, Dec_Aux3, Adf1 read, write, Adf1, Front
	enqueue	+, −, 0, 1, max, mod, PROG2, QROG2, aux1, aux2, aux3, Inc_Aux1, MInc1, Inc_Aux2, MInc2, Inc_Aux3, MInc3, Dec_Aux3, read, write, Adf1, arg1
	empty	+, −, 0, 1, max, mod, PROG2, QROG2, aux1, aux2, aux3, read, Adf1
	adf1	+, −, 0, 1, max, mod, PROG2, QROG2, arg1
Fitness Case	4 test sequences of 40 tests and one of 160 (Table 5.6). Values enqueued as Table 5.9 except F = 15.7 rather than 5.0	
	No program aborts	
Fitness Scaling	Pareto comparison with each operation and a memory penalty contributing separately. Operations score 1 per test passed and each memory cell used (above 15) scores −1.	
Selection	Pareto tournament of 4	
Hits	No. tests passed	
Wrapper	makenull	result ignored
	front	no wrapper
	dequeue	no wrapper
	enqueue	result ignored
	empty	result = 0 ⇒ TRUE, otherwise FALSE
	adf1	n/a
Parameters	Population = 10,000, G=50, program size ≤ 250	
Success Predicate	320 hits, i.e. all tests passed	

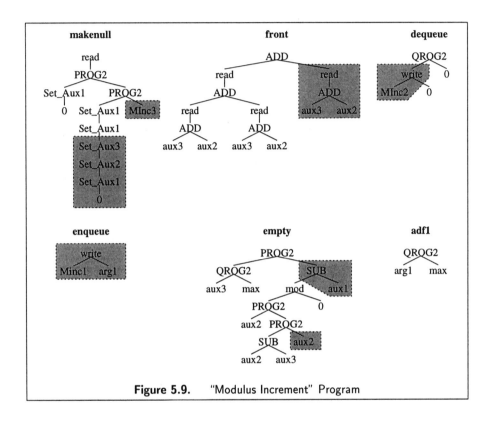

Figure 5.9. "Modulus Increment" Program

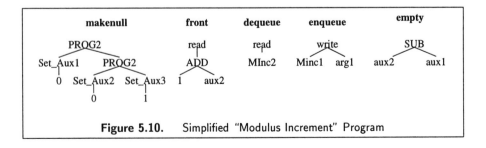

Figure 5.10.   Simplified "Modulus Increment" Program

Table 5.8.   Changes between Shuffler experiment and evolving a queue given MIncn

The six trees that form each program were split into various categories: ■ those that initialise things (makenull)   ■ those that change the queue (makenull, dequeue, enqueue),   ■ subroutines (adf1).   Using these categories the primitives were restricted to particular trees: ■ Set_Auxn can only be used by makenull   ■ The primitives which change things (write, Inc_Auxn, Dec_Auxn, MInc_Auxn) can only appear in tree where change is expected   ■ Allow arg1 only in trees which have arguments, i.e. enqueue and adf1.   ■ adf1 contains only primitives which perform calculations (+, −, max, mod, PROG2, QROG2). I.e. do not have side effects.   ■ dequeue can call front
Add a third variable Aux3 and associated primitives (i.e. Set_Aux3, Inc_Aux3 and MInc3).
Add PROG2 and QROG2. dequeue requires two actions to be performed (return result and remove item from queue), QROG2 naturally allows this and allows the first action to be the one yielding the overall result.
Dec_Aux1 and Dec_Aux2 are removed. By removing decrement it was hoped to avoid clashes when crossing over between similar programs whose exact operation was incompatible. I.e. one program causes queue head to move up one enqueue but a similar one causes it to move down and to encourage "hybrid" solutions in which: ■ aux3 can be used as a count of queue length as it has both increment and decrement primitives.   ■ Aux1 and Aux2 can still be used as head and tail pointers.   ■ PROG2 and QROG2 can readily link together partial solutions. It had been noted that many partial solutions used primitives (especially mod) to link together partial solutions where the primary effect of the primitive appears to be a nuisance).
No memory abort
Pareto fitness scaling, see Section 5.10.1
Change to 5th test sequence to produce a more even spread of queue lengths (Table 5.6).
Change to range of values in the queue (by changing F from 31.4 to 15.7, see Section 5.8)
A new individual is not inserted in the population if it is worse than the member of the population it is replacing. This change later removed, as it seemed to encourage premature convergence.

5.10   CIRCULAR BUFFER – EVOLVING MODULUS INCREMENT

In this section we describe an experiment which shows that it is possible to evolve a
queue as we did in the previous section, however in this experiment we do not provide
the GP with problem specific primitives. Instead we show that such primitives can be
evolved, using ADFs, as the GP solves the problem. However first it is necessary to
explain some of the techniques used. (Complete parameters are given in Table 5.10 and
Table 5.11 summarises the changes between this experiment and those in the previous
section).

5.10.1   Pareto Fitness

The fitness function should be able to discriminate accurately between programs
through out the evolution of the population. That is both at the beginning, when
the population contains random (poor) programs and later when the population should
contain better programs. To do this the test case was designed to cover all parts of the
trial programs with tests of a range of difficulties. So early on the easy tests would
discriminate between poor and very poor programs (all programs failing the harder
tests). Later on, when better programs have evolved, it is expected that most programs
will pass the easy tests and so the harder tests will be used to discriminate.

A future area for research would be to investigate dynamically choosing which tests
to use, so as to accurately discriminate between programs. Potentially far fewer tests
need be run to discriminate between members of a tournament, rather than between
members of the whole population. This could be incorporated into tournament selection
so fitness evaluation was at selection rather than when new trial programs are created.
The tradeoff between accurately assessing the value of an individual (and the number
of fitness tests that it must execute) and how well the evolutionary process performs
is also worthy of investigation. Co-evolution provides a mechanism for automatically
dynamically changing which fitness tests are used. Whilst an active research area
co-evolution and dynamic fitness functions are fields of research in their own right and
are too much of a distraction from data structures too consider in detail here. Therefore
our experiments use only fixed fitness functions. (Current research on both topics is
surveyed in Section 2.4.2).

A single fitness function is used to decide how well all components of a program
are performing and produce a single objective value for this. It has already been noted
that certain parts of the problem (i.e. makenull and enqueue) are easier than others
and so a scaling factor (0.05) was included to increase the impact of more difficult
parts of the test case. Despite this it was noted that sometimes the GP population
traded improvement on one part of the test case against improvement on others. That
is improvement in one part of the program was lost from the population as it was
displaced by improvement in another which produced a higher fitness. If the first
improvement is critical for an overall solution the GP is forced to rediscover it later.
Rather than explore increasing complex weightings for the various components of the
fitness function it was decided to use Pareto fitness.

Pareto optimality (cf. Section 3.9) offers a way of comparing individuals within the population using multiple criteria without introducing an arbitrary means of combining them into a single fitness. Six criteria are used:

1. number of makenull tests passed

2. number of front tests passed

3. number of dequeue tests passed

4. number of enqueue tests passed

5. number of empty tests passed

6. number of memory cells (above a minimum) used (NB this is a penalty)

(In this section the whole test case is always used, i.e. programs don't abort, so all programs pass all makenull and enqueue tests therefore criteria 1. and 4. don't help to differentiate between programs).

Whilst Pareto fitness has been used with linear chromosome GAs this is the first use of it with genetic programming. (Experiments in later chapters include explicit niching measures to reduce population convergence but they were not used here).

5.10.2   Demic Populations

In this and the previous section the GP population is divided into separate demes which constrain parents to be near to each other. Dividing the population limits the speed at which it converges and so may reduce the impact of premature convergence and improve the quality of the solutions produced. The technique used is described in Section 3.8.

Figures 5.11 to 5.14 show the spread of programs with a certain useful characteristic through the population. The characteristic chosen, is that adf1 should perform an operation like modulus increment.

For the purposes of these graphs, a cycle length is defined. Each adf1 is called with the value it returned previously starting with zero, until either it returns a value outside the legal range of memory addresses (in which case the cycle length is zero) or a value it has already returned. In the latter case the cycle length is the number of calls required to make adf1 return the same value as before. If the program uses adf1 as a simple modulus increment operator, a cycle length of at least 10 is required to pass all 320 tests. Therefore, it was felt, this would be a good metric. Indeed all the solutions do have a cycle length 10 or more. However as Figure 5.11 shows, it is possible for a GP to fail to solve the problem even after it has evolved this building block.

Figure 5.13 does shows the "adf1 cycle length" building block spreading through neighbouring demes. An alternative view is it lay hidden (perhaps within "introns") and at about generation 50 changes in the population made it beneficial to express it. (Figure 5.11 shows it was present in reasonable numbers in the initial population).

Figure 5.13 shows separate regions of the population but the separation is not as marked as described in [Collins, 1992, page 128] where large homogeneous regions form within the population, separated by narrow "hybrid bands". The lack of clear

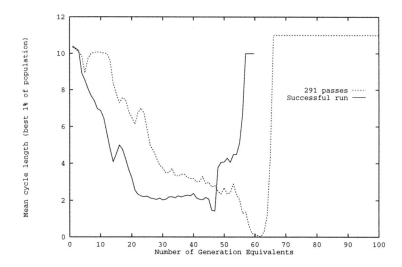

Figure 5.11. Evolution of adf1 cycle length in two runs of the Queue problem (when evolving modulus increment). The successful run produced Queue 2. (Graphs plot mean cycle length of the 1% of population with the longest cycles).

separation may be an advantage since "almost no evolution" occurs within the homogeneous regions but instead "almost all the genetic diversity and evolutionary innovation occurs in the hybrid bands". If the bands are very small they occupy only a small part of the population and so much effort is wasted on breeding in the homogeneous regions. The best compromise between avoiding the whole population converging to a single solution and the population forming very well defined regions separated by narrow hybrid bands may be (as we have here) ill defined regions with large overlaps.

There are many differences between this work and [Collins, 1992, Figure 7.6]; the population is smaller (which makes it harder for demes to achieve isolation) and the length of the evolutionary process is shorter but also the GP is not obliged to choose between two complementary genotypes. Collins' demes are similar but were designed to achieve high performance on a particular parallel machine architecture (Connection Machine-2).

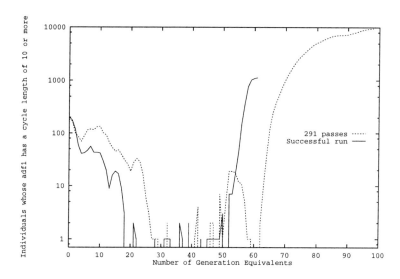

Figure 5.12.   Number of individuals in the population whose adf1 has a cycle length of 10 or more in two runs of the Queue problem (when evolving modulus increment). Successful run produced Queue 2.

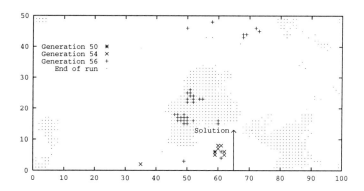

Figure 5.13.   Spread of individuals whose adf1 has a cycle length $\geq$ 10 near end of successful run (2) of Queue problem (when evolving modulus increment).

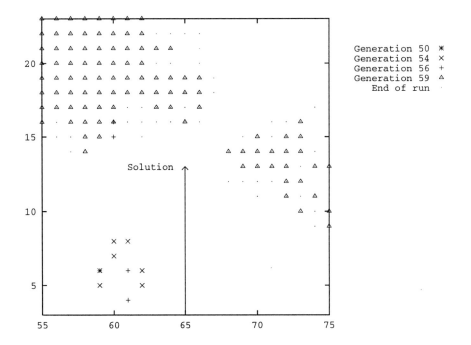

Figure 5.14. Spread of individuals whose adf1 has a cycle length ≥ 10 near to where successful Queue (2) individual evolved.

5.10.3   Good Engineering Practice

There is increasing interest in directing the GP genetic operators to increase the viability of offspring, a number of active approaches have been described in Section 3.7. This section describes measures taken to ensure the ADF is "sensible". (The use of a fitness penalty for excessive memory usage was described in Section 5.8). Both creation of the initial random population and the crossover operator were changed to ensure every adf1 has the following properties:

- It does not yield a constant i.e. the same value regardless of its argument

- It transforms its input, i.e. its output is not equal to its input.

These constraints are implemented by testing the adf1 part of a whole program independently of the rest of the program. (This can readily be done, as adf1's primitives do not have side effects). These tests are in addition and separate to the five test sequences already described. adf1 is tested with the values 0, 1, ... 9 and each answer given by adf1 with these values. I.e. if (adf1 9) = 10, then adf1 will also be tested with a value of 10. The proposed adf1 tree is rejected (so causing a new one to be generated for testing) if either:

- all the answers returned by adf1 are the same, or

- any value returned by adf1 is the same as its input

5.10.4   Pass by Reference

In order to allow a primitive modulus increment primitive (cf. MInc$n$) subroutine to evolve, adf1 was changed to use the pass-by-reference mechanism described on pages 90–91 which allows it to update its the argument.
Examples:

1. If initially aux2 has the value 8 and adf1 increments its argument (adf1 aux2) would change aux2 to have the value 9.

2. (adf1 (QROG2 (ADD (read 1) 1) aux2)) passes the value of the expression "$store[1]+$ 1" to adf1. When adf1 has finished its calculations on this value, the result will be both stored in $store[1]$ and returned by adf1.

5.10.5   Results

In one set of 57 runs, six passed the whole test case. Subsequent analysis shows that three of these are entirely general solutions to the stack problem, i.e. will pass any legal test sequence. Further, given suitable redefinition of max and sufficient memory, all three could implement an integer queue of any reasonable length.

Analyzing the other three programs shows that whilst they pass all 320 tests, they exploit holes in the test sequences. That is, they are not general and other test sequences could be devised, which they would fail.

Table 5.9.   Range of data values enqueued (F = 5.0) when evolving "Modulus Increment"

	<	-10	-9	-8	-7	-6	-5	-4	-3	-2	-1	0	1	2	3	4	5	6	7	8	9	10	>
							enqueue arguments																
No.	9	1	3	1			2	2	1	1	4	3	18	5	8	8	5	6	3		2	2	20
Total	104																						

Table 5.10.   Tableau for Evolving a Queue: Circular buffer solution found

Objective	To evolve a first-in first-out queue	
Architecture	Five separate trees, plus single ADF	
Primitives	makenull	+, −, 0, 1, max, mod, PROG2, QROG2, aux1, aux2, read, write, Set_Aux1, Set_Aux2
	front	+, −, 0, 1, max, mod, PROG2, QROG2, aux1, aux2, read
	dequeue	+, −, 0, 1, max, mod, PROG2, QROG2, aux1, aux2, read, write, Adf1, Front
	enqueue	+, −, 0, 1, max, mod, PROG2, QROG2, aux1, aux2, read, write, Adf1, arg1
	empty	+, −, 0, 1, max, mod, PROG2, QROG2, aux1, aux2, read
	adf1	+, −, 0, 1, max, mod, PROG2, QROG2, arg1
Fitness Case	4 test sequences, of 40 tests and one of 160 (Tables 5.6 and 5.9)	
	No program aborts	
Fitness Scaling	Each operation scored independently using Pareto comparison (1 per test passed), Memory usage above minimum (12 cells) penalized	
Selection	Pareto tournament of 4	
Hits	Test passed	
Wrapper	makenull	result ignored
	front	no wrapper
	dequeue	no wrapper
	enqueue	result ignored
	empty	result = 0 ⇒ TRUE, otherwise FALSE
	adf1	n/a
Parameters	Population = 10,000, G=100, program size $\leq$ 250, deme = 3 × 3	
Success Predicate	320 hits, i.e. all tests passed	

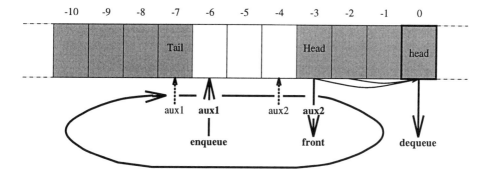

Figure 5.15. Execution of Queue program 2. Data are enqueued in cell indicated by aux1. Data is dequeued from the cell indicated by aux2 by first copying them to cell zero. (Cell zero is overwritten as the data values are extracted from it). Labels in bold indicate current values, dotted show previous values.

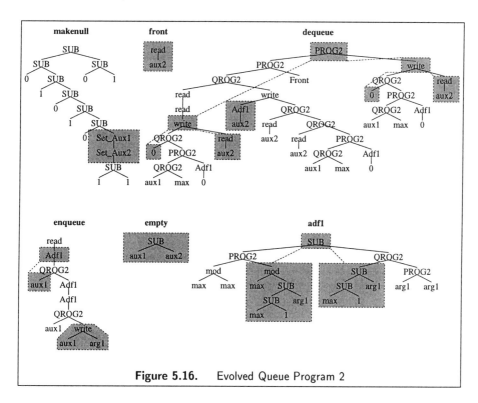

Figure 5.16.   Evolved Queue Program 2

Figures 5.15 to 5.21 show two of the correct programs. Figure 5.17 and 5.21 show simplifications of them and Figure 5.15 shows how the first implements a circular queue of up to nine integers. The second (Figure 5.18) allows ten integers.

Figures 5.23 and 5.24 show one of the programs that passes all the tests but which could fail a different test sequence. The program contains a small bug which the test

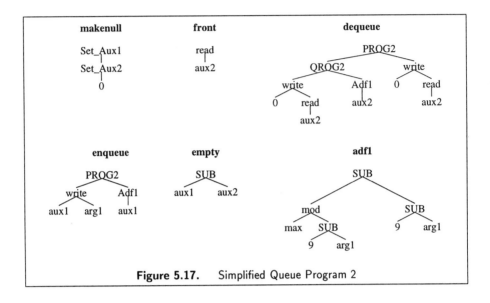

Figure 5.17.   Simplified Queue Program 2

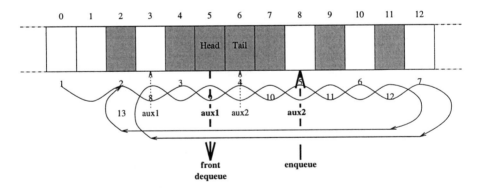

Figure 5.18.   Execution of Queue program 4. Whilst also a circular queue implementation, in this case adf1 increases it's argument by two and arranges on overflow to use the cells it previously skipped (numbers on the arrows indicate order cells are used in). Cell zero is only used once, but other cells are re-used.

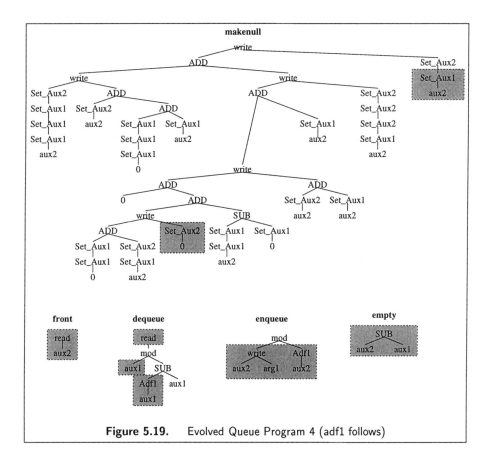

Figure 5.19.   Evolved Queue Program 4 (adf1 follows)

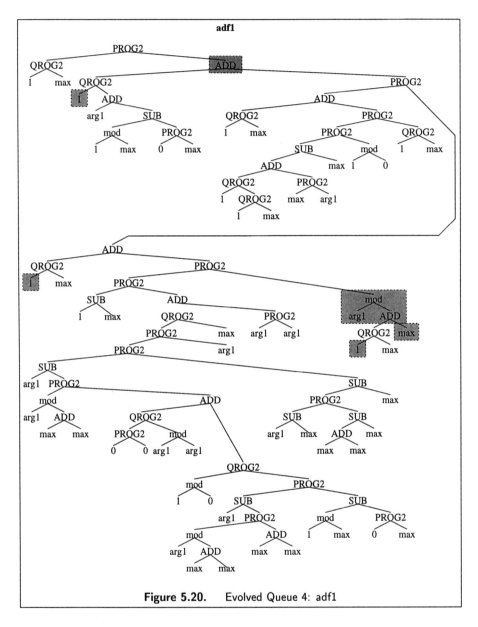

Figure 5.20.   Evolved Queue 4: adf1

makenull	front	dequeue		enqueue		empty		adf1	
Set_Aux2	read	QRQG2		PROG2		SUB		ADD	
Set_Aux1	aux2	read Adf1		write Adf1		aux2 aux1		2 mod	
0		aux1 aux1		aux2 arg1 aux2				arg1 11	

Figure 5.21.   Simplified Queue Program 4

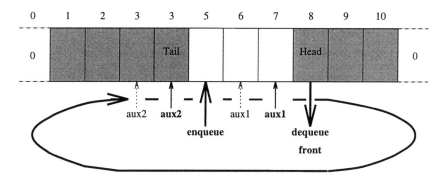

Figure 5.22. Execution of near perfect queue program (3) (can you spot the bug?). Data are enqueued to the cell in front of the one indicated by aux2 and dequeued from the one in front of that indicated by aux1. Shaded cells contain data.

case did not detect. The bug arises because the Front tree access aux1 directly but doesn't allow for the wrap-round required in a circular queue. If it had evolved to use adf1 this bug would not have appeared. Figure 5.25 shows a simplification of this imperfect program and Figure 5.22 shows its operation.

Using the formula for the number of runs required (Equation 4.1 page 75) and $\epsilon = 0.01$ and $P(10^4, 100) = 3/57$ yields 86. I.e. 86 independent runs, with each generating up to 1,000,000 trial solutions, will (assuming the probability of solution is 3/57 i.e. 1/19) ensure that the chance of producing at least one solution is better than 99%. This would require a total of up to $1,000,000 \times 86 = 86,000,000$ trial programs to be tested.

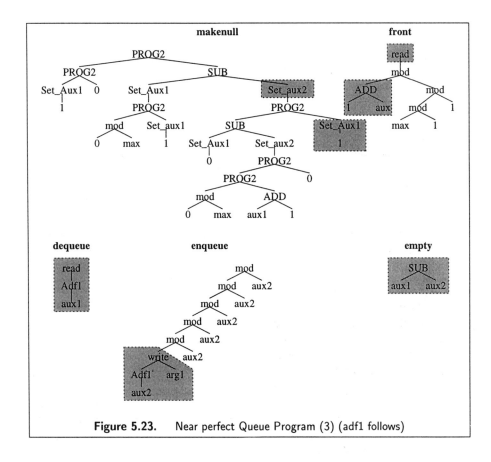

Figure 5.23.   Near perfect Queue Program (3) (adf1 follows)

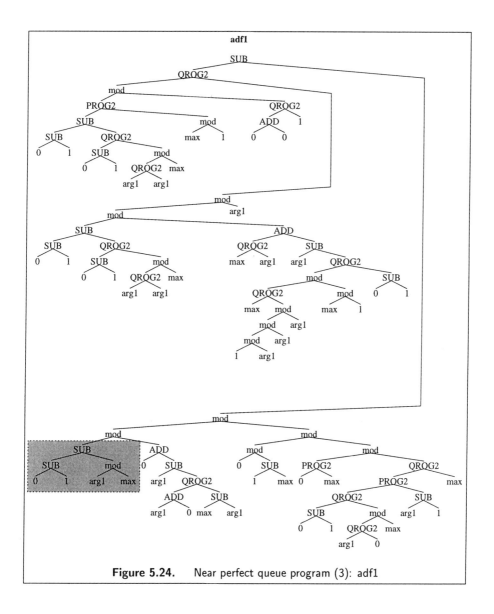

Figure 5.24.   Near perfect queue program (3): adf1

makenull	front	dequeue	enqueue	empty	adf1

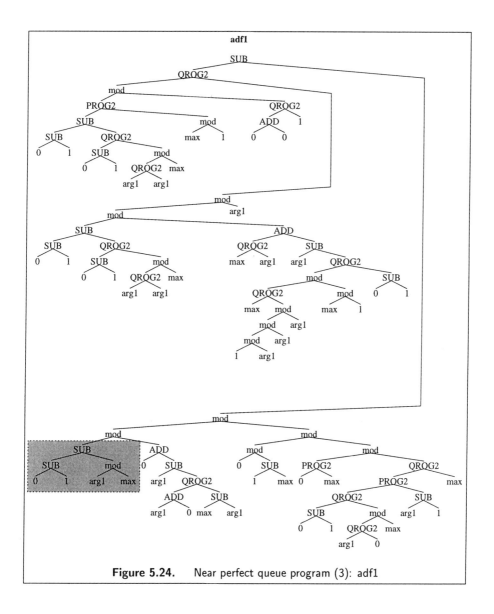

Figure 5.25.   Simplified Queue Program (3)

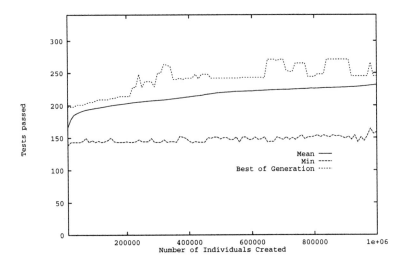

Figure 5.26. Evolution of the number of fitness tests passed in a typical run of the Queue problem (when evolving modulus increment).

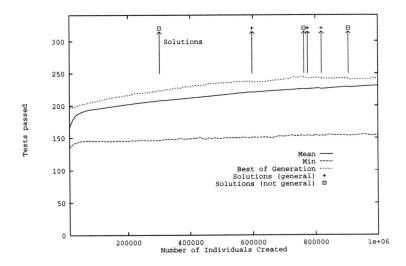

Figure 5.27. Evolution of the number of fitness tests passed. Means of 57 Queue runs (evolving modulus increment). The discovery of the six programs which pass all the fitness tests is also plotted.

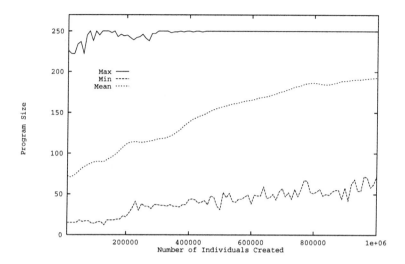

Figure 5.28. Evolution of program size in a typical run of the Queue problem (when evolving modulus increment).

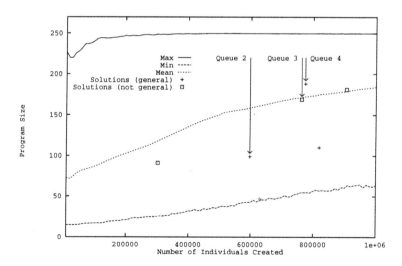

Figure 5.29. Evolution of program size. Means of 57 Queue runs (evolving modulus increment). The sizes of the six programs which pass all the fitness tests and when they were found are also plotted.

Table 5.11.   Changes between experiments evolving a queue given MIncn and evolving it

The population is divided in to 3 × 3 overlapping demes (Section 5.10.2). As this slows the rate of convergence, runs were continued for 100 generation equivalents (rather than 50).
Replace MIncn and Inc_Auxn primitives by the following changes to adf1 and how it is used.

- Each new adf1 is checked to see it is "sensible" (Section 5.10.3).

- adf1 uses pass by reference (Section 5.10.4)

- As adf1 now changes its argument, it is no longer allowed in the front or empty trees (which are restricted to use only read-only primitives, Section 5.10).

- Allowing adf1 to be used by makenull seemed to be causing a conflict with its use by dequeue and enqueue. As it is not required by makenull, makenull was changed so that it could no longer call it.

- Cache of results of calling adf1 is maintained. This produced a reduction in run time of about 30%.

- Reduce F from 15.7 to 5.0. This may be too small, as each of the "buggy" programs which pass the whole of the test case, are only able to do so because a critical element in the queue has the value zero.

- Apply memory penalty above 12 words of indexed memory used, rather than on 16 or above.

- When applying the memory penalty only include cells actually written to rather than counting all cells between the highest and lowest address used (either read or written). It was hoped that this would allow looser patterns of memory usage and so ease the evolution of the corresponding adf1.

- Reduce number of memory cells from 63 to 31.

Remove Aux3.

5.11   DISCUSSION: BUILDING BLOCKS AND INTRONS

In this section we return to the shuffler solution evolved in Section 5.8 and then discuss possible reasons for "introns" (i.e. code within the trees which does not affect the trees performance) and implications for a GP "building block hyposthesis". The shuffler solution evolved in Section 5.8 is interesting for several reasons:

1. GP solved the problem in an unexpected way, i.e. a way we would not expect a human programmer to use. However the solution is entirely correct.

2. As Figure 5.5 shows, the shuffler solution correctly implements a first-in first-out queue of up to nine items. However unlike the other correct evolved solutions presented in this book, it is not generic, i.e. it cannot implement queues of arbitary length. The code is composed of a fixed number of repeating units, and this number determines the maximum queue length. Presumably, should longer queues be required, they could be readily evolved from this solution.

3. The program is clearly composed of repeating units (write Inc_Aux2), cf. Figure 5.6. As each unit is added, the solution is able to correctly process longer queues and so pass more of the fitness test case. I.e. each unit increases the fitness of the solution. It appears the solution has evolved by being assembled from "building blocks" by crossover.

Many evolved solutions in this book contain repeated units of code but usually only one instance of the unit contributes to the operation of the program and the others have no effect of fitness, i.e. they are introns. For example the makenull tree of queue 4 (see Figure 5.19) contains the subtree (Set_Aux1 aux2) eight times but only one of these is important to the operation of the solution. The other seven are introns. The subtree (Set_Aux1 aux2) in the makenull tree is vitally important to the fitness of the whole program and so can be expected to be positively correlated with fitness. Thus we would expect crossover and selection to ensure that the subtree was spread rapidly through the population. In a fixed representation genetic algorithm this would mean, increasing the number of members of the population which contain the building block, but in a varible length representation such as GP, there is an alternative; increasing the number of times the building block occurs in each individual. Often repeating a code fragment in a single program will have a deleterious effect on the program's fitness and individuals carrying more than one instance of the code will be swept from the population by selection. However when it is not harmful, the number of copies of it can be expected to grow. In a few cases, such as (write Inc_Aux2) in the shuffler, the additional code can be beneficial and so will spread both into more individuals and also each individual will contain more copies of it. However in most case, it appears the best that can be expected is that, the code fragment is not harmful. NB this does not prevent it spreading. Provided it is useful at some point in the program, multiple useless copies of it (i.e. introns) can be expected. The observation that multiple units of code are seldom beneficial implies that such units cannot be thought of a "building blocks". Chapter 8 shows the correlation between code fragments and fitness can be used to quantitatively predict how many copies of the code can be expected in subsequent generations.

While nature does occasionally duplicate genes, this seems to be a relatively rare event, in contrast in GP duplication of code seems to be rampant. It would be interesting to consider forms of crossover (or homologous crossover) which discourage or even prevent code duplication. This could take the form of a rule which prevented crossover inserting code which duplicated code already in the tree. This would add a bias away from very small crossover fragments (as single terminal are likely to exist in most trees). A check that a large fragment was not carrying repeating smaller fragments might also be needed. (One-point and context preserving crossover, cf. Section 2.4.6, are steps in this direction).

5.12 SUMMARY

This chapter (which was published in part in [Langdon, 1995b]) has presented a series of experiments which show genetic programming can automatically generate programs which implement integer queue data structures from randomly addressible memory when guided by a small fixed test case. Further each of the correct solutions evolved (in Section 5.10) is generic, in that they could (with sufficient memory and change of parameters) provide the abstract data structure of any size.

Conceptually a queue is scarcely more complex than a stack and yet GP has found it far harder to evolve implementations of queues than was the case with stacks. There are many reasons why this may be the case; the perceived difference (938,000 trial programs versus 86,000,000 in the last experiment in this chapter) may be due to the details of the two experiments, e.g. some aspect of the fitness function suits the stack but the fitness functions used in this chapter were not well suited to the queue. However other possibilities are:

- In the stack problem the GP was provided with appropriate cursor primitives (i.e. inc_aux and dec_aux) and these made the task very much easier. A comparison of Section 5.9 and 5.10 provides support for this argument. In Section 5.9 cursor primitives suitable for a circular queue implementation were provided and the GP found programs which passed all the tests much more readily than in Section 5.10 where it was obliged to evolve such primitives.

- The small difference in apparent problem difficulty may not be the cause of the difference, instead the important difference may be the number of different ways of solving (or partially solving) the problem. In Chapter 4 there are two similar basic ways to implement a solution (either a push-down or a push-up stack). However there are three fundamentally different ways to implement a queue (circular buffer, packed array and linked list) as well as the "caterpillar" partial solutions found in Section 5.7. Each of which can be implemented in two or more distinct ways corresponding to the push-up push-down choice.

This could be viewed as meaning there are more solutions (any one of which would be acceptable) in the search space and so the problem is easier. But what seems to happen is the GP population converges to a partial solution which has initially relatively high fitness and finds it difficult to evolve past this to complete solutions.

- Genetic programming scales badly so a slightly more difficult problem becomes very much more difficult for GP.

From an information theory perspective, genetic programming has converted the information held in the test cases (the specification) into the information held in a program (the solution). The information content of the test cases is about 1436 bits, whereas that of the solutions (including redundant code) is less, e.g. 405 bits for queue 2 (this reduces to 160 bits if the simplified code is considered). So as with the stack, the GP has produced a more concise definition of the problem than the test case it was given. The difference is not as great as was the case with the stack as the evolved program contains redundant code. (The queue programs may contain more redundant code simply because the solutions took longer to find which gave greater time for redundant code to form and spread).

An implementation which incorporates "pass by reference" into the ADF framework has been described.

This chapter has shown "good engineering practice" can be incorporated into GP, via the test function, syntax and genetic operations.

It has shown results can be obtained using Pareto optimality within GP.

In these experiments the GP showed a marked tendency to converge to non-optimal solutions even with the large (10,000 individuals) populations. Thus these problems would appear to be "GP deceptive".

This chapter provides additional support for partitioning large populations. The model used is that of demes.

Table 5.12.   Differences Between Stack and Final Queue Experiment

	Page
Pareto scoring, including excessive memory usage penalty (to discourage caterpillar)	102
Population of 10,000 rather than 1,000 (5.5.1).	89
Use of 3 × 3 demes rather than completely mixed population (5.10.2).	103
Wrapper on empty true is defined as 0 rather than > 0(5.4).	88
31 memory cells instead of 63 (to discourage caterpillar).	118
Continue on memory error (5.3.1).	86
320 tests rather than 160. Additional test sequence to discourage caterpillar.	94
Last test sequence ensures all legal queue lengths are tested (Tables 4.4 and 5.6).	98
enqueue argument given by $5.0 \tan \text{rand}(\pi)$ rather than $\text{rand}(2000) - 1000$ (5.8).	94
New primitives (5.3) ■ Aux2 ■ (no inc_aux or dec_aux) ■ Write_Aux$n$ replaced by Set_Aux$n$ ■ mod ■ PROG2, QROG2	84
Primitives restricted as to which tree they may occur in (5.6).	90
Automatically Defined Functions (5.6) (including pass by reference 5.10.4).	90, 107
Front callable by dequeue (5.2).	85
Check adf1 is "sensible" (5.10.3).	107
adf1 cache (Table 5.11 and Section D.6)	118

6 EVOLVING A LIST

The list is one of the basic data models used in computer programs [Aho and Ullman, 1995, page 286]. This chapter shows it is possible using genetic programming (GP) to evolve a list data structure from basic primitives. There are many ways in which a list can be implemented ([Aho et al., 1987] suggest three fundamentally different ways, each of which has many variations) but GP is able to co-evolve all the list components so they form a single working implementation.

This chapter describes a case where loops have been successfully evolved. A CPU penalty component of a niched Pareto fitness function (Section 6.5.1) was introduced to contained run time which otherwise might have become excessive. Similarly syntax restrictions were used to limit run time, e.g. by preventing nested loops (Section 6.4.2) and, inconjunction with execution directed crossover (Section 6.6), to guide the genetic search. A call by reference mechanism is introduced to GP and used inconjunction with Automatically Defined Functions (Section 6.3). The last experiment in this chapter (Section 6.9) presents a candidate model for maintaining evolved software and demonstrates it on the list problem.

6.1 PROBLEM STATEMENT

An integer list data structure [Aho et al., 1987] has ten component operations which are summarised in Table 6.1. Whilst each of the ten operations is relatively simple, the complete problem represents a sizable increase in complexity from Chapter 5. Note that a list is a generalization of a stack and a queue (which we met in Chapters 4 and 5). A stack can be formed from a list by restricting access to just one end of it, while

Table 6.1.   Definitions of the Ten List Operations

Makenull	Make the list an empty list and return position given by End.
Retrieve(p)	Return the element at position p.
Insert(x, p)	Insert x at position p, moving elements at p and following positions to the next higher position.
Delete(p)	Delete the element at position p, moving elements at $p+1$ and following positions to the previous lower position.
End	Return the position following the last element of the list.
First	Return the position of the first position. If the list is empty, return the position given by End.
Next(p)	Return the position following position p.
Previous(p)	Return the position before position p.
Locate(x)	Return the position of the first element containing value x. If x is not in the list at all then return the position given by End.
Printlist	Print the elements in their order of occurrence.

a queue is a special type of list where access is restricted to both ends. Items being added to one end of the list and removed from the other.

The immediate goal is to evolve a list which works correctly with a limited number of elements. Nine (NB the same as Chapter 5) was chosen as sufficient to demonstrate the principle but as we shall see (in Section 6.8) GP is capable of evolving lists of any finite size.

6.2   ARCHITECTURE

The multi-tree architecture and multi-tree crossover described in Section 3.6 and successfully used in Chapters 4 and 5 was extended to include ten trees (one for each of the ten list operations) plus five other trees, one for each Automatically Defined Function (ADF).

6.3   AUTOMATICALLY DEFINED FUNCTIONS

Work on the queue has shown that co-evolving code which has some functionality in common can be eased if there is a shared ADF which can evolve to provide common code for the common functionality. This appears to be far easier than expecting the same functionality to evolve twice in separate locations (Section 5.10). (See Section 2.3.2 for an introduction to ADFs).

Analysing Table 6.1 we see a common requirement is for an addressing scheme for the list elements, however End, First, Next and Previous already collectively provide addressing actions. To take advantage of this, other parts of the list are allowed to call them, i.e. their code both implements the operation and is an ADF (cf. Front, Section 5.2). Chapter 5 indicates that it may be beneficial for functions which calculate the next value of their argument to use a pass by reference calling mechanism (Sections 5.6 and 5.10.4). This avoids evolving code to write the return value into the argument

Table 6.2.   Summary of the Properties of List Operations and ADFs

	Treat as ADF	Returns value	Arguments	Pass-by-reference	Directly testable	Sufficient testing
Makenull	×	√				
Retrieve	×	√	1		√	√
Insert	×	×	2			
Delete	×	×	1			
End	√	√				√
First	√	√				√
Next	√	√	1	√		√
Previous	√	√	1	√		√
Locate	×	√	1		√	
Printlist	×	×			√	√
Adf1	√	√	1	×		
Ins_adf	√	√	1	×		
Del_adf	√	√	1	×		
Loc_adf	√	√	1	×		
Prt_adf	√	√	1	×		

after every call. Therefore all of the operations that can be treated as ADFs and that have arguments (i.e. Next and Previous) update them directly using the pass by reference mechanism (Table 6.2 summarises characteristics of operations and the ADFs).

Again from Table 6.1 we see four operations (Insert, Delete, Locate and Printlist) may need to process multiple elements of the list. A single ADF was provided in the hope that it would evolve to meet this common need. As each operation processes list elements differently the ADF is parameterised, using a private ADF for each operation (see Figure 6.1). When the main ADF is called, it is passed a reference to the corresponding private ADF, which it in turn may call (using the reference). To avoid additional arguments each private ADF may have access to the arguments of its operation as well as its own (effectively it is in the scope of its operation). As before (cf. Section 5.6) the ADF hierarchy was chosen so recursion cannot arise.

6.4 CHOICE OF PRIMITIVES

The terminals and functions were chosen to make the task of evolving a list as easy as possible and follow on from those used when solving the queue problem. Tables 6.3 and 6.4 show where they may be used and describe what they do.

Thirty one memory cells are provided, which should suffice for lists of up to nine elements. These are numbered $-15 \ldots 15$, which allows evolved code to use negative as well as positive addresses. Code may also use the auxiliary variable (aux1), possibly to store the length of the list.

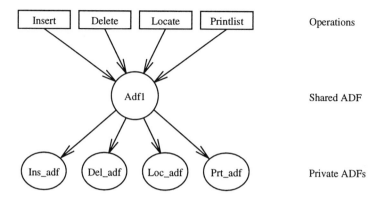

Figure 6.1.   ADF Calling Hierarchy Available to Solve the List Problem

6.4.1   Iteration

The requirement to process multiple list elements means the GP must support iteration (loops) or recursion, either implicitly (e.g. using block memory move functions) or explicitly. It was decided not to use high level functions but instead to require the GP to explicitly evolve iterative structures. Fears that the loop primitive, forwhile, could cause excessive run time lead to: forbidding nested loops; loops only being allowed where they appear to be required (i.e. Adf1); and a limit (32) on the number of iterations. The limit was set as low as possible but still allows loops to span all the available memory. (Section 2.4.2 surveys other GP work in this area).

6.4.2   Syntax Restrictions

Syntax rules were imposed with the aim of aiding the evolutionary process by forbidding exploration of apparently infeasible programs without the cost of evaluating their fitness and also ensuring essential primitives are not lost from the population. (Section 6.6 describes other work on using syntax rules to aid GP).

Whenever a new individual is created (i.e. either by crossover or in the initial random population) it is compared with the syntax rules. If it violates any of them, it is discarded and a new one is created to replace it. If crossover creates an illegal individual then the new one is created by re-selecting crossover points within the same tree within the same parents. In contrast to Section 5.10.3, these rules are enforced by analysing the program source code and it is not necessary to execute any part of the program to verify they are obeyed. The rules were:

- Prt_adf must contain at least one print function.

- The loop index, i0, may only appear inside the third argument of forwhile, i.e. the loop.

- Loops may not appear inside the third argument of other loops (i.e. no nested loops).

- Adf1 must contain at least one loop, which must contain at least one i0.

Table 6.3.   Tableau for Evolving a List

Objective	To evolve a list	
Architecture	Ten separate trees, plus five ADFs	
Primitives	Makenull	PROG2, write, Set_Aux1, End
	Retrieve	arg1, read
	Insert	PROG2, aux1, adf1, Next, ARG1, ARG2, write
	Delete	PROG2, aux1, adf1, Next, ARG1, Prev
	End	aux1
	First	aux1
	Next	arg1
	Previous	arg1
	Locate	adf1, First, ARG1
	Printlist	adf1, First
	Adf1	arg1, aux1, forwhile, i0, FUNC, End
	Ins_adf	arg1, swap
	Del_adf	arg1, swap, ARG1, Next
	Loc_adf	arg1, ARG1, read
	Prt_adf	arg1, read, print
	All trees may contain +, −, 0, 1 and max	
Fitness Case	538 trees run in 21 sequences. 167 consistency tests. Tangent test data distribution (F = 15).	
Fitness Scaling	Each tree scored independently using Pareto comparison, memory usage above minimum (12 cells) and CPU usage above 120 per test run are Pareto fitness penalties.	
Selection	Elitist Pareto Tournament group 4, Niche population sample size 81.	
Hits	Number of consistency checks passed	
Wrapper	Insert, Delete and Printlist result ignored, otherwise no wrapper.	
Parameters	Population = 10,000, G=100, program size ≤ 500, Max initial tree size 50, 90% directed crossover.	
Success Predicate	167 hits, i.e. all tests passed	

Table 6.4.   Actions Performed by Terminals and Functions

Primitive	Purpose
max	constant 10 ($\geq$ max list size).
PROG2(*t*,*u*)	evaluate *t*; **return** *u*
arg1	argument of current operation or ADF, but:
ARG1, ARG2	arguments of Insert, Delete, Locate or Printlist.
aux1	an auxiliary variable (i.e. in addition to indexed memory).
Set_Aux1(*x*)	aux1 = *x*; **return** aux1

forwhile(*s*,*e*,*l*)	**for** i0 = *s*; i0 $\leq$ *e*; i0++
	    if timeout (32) **exit loop**
	    if *l* returns zero **exit loop**
	return i0

FUNC	call private ADF of operation which called Adf1.
print(*d*)	**if** room in print buffer copy *d* into it; **return** number of items in it **else** evaluate *d*; **return** 0
Indexed memory is held in store[$-l$ ... $+l$], where $l = 15$, i.e. a total of 31 cells.	
read(*x*)	**if** $|x| \leq l$ **return** store[*x*] **else return** 0
write(*x*,*d*)	**if** $|x| \leq l$ store[*x*] = *d*; **return** original contents of store[*x*] **else** evaluate *d*; **return** 0
swap(*x*,*y*)	**if** $|x| \leq l$ **and** $|y| \leq l$ exchange contents of store[*x*] and store[*y*] **if** $|x| > l$ **and** $|y| \leq l$ store[*y*] = 0 **if** $|x| \leq l$ **and** $|y| > l$ store[*x*] = 0 **return** 1

- It would appear to be sensible for code to use its arguments. Where feasible, syntax checks are used to encourage this. Thus Retrieve, Next, Previous, Adf1, Ins_adf, Del_adf, Loc_adf and Prt_adf must contain at least one arg1 terminal and Adf1 must contain at least one FUNC (cf. Table 6.4) primitive.

6.5 FITNESS FUNCTION

6.5.1 Pareto Optimality and Niches

Pareto fitness was described in Section 3.9 and used in some queue experiments (cf. Section 5.10.1). Pareto scoring means individuals which make an improvement on any part of the problem tend to be preferred, whereas a scalar fitness will tend to require each improvement to match or exceed any deterioration in all other parts of the problem. Whether an improvement is more important than a deterioration is given by scaling parameters within the fitness function. Consequently setting them is complex and must be done with care. To some extent Pareto fitness avoids this problem.

With Pareto scoring, a single population can contain several hundred different fitness values (or niches) each of which is the best in the sense of not being dominated by any other member of the population. This encourages crossover between individuals that are good at different parts of the problem, which may produce offspring that are relatively fit on more of the problem. However unless there is some selection pressure to maintain multiple niches, the population will tend to reduce the number of niches it occupies. This is an aspect of "genetic drift" is particularly important in small populations [Horn et al., 1993]. To maintain a large number of niches the fitness sharing scheme described in Section 3.6 was used.

Where a selection tournament is unable to discriminate between two or more candidates (either because they have identical fitness or no fitness value dominates all the others) then these candidates are compared with a sample of the rest of the population. The one that is dominated by or has identical fitness to the fewest other members of the population wins the tournament. This creates a secondary selection pressure in favour of individuals that occupy relatively unpopulated niches, which tends to prevent the population converging and instead it contains many different non-dominated fitness niches.

Figure 6.2 shows a typical run of the list experiment. When fitness sharing is used the number of non-dominated fitness values within the population (i.e. occupied points on the Pareto surface) evolves to be about 100–150, with on average 6–9 programs per niche. In contrast where comparison with the rest of the population is not used the number of non-dominated fitness values in the population falls rapidly, stabilising at about 10. However the population eventually converges to a few of these so that they contain about $\frac{3}{4}$ of the population. Without comparison with the rest of the population, the proportion of the population with one of the best fitness values is also more erratic.

6.5.2 Fitness Test Case

The fitness of each individual is determined by running it on 21 fixed test sequences containing in total 538 operations. Tests are grouped into (a total of 167) subsequences which call several operations and cross check the values returned by them. If the checks

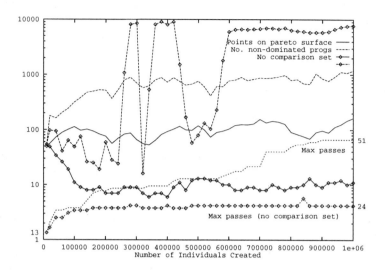

Figure 6.2. Evolution of the number of fitness niches occupied with and without comparison with the rest of the population ($\Diamond$ indicates run without comparison set). Typical list runs (starting from identical initial populations). All plots, except the maximum number of tests passed, are plotted on a log scale.

are passed we increase the program's fitness along each dimension corresponding to an operation in the subsequence. However if a check is not passed no further tests from the test sequence are made and the next sequence is started. This has the advantage of reducing run time by reducing the number of operations that are executed but perhaps encourages premature convergence by stressing the tests that occur at the start of each sequence which tend to be easier and possibly susceptible to solution by simple but highly test specific code.

No preset design or pattern of memory usage is imposed by the fitness tests. This undoubtedly makes the problem more difficult but we wish to show an implementation can be automatically generated. This flexibility makes testing more complex as often it is impossible to say the answer returned by an operation is correct, until it can be compared with answers returned by other operations (cf. column six in Table 6.2).

As in Chapters 4 and 5, the tests only cover correct operation of the list. I.e. error trapping, such as detecting the deletion of non-existing list elements, is not covered.

Again like Chapters 4 and 5 all storage, i.e. the indexed memory and aux1, is initialized at the start of each test sequence (i.e. 21 times). In half the test sequences the indexed memory is initialized to zero (aux1 is always set to zero). In the other half (unlike Chapters 4 and 5) the indexed memory is initialized to a random but fixed data pattern, which is different for each test sequence. This is to discourage the GP from evolving partial solutions which exploit the value zero to indicate memory cells are unlikely to have been written to and so are empty. In earlier experiments (cf. Section 5.4.1) such programs had been found, they appeared to work until they inserted zero into the data structure. The random data patterns have the same distribution of values as that inserted into the list. In most other published work indexed memory is initialised to zero (as in Chapters 4 and 5) however [Jannink, 1994, page 436] describes a regular non-zero initialization pattern. [Crepeau, 1995, page 132] "memory locations (are) initially filled with random 8 bit values" as this makes it "highly probably" that problem specific values needed to solve the problem "are somewhere in memory".

Test Data Values. Values to be entered into the list are specified in the test sequence. The "tangent" distribution of test data values with its wide range of positive and negative values both large and small, described in Section 5.8 was used again. The scaling factor F was set to 15, so that about half the data values inserted in the list lie in the range of legal memory indexes (i.e. ±15).

6.5.3   CPU and Memory Penalties

CPU Penalty. The number of instructions (i.e. function calls and terminals evaluated) are counted as each individual is tested. The mean number per operation used is calculated and becomes a penalty component in the Pareto fitness. However individuals which use less than 120 instructions per operation have zero penalty.

This scheme was introduced as it was anticipated that the forwhile loop could lead to very time consuming fitness evaluations and so excessively long run times. Figure 6.3 shows when the CPU penalty is applied most program evolve to use less than or near to the CPU threshold during their fitness testing. As each program takes less CPU to test the total run time is reduced. The penalty also causes the evolution of near parsimonious code (Figure 6.8). This is in dramatic contrast to the queue (which had no CPU or space penalties, cf. Figure 5.29, page 117) where programs rapidly grew to the limit of the available space. This growth is widely seen in GP and is often referred to as "bloat", cf. Section 2.4.2. However the threshold was chosen with care to avoid over penalizing constructs (like loops) which have a high CPU cost but may not appear to help achieve higher fitness levels until later in the evolutionary process. Therefore the threshold was deliberately set high at about 8 × fastest program that might evolve.

This is thought to be the first use of an explicit CPU penalty in the fitness function, however both Teller's PADO and [Maxwell III, 1994] include implicit run time as part of fitness evaluation and there are many case where program size is included as part of the fitness calculation, e.g. [Iba et al., 1994a; Zhang and Mühlenbein, 1995a] (where the language does not include program branching, subroutines or iteration, program size and number of primitives evaluated are the same, i.e. a CPU penalty is equivalent to a size penalty).

Memory Penalty. When evolving a queue, memory hungry partial solutions evolved (cf. Section 5.7). Therefore an excessive memory usage penalty was introduced to dissuade the population from evolving down this blind alley. A threshold of using 12 cells must be passed before this penalty applies (12 being sufficient for queue of nine items). This penalty was retained for the list and such memory hungry behaviour has not been observed. This might mean the penalty is working or such solutions are not common in which case the penalty may be unnecessary or too restrictive.

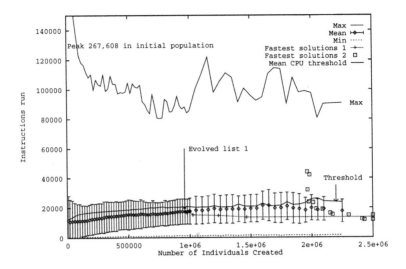

Figure 6.3. Evolution of the number of primitives executed during fitness testing on the List problem, means of 56 runs. Error bars indicate one standard deviation either side of the population mean. The fastest solutions evolved during the two successful runs and the population mean of the threshold above which the CPU penalty is applied are also shown. The minimum number of instructions are executed by relatively unsuccessful programs as these are run on few tests.

Increased Penalties Following Finding a Solution.   In order to search for faster solutions or ones that use less memory, after the first solution has been found in a run, both penalties are increased by setting their thresholds to zero. The new fitness function is applied to members of the existing population as well as newly created individuals.

6.5.4   Locating Errors with Fitness Testing

In any multi-component problem there will be some ambiguity between which parts are performing well and which contain errors, however the fitness tests were designed to try and reduce this by indicating those operations which pass sufficient tests so that they are probably correct. That is, failure to pass the whole test case is probably due to errors elsewhere in the program. This has the potential advantage of reducing the number of active dimensions in the fitness function and the information is also used in the following section.

Various points in the test case were chosen to indicate one or more operations have been tested sufficiently so that if no errors have occurred up to this point we are confident they are working correctly. Naturally this must be done with care so operations are not said to be correct when they still contain errors. This is implemented by marking the chosen points in the fitness test sequences with the operation's name. If they are reached without any errors occurring this is taken to mean testing of that operation is complete. Regardless of any subsequent errors (which are assumed to be the fault of one of the other operations) the operation is given its maximum possible score (i.e. the score it would have if every consistency check was passed). This is applied to Retrieve, End, First, Next, Previous and Printlist. This does not change the execution of the fitness test case but in principle this information could be used to avoid retesting operations which are believed to be correct. (However often it is necessary to run "correct" operations again in order to be able to test other parts of the code).

6.6 DIRECTED CROSSOVER

As Figures 6.4 and 6.5 show, GP solves the different parts of the list problem at different times. If it were known that a fragment of code was working well it would seem wasteful to perform crossover in it. Of course GP does not know for certain if code is correct, however the crossover location can still be guided by the program's current behaviour (as this may be misleading 10% remain unguided). As discussed in Section 3.7 a number of papers show (albeit on very different problems) benefits in using either current behaviour [Rosca and Ballard, 1996] program syntax [Gruau, 1996b; D'haeseleer, 1994] or evolving program syntax [Whigham, 1995b] to bias crossover or other genetic operators. Our mechanism succeeds in dynamically redistributing crossover locations to code in need of improvement as the population evolves. It only considers code at the level of individual operations or ADFs but could be refined.

The mechanism uses knowledge of the first parent's fitness and the number of times the trees in it were executed and whether they appeared to be successful or not to probabilistically bias the choice of which tree the crossover occurs in. It avoids trees which are believed to be correct (as defined in Section 6.5.4), that have never been executed (NB if the only difference between a parent and its offspring is in non-executed code, then that code will not be executed in the offspring either and the offspring will behave identically to the parent) or those that passed all their fitness tests. Otherwise it is biased to choose trees that appear to fail most often (details given in [Langdon, 1995a]).

An alternative worth exploring would be a more incremental approach aiming program modification at code that is closest to working, avoiding code that is performing badly until other code is working. However such an approach was not taken as being more complex but also for fear that it would encourage the evolution of specialist programs which could not evolve to solve the entire problem.

6.7 PARAMETERS

The default values for parameters given in Section D.3 were used except for, the population size (10,000), the maximum program length (500), maximum size of each individual tree in the initial population (50) and the length of each run (≥ 100 generation equivalents, cf. Table 6.3).

6.8 RESULTS

In a group of 56 runs, two produced solutions which passed all the tests. All runs completed at least 100 generation equivalents with the promising ones being continued (the longest run being 300 generations).

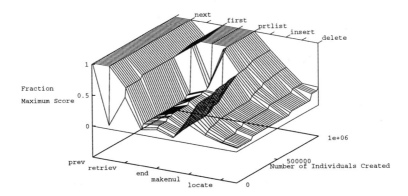

Figure 6.4.   Evolution of the Maximum Score in the Population for Each List Operation, Typical Run

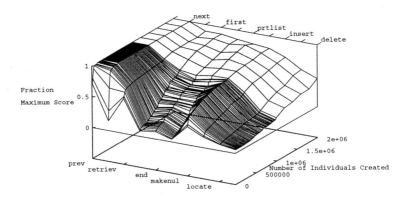

Figure 6.5.   Evolution of the Maximum Score in the Population for Each List Operation, Means of 56 Runs

Like the stack and the queue, solutions have been found which not only pass all the tests, but subsequent analysis shows to be correct and general, i.e. given sufficient memory would correctly implement a list of any finite size. Figure 6.6 shows the first program to pass all the test case (evolved after 95.7840 generation equivalents) which is also a general and generic solution to the list problem.

Figure 6.7 contains simplified equivalent pseudo code for four of the operations and shows GP has implemented the list as an array, with Insert opening a gap for the new data element by moving part of the list up one memory element. Delete moves the top part of the list down one element overwriting the element to be deleted.

Solutions were also found which exploit the finite size of the test set, in that they are able to pass all of the tests but are not entirely general. Interestingly the same GP run found solutions which are general less than five generations later. Each program contains redundant code, i.e. code that can be removed yielding a shorter program but with the same functionality. In Figure 6.6 the essential code is highlighted by shaded boxes.

On continuing the evolutionary process, shorter solutions with reduced CPU cost were found, see Figures 6.3 and 6.8. (The data after generation 100 are more sparse. To avoid excessive variability in Figures 6.3, 6.5 and 6.8 only data referring to fifteen or more runs are plotted). In the first successful run reductions of 20% in program length and 30% in the number of instructions required to complete the test sequences were produced. In the second case the changes were more dramatic with program length falling by two thirds and number of instructions to about a quarter of the first solution found. The shortest solutions reported by both runs have similar lengths and execute about the same number of primitives during the fitness test case. The evolution of solutions which use fewer instructions is exactly what the increase in the CPU penalty (described in Section 6.5.3) was designed to achieve. However if the penalty was not increased there was some reduction due to random fluctuations. The increase in penalty produced bigger effects in these runs but it is not known if this is generally true.

Figure 6.9 shows the number of various primitives in a typical population as it evolves relative to their abundance in the initial random population. It shows a number of primitives become very rare and indeed nine are lost entirely from the population. In 27 runs out of the 56 after 100 generations less than 10% of the population contained a primitive required in the solutions that were found. Of these 27, 16 runs lost all of one or more such primitives. That is in about half the runs loss (or scarcity) of one or more primitives prevents (or makes unlikely) finding a solution similar to those found. (Chapter 8 discusses why primitives may become extinct).

From Figure 6.8 a crude estimate of the probability of a solution being found by generation 200 when using a population of size 10,000, can be estimated at 2/56. Using Equation 4.1 (page 75) the number of GP runs required to be assured (with 99% probability) of obtaining at least one solution can be estimated to be 127. This would require a total of up to $2 \times 10^6 \times 127 = 2.54 \times 10^8$ trial programs. NB this must be treated as an estimate, not an exact figure.

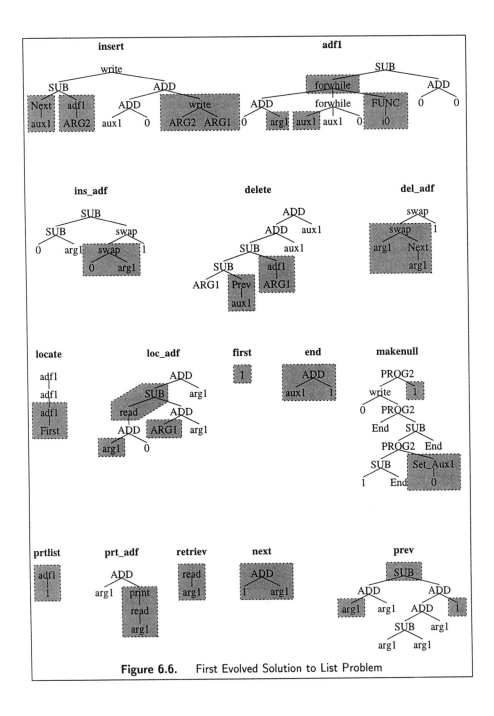

Figure 6.6.   First Evolved Solution to List Problem

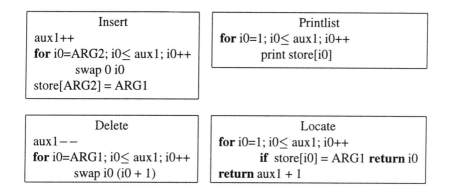

Insert
aux1++
for i0=ARG2; i0≤ aux1; i0++
swap 0 i0
store[ARG2] = ARG1

Printlist
for i0=1; i0≤ aux1; i0++
print store[i0]

Delete
aux1 − −
for i0=ARG1; i0≤ aux1; i0++
swap i0 (i0 + 1)

Locate
for i0=1; i0≤ aux1; i0++
if store[i0] = ARG1 **return** i0
return aux1 + 1

Figure 6.7. Simplified Pseudo Code Equivalent to First Evolved Solution to List Problem

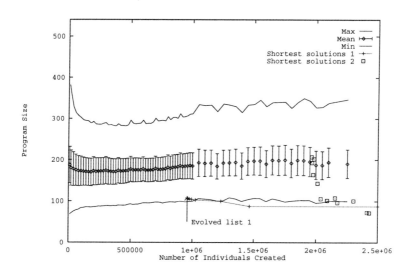

Figure 6.8. Evolution of program size, means of 56 runs. Error bars indicate one standard deviation either side of the population mean. The shortest solutions evolved during the two successful runs are also shown. (Program size limited to 500).

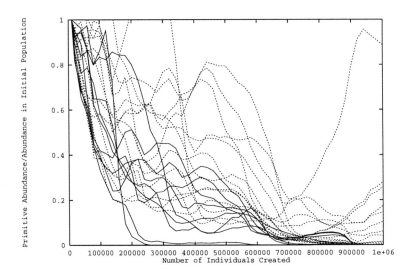

Figure 6.9. Evolution of the frequency of rare primitives (i.e. terminals and functions where the number of them in the population falls below 10% of its original value. NB the many case where primitives did not fall dramatically or increased in number are not shown). This graph plots the ratio of the number of them in the population to the number of them in the initial population for a typical run. The nine primitives which are lost completely from the population are shown as solid lines, the others are shown as dotted lines.

6.9 SOFTWARE MAINTENANCE

Software maintenance is the problem of ensuring existing code continues to operate effectively. This may involve correcting bugs in existing code or adapting code to new requirements. In the software industry maintenance is a major task but has as yet attracted little interest from GP. [Petry and Dunay, 1995] is one exception and [Andre, 1994c] considers using GP to extend the functionality of human written optical character recognition programs (i.e. maintain them).

Automatically generated code (such as produced by a high level language compiler) may be difficult to maintain at the code level and it is common practice to change the inputs to the code generator (i.e. the source code) and run it again. It is anticipated that evolved code will also be difficult to maintain, so maintenance may be performed by changing the inputs to the automatic code generator (i.e. the GP) and running it again.

This section uses the list problem to demonstrate the following model for maintaining evolved code:

1. Start with the original fitness function and the population that contained the solution to the original problem (this should avoid solving the new, possibly harder, problem from scratch),

2. Write additional fitness tests for the new functionality,

3. Expand the existing individuals within the population to include random code for the new functionality,

4. Evolve the expanded population with both the original and new fitness tests.

To use the list problem as a test bed for this model, it is split into two, one part representing the original problem and the other the new requirements. The first is all the operations except Locate and Delete, which represent the new requirements. Locate and Delete were chosen in the expectation that once Insert and Printlist operations are working, being similar, Locate and Delete could be readily added. As they are also the most difficult operations (see Figures 6.4 and 6.5), removing them from the first phase should have the advantage of speeding it up allowing more time to be spent on the maintenance phase.

Each GP run starts as before (Sections 6.2 to 6.8) except in the first phase the new fitness function does not test either Delete or Locate (it comprises 14 test sequences and a total of 426 operation calls and 118 consistency checks). After a solution to the smaller problem has been found, solutions are allowed to spread through the population by continuing the run until at least 1,000 other individuals which solve the smaller problem (i.e. pass all 118 checks) have been found before proceeding to the second phase.

At the start of the second phase the trees for Delete and Locate (and their associated ADFs) in every individual in the population are re-created at random. The other eleven trees in each individual are not changed. So we start the second phase with every individual being a hybrid of code that is adapted to the smaller problem (but need not be an exact solution to it) and random code. In the second phase, the first 14 test sequences are augmented by 7 more designed to test Delete and Locate, they contain 113 operation calls and 41 consistency checks. The population is allowed to evolve as before. The directed crossover mechanism (Section 6.6) ensures crossovers are allowed in every tree but are weighted towards the newly introduced random code.

This use of a substantially adapted population as a starting point can be compared to Perry's [Perry, 1994] use of an initial population which is primarily random but also contains a small number of partially adapted individuals. On a learning task (rather than maintenance) he shows it gives a performance improvement. [Ferrer and Martin, 1995] also reports improved performance from seeding the initial population with previously found good solutions. While [Kraft et al., 1994] construct the initial population to contain a high proportion (80% or more) of terminals which the user has chosen as likely to be relevant. (Seeding is also used on the South Wales problem, cf. Section C.9.4).

6.9.1   Results

In a group of 59 runs, five produced solutions which passed the first set of tests. In these five, evolution was allowed to continue for between 40 and 88 generations, during which two runs found programs which pass the second phase of testing. Both runs produced general programs which implement a list and have a similar structure to those produced in the first experiment. As with the first experiment, on continuing the evolutionary process (with increase CPU and memory penalties) both runs found shorter solutions and solutions which took fewer instructions to complete the test cases.

From finding the first solution to the first part of problem to starting the second took between 3.8 and 7.2 generation equivalents and the first solutions to the whole problem appeared 8.2 and 13.4 generations later (i.e. 16.3 and 25.8 after the first solutions to the first part).

The probability of a solution being found by generation 25.8 when using a population of size 10,000, is estimated to be 2/5 (further work is needed to verify this estimate). Using this, the number of individuals which need to be evaluated in order to be 99% sure of at least one solution is $2.58 \ 10^6$. Or $1/100^{th}$ of the effort to solve the whole problem.

Whilst [Bruce, 1996] does not deal with program maintenance, he reports a similar impressive reduction effort required to evolve a complete solution when individual (five) components are evolved sequentially rather than simultaneously. However unlike our approach, to effect sequential evolution the action of each operation on internal memory is specified by the user and forms part of the fitness function.

6.10   DISCUSSION

While genetic programming appears to find the list problem hard, in terms of the number of individuals generated, it is only about three times more difficult than the queue, despite requiring the co-evolution of ten operations rather than five. There are many differences between the GPs used to solve these problems (such as the syntax restrictions, Section 6.4.2) which no doubt play a part in the difference; none the less so small a rise in problem difficulty given the change in size is interesting.

It is tempting to ascribe the GP's difficulty in finding solutions to the many cases where vital primitives are removed by evolution from the population. The size of the population makes it very unlikely that the complete loss of a primitive from the population (Section 6.8) is due to random chance (known as "genetic drift"). However this should be regarded as a symptom of a deeper problem: they are not justifying their presence in the *current* population.

Their loss indicates they have below average fitness, i.e. in many populations, the fitness function is being deceptive and leading the GP towards some local optima and away from correct solutions. Thus simply adding more of them to the population via a mutation operator would not be expected to solve this problem directly. (However mutation might be beneficial by allowing the population to retain them whilst it evolves beyond the deceptive local optima or via other effects such as incorporating an element of hill climbing, see [O'Reilly and Oppacher, 1996] and [Iba et al., 1994b]). Their below average fitness may be associated with the CPU penalty, which introduces a small selection pressure against "introns" (see [Nordin et al., 1996]) or code of no immediate purpose and this may eventually succeed in removing all of certain primitives.

Measures to retain population diversity such as fitness niches or demes appear to be necessary to give the evolutionary process time to assemble the primitives into high value building blocks from which complete solutions can be assembled so enabling it to escape from local optima. Overlapping demes, which constrain mates to be selected only from near neighbours (similar to those in [Tackett and Carmi, 1994]) succeeded in delaying the lost of primitives but spreading the population out across the fitness landscape using a "fitness sharing function" [Horn et al., 1993] was more effective in delaying the losses for longer and so was used.

While fitness niche appear to combat the effects of deceptive fitness functions to some extent, the many non-dominated solutions within the population mean the primary selection pressure is to find relatively unpopulated fitness niches, rather than better ones. It also means almost all crossovers occur between disparate individuals. It is unclear how beneficial this is. [Ryan, 1994] suggests benefits for disassortive mating, while [Harvey, 1992] suggests (for a variable length but linear GA) better results may be obtained by breeding between similar programs. He suggests this will produce smaller improvements at each stage but more progress in the long run.

One of the lessons, for multi-part programs, from the queue was while ADFs are useful, it may be better to ensure the evolutionary pressures on them do not pull in more than one direction by avoiding an ADF being used in two completely different ways. For example in the queue problem the enqueue and empty operations have little in common, when they shared the same ADF it appeared to try and satisfy both and so failed to develop any clear functionality and no overall solutions were found. Accordingly the use of ADFs was constrained (Table 6.3). This up front GP design and the use of syntax restrictions (Section 6.4.2) was intended to help the GP, it would be interesting to see how far the GP would get with fewer restrictions.

6.11 CONCLUSIONS

The importance of abstract data structures to software engineering is well recognised. Our experiments (which were published in part in [Langdon, 1996b]) show genetic

programming, using indexed memory, can automatically implement integer list structures, co-evolving all ten components simultaneously. The list data structure is a
generalisation of the stack and the queue data structures (which have already been
evolved) however it is more complex than either.

As with earlier work, generic programs have been automatically created that not
only solve the problem on which they were trained but which (with sufficient memory)
implement the abstract data structure of any size.

A model for maintaining evolved software based on population re-use has been
demonstrated and (in one example) considerable savings shown compared to evolving
a solution to the new requirement from scratch.

Program execution time can be included as a Pareto component of fitness and leads
to shorter and more efficient programs. It has been shown that a genetic programming
population using Pareto tournament selection, in conjunction with comparison with (a
sample of) the rest of the population can stably support many fitness niches.

Whilst this work has shown fitness niches, CPU penalties and biased choice of
crossover points were effective when evolving a list, further work is required to demonstrate to what extent they are generally useful.

7 PROBLEMS SOLVED USING DATA STRUCTURES

In this chapter we show that data abstraction can be beneficially used within genetic programming (GP). Work so far [Teller, 1994a; Andre, 1994b; Brave, 1995; Jannink, 1994] shows GP can automatically create programs which explicitly use directly addressable (indexed) memory to solve problems and Chapters 4, 5 and 6 demonstrate that GP can automatically generate abstract data structures such as stacks, queues and lists. In this chapter we show that GP can evolve programs which solve problems using such data structures. In two cases we show better GP performance when using data structures compared to directly addressable memory. In the remaining case (which is the first problem presented) the evolved solution uses an unexpected data structure which is appropriate to the problem rather than indexed memory when both are available. Section 7.4 reviews published GP work where explicit memory is used and concludes that in most successful cases data structures appropriate to the problem have been provided for the GP (although the experimenter may not have used the term "data structure").

Three example problems are presented. In each the task is to induce a program which processes a context free language given training samples of the language. We chose problems that should be solvable using stack data structures as stacks were the easiest of the data structures investigated in Chapters 4, 5 and 6 to evolve. In general, data structures at least as powerful as stacks are required to process context free languages.

In Section 7.1 GP evolves a program which classifies sequences of brackets as being correctly or incorrectly nested. Section 7.2 evolves programs which classify sequences of multiple types of bracket as being correctly nested or not (a Dyck language) and Section 7.3 evolves programs which evaluate Reverse Polish (postfix) expressions. The structure of Sections 7.1, 7.2 and 7.3 is based on the structure of Chapters 4, 5 and 6. For example Sections 7.1.1, 7.2.1 and 7.3.1 each contain the problem statement for one of the three problems. Section 7.5 summarises this chapter.

7.1   BALANCED BRACKET PROBLEM

Other work on GP evolving language recognizers has concentrated upon using GP to evolve tree based specifications for abstract machines, such as finite state machines [Dunay et al., 1994; Longshaw, 1997; Slavov and Nikolaev, 1997], deterministic push-down automata [Zomorodian, 1995], machines composed of simple Turing machines [Dunay and Petry, 1995; Petry and Dunay, 1995] or special memory nodes within the tree [Iba et al., 1995]. While [Falco et al., 1997] uses GP to generate a number of formal languages. However [Koza, 1992, page 442] recasts a simple language recognition problem in terms of classifying DNA sequences as *introns* or *exons* and shows GP can evolve a correct program for this task and [Wyard, 1991; Wyard, 1994; Lucas, 1994] use GAs operating on formal grammar rules of various types to induce grammars for a number of regular and context free languages. In contrast we wish to use the task of evolving a language recogniser to investigate the impact of providing data structures versus indexed memory, and so we follow normal GP practice and our GP executes the GP tree directly i.e. treats it as a program.

In this section we show GP can solve the balanced bracket problem directly when given an appropriate data structure ([Zomorodian, 1995] previously solved this problem using GP to evolve a specification for a pushdown automaton, [Wyard, 1991] used a GA operating on formal grammar rules to induce a grammar for it and [Lankhorst, 1995] used a fixed representation GA to specify a pushdown automaton, while [Sun et al., 1990] solved it by training a neural network in combination with a stack). The balanced bracket language is a context free language and so can be recognised by a pushdown automaton (which implies use of a stack) and not a regular language, which could be recognised by a finite state machine. However a pushdown automaton is not required, the balanced bracket language can be recognised by an intermediate machine, a finite state automaton with a counter. The solution found by GP was of this form. In a run where both index memory and register memory were available, the evolved solution used the register memory, NB GP selected the appropriate data structure for the problem.

7.1.1   Problem Statement

The balanced bracket problem is to recognise sentences composed of sequences of two symbols, (and), which are correctly nested. E.g. (( )) is correctly nested but ( )) is not. A limit of ten symbols per sentence was assumed.

7.1.2   Architecture

Two automatically defined functions (ADFs) (see Section 2.3.2 for an introduction to ADFs) are available to assist the main result producing branch (or tree). The first,

Table 7.1. Tableau for Balanced Bracket Problem

Objective	Find a program that classifies sequences of ((represented by 1) and) (-1) as being correctly nested or not.
Architecture	Main tree, adf1 (no arguments) and adf2 (one argument)
Primitives (any tree)	ADD, SUB, PROG2, IFLTE, Ifeq, 0, 1, -1, max, forwhile, i0
(rpb, adf1)	adf2, aux1, read, write, swap, Set_Aux1
(rpb, adf2)	arg1
(rpb only)	adf1
Max prog size	4 × 50 = 200. In initial population each tree is limited to 50 primitives.
Fitness case	175 fixed test examples, cf. Table 7.2
Fitness Scaling	Number of test examples correctly classified (scalar).
Selection	Tournament group size of 4 used for both parent selection and selecting programs to be removed from the population. Steady state population (elitist).
Hits	Number test sentences correctly classified
Wrapper	Zero represents False (i.e. not in language) otherwise True.
Parameters	Pop = 10,000, G = 50, 3 × 3 demes, no CPU penalty, no aborts.
Success predicate	Fitness ≥ 175

adf1, has no arguments and has the same terminal and function sets as the main tree. However as it does not have any arguments, it does not use the primitive arg1.

The second, adf2, has one argument but cannot contain terminals and functions with side effects. This allows a cache of previous values returned by it to be maintained, thus reducing run time. (Caches of ADF values were also used in Chapter 5, cf. Table 5.11 (page 118). See also Section D.6).

7.1.3   Choice of Primitives

Table 7.1 shows the parameters used and the terminals and functions provided, NB they include indexed memory but not stacks.

For ease of comparison the same sized indexed memory and stacks were used in all three sets of experiments in this chapter. Both were deliberately generously sized to avoid restricting the GP's use of them. The indexed memory consisted of 127 memory cells, addressed as $-63 \ldots +63$, and the stack allowed up to 99 32-bit signed integers to be pushed. As in the previous chapters, memory primitives had defined behaviour which allows the GP to continue on errors (e.g. popping from an empty stack or writing to a non-existent memory cell). All stored data within the program is initialised to zero before the start of each test sentence. Tables 7.9 and 7.10 (pages 165–166) give the actions of terminals and functions used in this chapter.

Table 7.2. Number of correctly nested and incorrectly nested bracket test sentences of each length used in the nested bracket test case. Longer incorrect sentences were chosen at random from all the possible incorrect sentences of the same length.

Length	Positive		Negative	
1			all	2
2	all	1	all	3
3			all	8
4	all	2	all	14
5			random	4
6	all	5	random	5
7			random	5
8	all	14	random	14
9			random	14
10	all	42	random	42
Totals		64		111

7.1.4 Fitness Function

The fitness of each trial program was evaluated on a fixed set of 175 example sentences containing both correctly nested (positive tests) and incorrectly nested brackets (negative tests). The test case includes all the positive cases up to a length of ten symbols and all the negative examples up to a length of four. The number of negative examples grows rapidly with sentence length and so above a length of four a limited number negative examples were chosen at random (see Table 7.2). The program is run once for each symbol in the sentence. Thus each program is run 1403 times (674 for (and 729 with an argument of)). The value returned by the program on the last symbol of the sentence gives its verdict as to whether the sequence is correctly nested, i.e. the value returned by the program is ignored, except on the last symbol of each test sentence.

This test case and the test cases used in Sections 7.2.4 and 7.3.4 are available via anonymous ftp. Section D.9 gives the network addresses.

7.1.5 Parameters

The default values for parameters given in Section D.3 were used except the population size and the maximum program length. The parameters used are summarised in Table 7.1.

Earlier work (cf. Chapter 5) had shown even a large population had a great tendency to converge to partial solutions which effectively trapped the whole population preventing further progress. In this (and the following section) the population was partitioned into demes so crossover is restricted to near neighbours in order to reduce the speed of convergence (see Section 3.8). As in Chapter 5 the population is treated as a 50×100 torus with two members of the population per square on its surface. Each time a new individual is created, a 3×3 square neighbourhood on the torus (known as a deme) is selected at random. Parents and the individual their offspring will replace are selected from this deme rather than from the whole population [Tackett, 1994; Collins, 1992].

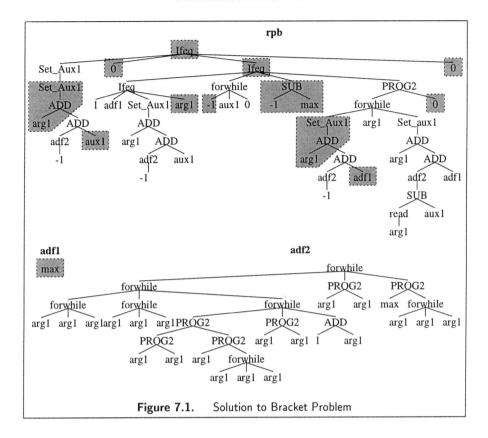

Figure 7.1.   Solution to Bracket Problem

7.1.6   Results

In the first run a general solution was produced by generation 19, which contained 88 primitives. This is shown in Figure 7.1 and a simplified version is shown in Figure 7.2.

In contrast to earlier work [Zomorodian, 1995], where GP was obliged to evolve pushdown automata, the evolved solution is effectively a finite state machine with a counter (NB less powerful than a pushdown automaton). The evolved solution (cf. Figure 7.2) only uses a single integer memory cell (aux1), in which it counts the depth of nesting. At the end of a legal sentence this count must be zero. Further, should the brackets be unbalanced before the end is reached, this is recognised and aux1 is also used as a flag indicating this. This solution not only passes all the fitness tests and is a general solution to the problem but (given suitable redefinition of max) is a solution for sequences of any length.

To find the solution given in Figure 7.1 required $19 \times 10,000 = 190,000$ individuals to be processed. This is similar to that required in [Zomorodian, 1995] where a solution was found in generation 24 with a population of 3,000. ($24 \times 3,000 = 72,000$).

Given the readily found general solution did not exhibit stack like behaviour it was decided not to repeat this problem with a GP that had stack primitives.

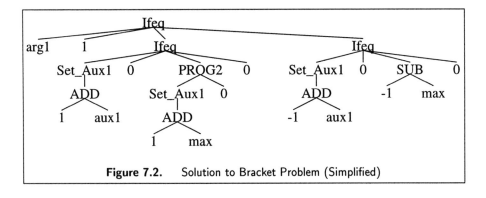

Figure 7.2.   Solution to Bracket Problem (Simplified)

7.2 DYCK LANGUAGE

In this section we apply genetic programming to a solve a new problem, that of recognising a Dyck language. Two sets of experiments were conducted, the first provided the GP with primitives which implement a stack for it and the second provided indexed memory and other primitives like those from which it has been shown GP can evolve stack data structures, cf. Chapter 4. The same fitness function, population size and other parameters were used in both sets of experiments. Solutions were readily found when the GP was provided with a stack data structure but no solutions have been found when using indexed memory.

The Dyck problem was chosen as Dyck languages are context free languages and require machines at least as powerful as pushdown automata (i.e. stacks) to solve them. Dyck languages are generalisations of the balanced bracket problem to multiple types of bracket.

7.2.1 Problem Statement

The problem is to recognise which sentences are correctly bracketed, however there are now four types of bracket pairs, (,), [,], {, }, `, '. E.g. {} [] is correctly bracketed but [} is not. As with the nested brackets problem, a limit of ten symbols per sentence was assumed.

7.2.2 Architecture

In the first experiments (stack given) no ADFs were used, whilst in the second there are three ADFs, having 0, 1 and 0 arguments. It was hoped that these could evolve to operate like pop, push and top. Each could be called from the main tree, additionally the third (which it was hoped might evolve to act like top) could be called by the first.

7.2.3 Terminals, Functions and Parameters

The terminals, functions and control parameters used in these two experiments are as Section 7.1 except where given in Table 7.3. The differences between the two experiments in this section are shown in the middle and right hand columns of Table 7.3.

The five stack primitives are based on the definition of a stack given in Table 4.1 (page 63), however they have been made more rugged by ensuring their behaviour is defined in all circumstances, i.e. including errors such as popping from an empty stack. Their behaviour is defined at the end of this chapter in Tables 7.9 and 7.10.

This problem is more complex than that in Section 7.1 and so the test case is longer. To constrain the increase in run time, forwhile loops were not used.

7.2.4 Fitness Function

The fitness of every trial program is determined by presenting it with a series of symbols from test sentences and counting how many times it correctly classifies each

Table 7.3. Tableau for Dyck Language Problem

Objective	Find a program that classifies sequences of four types of bracket ((((represented as 5),) (71), [(13),] (103), { (31), } (137), ' (43) and ' (167)) as being correctly nested or not.		
Primitives	Common	Stack Given	Index Memory
All trees:	ADD, SUB, PROG2, IFLTE, Ifeq, 0, 1, max, aux1	Makenull, Empty, Top, Pop, Push	read, write, inc_aux1, dec_aux1
rpb: as all plus	ifopen, ifmatch, ARG1, Set_Aux1		adf1, adf2, adf3
adf1: as all plus			adf3
adf2: as all plus			arg1, arg2
Max prog size	Initial tree limit 50	50	4 × 50 = 200
Fitness Case	286 fixed test examples, cf. Table 7.4		
Fitness Scaling	Number of correct answers returned.		
Selection	Tournament size 4 (After first solution CPU penalty used giving a two dimensional fitness value, fitness niching used with a sample of up to 81 (9 × 9) nearest neighbours).		
Hits	Number test symbols correctly classified.		
Wrapper	Zero represents True (i.e. in language) and all other values False.		
Parameters	Pop = 10,000, G = 50, Pareto, 3 × 3 demes, CPU penalty only after first solution found, Abort on first error in sentence.		
Success predicate	Hits ≥ 1756, i.e. all answers correct.		

as to whether it is the last of a correctly balanced sequence. All memory is initialised to zero before the start of each test sentence.

Test Case. The number of possible test sentences of a particular length is much larger than in Section 7.1 and so it was not practical to include sentences longer than eight symbols and even for lengths of six and eight symbols it was necessary to select (at random) positive test examples to include.

In a correctly matched sentence there will be equal numbers of opening and closing brackets of each type but this is unlikely to be true in a random sequence of brackets. If the only negative examples are random sequences of symbols, a program could correctly guess most answers just by considering if there are equal numbers of each pair of bracket. We anticipate that such programs can be readily evolved, for example the program that evolved in Section 7.1 does this. However it may be anticipated that evolving complete solutions from such partial solutions will be very difficult. (Chapter 8 suggests the evolution of correct stacks is made harder by the presence of "deceptive" partial solutions). To penalise such partial solutions the test case included examples where there are equal numbers but which are not correctly nested (referred to as "Balanced" in Table 7.4).

As before it was not practical to include all cases and so longer negative examples (both balanced and not balanced) were selected at random. Even so the fitness tests are much longer than that in Section 7.1 and so to keep run time manageable the number of times each program must be run was reduced by:

- Only using the first half of the test case (i.e. tests up to length six). However if a program passes all the shorter tests then it was also tested on test sentences of length seven and eight. Thus most of the time the second half of the test case is not used. It is only used by programs that are nearly correct, which evolve later in the GP run.

- In the first experiments in this chapter, each program is only tested at the end of each test sentence. In these experiments the value returned for each symbol is used. If a wrong answer is returned the the rest of the sentence is ignored. This reduces run time as in many cases only part of the test sentence is processed.

Some shorter sentences are identical to the start of longer ones and so they need not be tested explicitly as the same actions will be performed as part of a longer test. Therefore such duplicates were removed from the test case. The test case after removing such duplicates are summarised in the right hand side of Table 7.4.

Symbol Coding. Initially brackets were coded as $\pm 1, \pm 2, \pm 3, \pm 4$ but general solutions proved difficult to find. Instead, despite the use of "balanced" negative examples, partial solutions based upon summing up symbol values dominated. Since the purpose of the experiment was to investigate learning correct nesting of symbols rather than learning which symbols match each other the problem was simplified by providing the GP with two new primitives (ifmatch and ifopen, cf. Table 7.10) which say which symbols match each other. To further discourage partial solutions based on summing symbol values the symbols were recoded as prime values with no simple relationships between them (cf. Table 7.3).

Table 7.4.   Number of correctly and incorrectly nested test sentences in the Dyck language test case. The incorrect test sentences are divided into those with the correct number of each type of bracket but which are in the wrong order (referred to as "Balanced") and others (referred to as "Rand"). Longer sentences were chosen at random. The right hand side of the table gives the number in each category actually used in the Dyck test case, i.e. after removing duplicates.

Length	Positive	Negative		After Removing Duplicates			
		Balanced	Rand	Positive	Balanced	Rand	Score
1		all 8					0
2	all 4	all 60				9	18
3			16			10	30
4	all 32	all 24	16	27	16		172
5			16			16	80
6	rand 32	rand 32	32	32	32	32	576
7			16			16	112
8	rand 32	rand 32	32	32	32	32	768
			Totals	91	112	83	1756

Evolving Improved Solutions.   The combination of Pareto fitness, a CPU penalty and fitness niches introduced in Chapter 6 (Section 6.5.3) was used in these experiments. Briefly after an individual which passes all the tests is found the GP run is allowed to continue using a modified fitness function which includes a CPU penalty. Each program's fitness now contains two orthogonal terms, the original score and the $\lfloor$mean$\rfloor$ number of instructions run per program execution. Tournament selection is still used for reproduction and deletion but now uses Pareto comparison (see Section 3.9), so passing tests and using little CPU are equally important. The fitness sharing scheme described in Section 6.5.3 was used. This introduces a secondary selection pressure to be different from the rest of the population so allowing high scoring and high CPU programs to co-exist with programs with lower scores but using less CPU. This may reduced premature convergence.

7.2.5   Results

In three runs given the stack primitives general solutions were evolved by generation 7 to 23 (in three identical runs but using simple non-demic (normal) populations, two runs produced solutions in generations 30 and 39). Evolution was allowed to continue after the first individual to pass all the tests was found. Under the influence of the CPU penalty faster but still general solutions were found (see Figure 7.3). Figure 7.4 shows the first solution to evolve in a run using demes and Figure 7.5 shows one of the fastest solutions produced in the same run after 50 generations. As in Section 7.1 the solutions are not only general solutions to the given problem, but given a deep enough stack would work with any sentences of any length.

   As all runs given stack primitives and using demes succeeded in finding a solution the best (i.e. most likely) estimate of the number of runs required to be assured (with

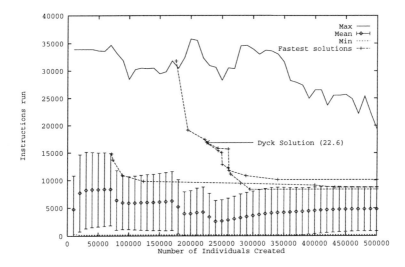

Figure 7.3. Evolution of the number of primitives executed during fitness testing on the Dyck problem, means of 3 runs using demes. Error bars indicate one standard deviation either side of the population mean. The fastest solutions evolved in each run are also plotted. The minimum number of instructions are executed by relatively unsuccessful programs as these are run on few tests.

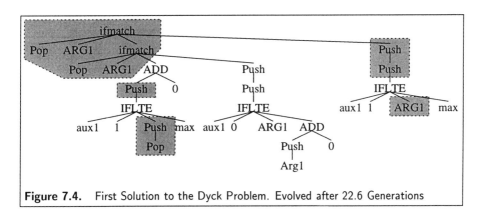

Figure 7.4. First Solution to the Dyck Problem. Evolved after 22.6 Generations

99% probability) of obtaining at least one solution is one. This would require a total of up to $23 \times 10^4 \times 1 = 2.3 \ 10^5$ trial programs.

In contrast none of 15 runs using the indexed memory primitives passed all the tests. (The probability of the difference between the two experiments being due to chance is $\ll 0.1\%$). Some of the more promising runs were extended beyond 50 generations up to 140 generations without finding a solution. The best (produced after 84 generations) still failed 3 tests (on sequences of up to six symbols). It showed some stack like behaviour which enables it to pass 13 of the tests of length seven and eight

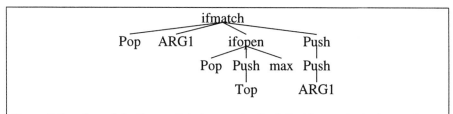

Figure 7.5.   One of the Fastest Solutions to the Dyck Problem evolved after 50 Generations

but also showed some signs of over fitting to the specific test case used rather than having learnt to solve the general problem.

A program which always returns zero (i.e. True) has a fitness of zero because it will always fail on the first symbol of each test sentence (a sentence of odd length must be unbalanced). In contrast a program which never returns zero will always be correct on the first symbol of each sentence and so will get the opportunity to be tested on the second symbol which it may also pass. For the actual test case used a program which never returns zero has a fitness of 714. While aborting a test sentence on the first error reduces the number of times programs are run, it may also make it more difficult to evolve a solution. In both experiments the GP population quickly learns not to return zero, but when using indexed memory it appears to be more difficult than when given a stack to escape this local optima and learn to return zero at some points.

7.3   EVALUATING REVERSE POLISH EXPRESSIONS

In this section we describe the final comparison of appropriate data structures and indexed memory. Once again solutions are readily evolved when the appropriate data structure is provided but no solutions have been found when using indexed memory.

Two sets of experiments were made, the first provided the GP with primitives which implement a stack for it and the second provided primitives like those from which it has been shown GP can evolve stack data structures.

7.3.1   Problem Statement

In this section the GP evolves a four function ($+$, $-$, $/$ and $\times$) calculator, i.e. evaluates integer arithmetic expression. The problem is simplified by presenting the expression in Reverse Polish Notation (postfix), which avoids consideration of operator precedence and by avoiding expressions which include division by zero. No limit on the length of expressions was assumed, however the expressions tested were between three and fifteen symbols long (see Table 7.6).

7.3.2   Architecture

The multi-tree architecture and multi-tree crossover described in Section 3.6 and employed in Chapters 4, 5 and 6 was used. This allows trees within each individual to evolve to specialise in solving one of the operations that form the complete calculator program. Each individual within the population consists of five separate trees (num, plus, minus, times and div) plus either zero or two ADFs. As in Sections 7.1 and 7.2 each test sentence is presented a symbol at a time to the GP, however in this case the appropriate tree is selected. E.g. if the symbol is an integer, then the num tree is executed with the integer as its argument. Each tree returns a value as the current value of the expression (num's answer is ignored).

In the first experiments (stack given) no ADFs were used, whilst in the second there are two ADFs, having 0 and 1 arguments respectively. It was hoped that these could evolve to operate like pop and push. Both ADFs could be called from the five main trees.

7.3.3 Terminals, Functions and Parameters

The terminals, functions and control parameters are as Section 7.2 except where given in Table 7.5.

Fears that run time might prove to be excessive led to the decision to remove some unnecessary primitives from the function and terminal sets. Since all storage including the supplied stack is initialised before the evolved programs can use it, the Makenull operation is not needed. Therefore the terminal set was simplified by not including Makenull and Empty (which is also not needed) in these experiments.

7.3.4 Fitness Function

In each individual in the population a separate score is maintained for its five operations (num, plus, minus, times and div) plus a CPU penalty. Each time the individual returns the correct answer (and it is checked) the score for each of its operations that has been used since the last time its result was checked is incremented. As in Section 7.2, these scores are not combined and each contributes as a separate objective in multi-objective Pareto selection tournaments.

Test Case.   The fixed test case was created before the GP was run. Part of the test case was devised by hand and the remainder was selected at random. However randomly selected data values (from the range $-99 \ldots +99$) proved to be unsatisfactory for expressions containing "/" because division of two randomly selected integers has a high chance of yielding zero or an integer near it and therefore data values were changed by hand. (Less than one in eight divisions of randomly chosen values will yield a value of 4 or more or -4 or less).

The following rules were used to create the test case:

- It was expected that as minus and divide are not commutative they would be the most difficult operations to evolve and therefore the test case include a higher proportion of minus and divide than the other two arithmetic operations (cf. Table 7.7).

- The test case was designed to include deeply nested expressions (cf. Table 7.8) as it was anticipated otherwise non-general partial solutions only able to evaluate simple expressions, which could be evaluated without using a stack, would predominate.

- To avoid consideration of exception handling, and its associated complexity, divide by zero was deliberately excluded from the test case.

Table 7.5. Tableau for Reverse Polish Notation (RPN) Expression Evaluation Problem

Objective	Find a program that evaluates integer Reverse Polish (postfix) arithmetic expressions.		
Primitives	Common	Stack Given	Index Memory
+ − ×/ trees:	ADD, SUB, MUL, DIV, PROG2, 0, 1, aux1, Set_Aux1	Top, Pop, Push	read, write, inc_aux1, dec_aux1, adf1, adf2
num: as ops plus	arg1		
adf1: as ops but			no adfs
adf2: as ops but			no adfs and add arg1
adf3: as ops but			no adfs and add arg1, arg2
Max prog size	Initial tree limit 50	$5 \times 50 = 250$	$7 \times 50 = 350$
Fitness Case	127 fixed test expressions, cf. Tables 7.6, 7.7 and 7.8.		
Fitness Scaling	Number of correct answers returned.		
Selection	Pareto tournament size 4, CPU penalty (initial threshold 50 per operation), fitness niching used with a sample of up to 81 other members of the population.		
Hits	Number of correct answers returned.		
Wrapper	Value on num ignored. No wrapper on other trees.		
Parameters	Pop = 10,000, G = 100, Pareto, no demes, CPU penalty (increased after 1st solution found), abort on first wrong answer given in expression.		
Success predicate	Fitness ≥ 194, i.e. a program passes all tests.		

Table 7.6. Length of reverse polish expressions at each point where answers are checked in the fitness test case.

length	1	2	3	4	5	6	7	8	9	10	11	12	13	14	15	Total
No. of cases			10	3	55	27	44	2	36	1	5		8		3	194

- Randomly generated data values were manually changed so that only a few divisions yield values in the range $-3 \ldots + 3$.

- To avoid problems with overflow, randomly generated expressions did not allow: arguments to addition or subtraction outside the range $-10^8 \ldots +10^8$ or arguments to multiplication or division outside the range $-65535 \ldots +65535$.

- Also to avoid overflow problems, data values set by hand were chosen so neither the product of two arguments of divide nor the square of the second argument exceeded 2,147,483,647.

- Most test expressions were well formed, with exactly the right number of data values for the number of operators (and vice-versa). (Since all four operators are binary this means there is one more data value than the number of operators in the expression). However, to test generality, one expression with fewer arithmetic operations was included. In this case there should be multiple data values left after evaluating the expression.

As before it was necessary to constrain run time. This was done by checking answers during the evaluation of each expression and aborting evaluation following the first error detected and removing test examples which essentially duplicated others. This left 127 test expressions which include 194 points where the trial program's answer is checked.

CPU Penalty. The long run times encountered with these experiments led to the decision to include a CPU penalty of $\lfloor$mean$\rfloor$ number of primitives executed per program run. Unlike the previous section, this CPU penalty was applied from the start of each run. However initially only programs with long run times are penalised (by ignoring the penalty where it was ≤ 50. This was implemented by setting the penalty is zero for such fast programs). Should a program be evolved which passes the whole fitness test case then the CPU penalty is increased by applying it to all programs.

7.3.5 Results

In eleven runs using stack primitives, six produced solutions which passed all the tests, these were found between generations 11 and 23 (see Figure 7.6). In four cases the first programs to pass all the tests were also general solutions to the problem. In the other two the first solutions failed special cases such as $1 - 1$ and $x/y = 0$ (which were not included in the test case), however in both runs general solutions were evolved less than 12 generations later (before 34 generations).

Table 7.7.   Number of times each tree occurs in reverse polish expression (RPN) test case
and the score it has when the whole test case is passed.

Operation	No.	Max Score
num	550	163
plus	67	58
minus	103	85
times	85	64
divide	156	127
	420	
Totals	970	497

Table 7.8.   Number of symbols (i.e. operators or numbers) used in the RPN test case for
each level of expression nesting. (Depth of nesting calculated after the symbol has been
processed).

depth	1	2	3	4	5	6	Total
No. of cases	387	390	149	31	12	1	970

Under the action of the increased CPU penalty, solutions which took about one third
of the CPU time of the first solution found were evolved. Figure 7.7 shows one of the
first general solutions to be evolved and Figure 7.8 shows one of the fastest solutions
evolved at the end of the same run.

In 59 runs with stack primitives replaced by indexed memory (see right hand side
of Table 7.5) no program passed all the tests. (NB the probability of the difference
between the two experiments being due to chance is ≪ 1%). The highest number
of tests passed (148 of 194) was achieved by a program which used the first ADF to
implement DIVR (i.e. standard divide but with the arguments in reversed order, see
Table 7.9) and the second to approximate both push and pop on a three level stack.
Other unsuccessful trials included adding a third ADF (with two arguments) in the
hope that this might evolve the DIVR functionality leaving the other ADFs free to
implement push and pop (best 102 in 33 runs, of which 16 ran out of time before 50
generations) and supplying SUBR and DIVR functions (in place of SUB and DIV)
where the best score was 116, in 38 runs.

The probability of a general solution being found by generation 23 when given the
stack primitives is best estimated at 4/11. Using Equation 4.1 (page 75) the number
of GP runs required to be assured (with 99% probability) of obtaining at least one
solution is 11. This would require a total of up to $23 \times 10^4 \times 11 = 2.53 \ 10^6$ trial
programs.

Discussion.   The non-commutative functions (− and /) appear to be more difficult
to evolve than commutative ones because the arguments on the stack are in the opposite
order to that used by the SUB and DIV functions. (The problem can be readily solved,

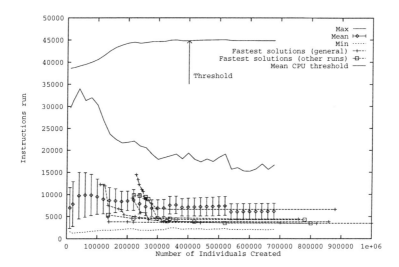

Figure 7.6. Evolution of the number of primitives executed during fitness testing on the calculator problem, means of 11 runs. (Average data is not plotted after generation 70 as several runs run out of time by this point). Error bars indicate one standard deviation either side of the population mean. The fastest solutions evolved during the six successful runs and the population mean of the threshold above which the CPU penalty is applied are also shown. The minimum number of instructions are executed by relatively unsuccessful programs as these are run on few tests.

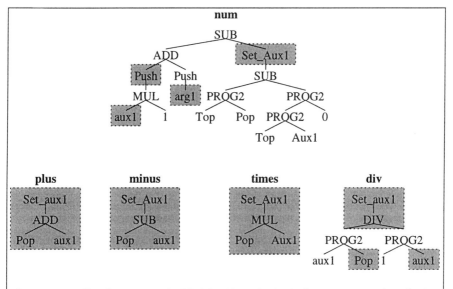

Figure 7.7. First Solution to the RPN Problem. Evolved after 11.0 generations (12240 instructions to complete test case)

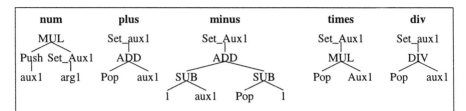

Figure 7.8.   One of the Fastest Solutions to the RPN Problem evolved after 76 generations (4842 instructions to complete test case)

when given the stack primitives, by replacing SUB and DIV by SUBR and DIVR which process their arguments in the opposite order, i.e. the order on the stack). The div tree has to use some storage (i.e. aux1) to reverse the order of the stack arguments (sub can simply negate the result of performing the operation in the wrong order to get the right answer). The need to use aux1 makes the problem deceptive, in that many programs can obtain high scores using aux1 as the top of the stack and only fail tests which require deeper use of the stack.

Some of the difficulty the GP with indexed memory found may have been due to trying to use aux1 both as stack pointer (for which inc_aux1 and dec_aux1 make it suitable) and as the top of stack (as evolved in many cases where the stack primitives were given). If this is case better results might be obtained by adding a second auxiliary variable (aux2) so these two uses could be split between two variables.

The top curve on Figure 7.6 shows the initial CPU penalty threshold, i.e. before a solution has been found. This shows on average the CPU threshold is higher than the average maximum CPU used by any individual in the population. While this means the CPU penalty has a small effect, the effect need not be negligible since any program which does exceed the threshold automatically has poor fitness and so is likely to be removed quickly from the population (and so not be included in these statistics). I.e. the penalty may still be effective in constraining growth in elapse time and program size (often described as "bloat").

Contrasting Figure 7.6 with a similar plot for the list problem (Figure 6.3, page 132) we see in the list the CPU penalty is much more constraining, despite the threshold being set at 120 per test rather than 50. This is probably simply due to the presence of the forwhile primitive in the function set but may also be due in part to the problem requiring more primitives to solve it (fastest evolved solution 29.1 per test versus 7.0 for the calculator).

7.4   WORK BY OTHERS ON SOLVING PROBLEMS WITH MEMORY

This section briefly reviews published work on solving problems using GP which includes memory primitives. In most successful cases data structures appropriate to the problem have been used although the term "data structure" may not have been. The principle exception is Teller's signal processing system PADO. This section groups publications according to memory structure, starting with the simplest and finishes with consideration of PADO.

7.4.1 Scalars

[Cramer, 1985] showed programs which use simple scalar memory could be evolved, however the paper concentrates upon program representation not use of memory. [Huelsbergen, 1996] solved the same problem, albeit with different primitives etc., but also uses simple scalar memory. Huelsbergen also shows the problem can be solved by random search in a practical time.

[Koza, 1992, page 470] presents an example where a single variable is used to maintain a running total during execution of a loop. While in [Koza, 1994, page 512] a small number of variables are used in a protein classification problem where the program processes proteins sequentially, a residue at a time. The variables provide the ability to store information about previous parts of the protein which is expected to be useful in this classification problem. NB in both cases programs were evolved using memory appropriate to the problem.

7.4.2 One Indexed Memory

Most of the published work on using GP where use of memory is explicitly evolved follows [Teller, 1993; Teller, 1994a] which introduced "indexed memory", i.e. a single multiple celled directly addressable memory, to GP. For example [Raik and Browne, 1996] use indexed memory to show that on a reactive task, GP with explicit memory performs better than GP with implicit memory. Indexed memory, as it allows random access, provides little "structure" and could be problem independent, however in [Andre, 1994b; Andre, 1995b; Andre, 1995a] the indexed memory is made problem specific by treating it as two dimensional and sizing it so that it is isomorphic to a small problem "world". That is the memory is given a structure appropriate to the problem. A similar approach is taken in [Brave, 1996c] where memory is isomorphic to a full binary tree "world".

The simple indexed memory used in [Crepeau, 1995] is not obviously structured in a problem specific manner. The author suggests the success of GP at evolving a "Hello.World" program by manipulating (a subset of) Z80 machine code may in part be due to initialising memory with random 8 bit values. Thus it is "highly probable" [Crepeau, 1995, page 132] that the needed ascii values are initially in the indexed memory.

Another GP system which evolves machine code, based this time on the SUN RISC architecture, allows large amounts of directly addressable memory, however [Nordin and Banzhaf, 1995] does not describe experiments using it. [Nordin and Banzhaf, 1996] describes experiments using the system for sound compression where indexed memory and structured memory (a stack) were tried. In these experiments "programs took longer time to evolve and performed worse in fitness but had a softer sound with less overtones" than experiments without memory. However other changes were simultaneously made which may have made the task more difficult. Therefore it is difficult to draw any conclusions regarding the benefits or otherwise of data structures from this paper.

[Jannink, 1994] includes 16 memory cells in one experiment to evolve programs which generate "random" numbers. This is said to give "the best average validation score", i.e. better than when the programs were not given access to memory. Details of how the evolved programs use memory are not given and no comparison with other memory sizes or structures is provided.

7.4.3   Case Base

[Spector and Alpern, 1995] presents a system which attempts to evolve music-making programs, specifically producing jazz improvisation responses to supplied "single-measure calls". "While we (Spector and Alpern) have not yet succeeded in inducing and recapitulating the deep structure of jazz melody" promising music generating programs have been evolved and the authors "believe that our framework holds promise for the eventual achievement of this goal."

While the authors refer to their memory system as "indexed memory" it is problem dependent. Consisting of 31 identical data structures, each of which is designed to hold a melody (expressed as 96 MIDI values). One data structure holds the input, another the output (i.e. the program's jazz "response") and the rest form a one dimensional array of 29 elements containing a case base of human written music. Only the output structure may be written to. Various problem dependent functions are provided for cutting and splicing segments of melodies but data values within the data structures cannot be directly manipulated.

7.4.4   Strongly Typed Genetic Programming

[Montana, 1995] presents two examples where GP is provided with local variables which it uses to solve problems (the two other examples don't allow explicit use of evolvable memory). The use of the strong typing framework means the variables must be typed. In both examples the variables are lists, which are either of the same type as the input or the same type as the output. That is with strongly typed GP data structures appropriate to the problem are readily chosen (STGP also prevents some kinds of abuse of the data structures).

7.4.5   Graph Data Structures

[Brave, 1995; Brave, 1996a] shows GP using a graph data structure which provides primitives to connect nodes and follow connections. Using this data structure the GP was able to solve a navigation problem which requires it to form a mental model of its world. This builds on [Andre, 1994b] but replaces a predetermined isomorphism between indexed memory and the problem "world" by a more complex data structure that is appropriate to the problem.

7.4.6   Linked List Data Structure

[Haynes and Wainwright, 1995] requires GP to evolve control programs for agents which have to survive in a simulated world containing mines. The agent's memory is a dynamically allocated linked list, with a new list element representing the current location being automatically allocated each time the agent enters a new location in the world. Read and write access is with respect to the current location, e.g. the current memory cell, the cell representing the location north of here, the cell north-east of that and so on. The list keeps track of the agent's path allowing it to backtrack along its path. (Since its path lies in a minefield a safe option is always for the agent to retrace its steps). NB the memory is structured in an appropriate fashion for the problem.

7.4.7 Tree Structured Memory for Temporal Data Processing

[Iba et al., 1995] introduces "special 'memory terminals', which point at any nonterminal node within the tree." The value given by a memory terminal is the value at the indicated point in the tree on the previous time step. While this structure is applicable to a range of signal processing problem, once again memory has been constrained for the GP into a structure appropriate to the problem.

[Sharman et al., 1995; Esparcia-Alcazar and Sharman, 1997] similarly use memory terminals to hold values previously calculated at nodes within the program tree, however the mechanism for connecting terminals to inner nodes is different; explicit "psh" functions within the program tree save the value at that point in the tree by pushing it onto a stack. The stack is non-standard as "psh" writes to the current stack whereas "stk$n$" terminals provide a mechanism to read the stack created on the previous time step. The stack is also non-standard in that the "stk$n$" terminals non-destructively read data inside the stack (rather than from just the top of stack).

7.4.8 Object Oriented Programming

Some confirmation of the experimental results of Chapters 4 and 5 is provided by [Bruce, 1995; Bruce, 1996]. Although Bruce casts his work in an object oriented light rather than in terms of data structures there is much that is similar to this work. The details of the data objects in Bruce's experiments on evolving stack and queue data objects are similar to the stack and queue data structures in Chapters 4 and 5. They differ principally by the inclusion of a "Full?" object method and the lack of top or front operations. Bruce also considers the evolution of a "priority queue". While this has some similarities with the list data structure evolved in Chapter 6 it is significantly simpler with only five data methods rather than the ten simultaneously evolved in Chapter 6.

The details of the genetic programming system Bruce uses are similar to those used in Chapters 4, 5 and 6. For example one tree per data method (making a total of five trees per individual, see Section 3.6), separating pointers from main indexed memory (cf. Section 3.5), and use of tournament selection (cf. Section 3.2) with a steady state population (cf. Section 3.3). However a population size of 1,000 is used throughout rather than increasing to 10,000 for the more difficult problems.

Bruce conducts six experiments per object type in which he investigates the impact of, evolving the data methods one at a time rather than simultaneously, allowing the inspection of the internal operation of the programs and the impact of using strongly typed genetic programming. As might be expected, evolving one thing at a time, including a comparison of evolved program behaviour with a prescribed ideal implementation in the fitness function, and ensuring the evolved program is type correct, all make the GP's task easier. If all three are avoided (as in our experiments), which he labels experiments "3a", then his GP was unable to evolve the data structure in 20 runs. (Typically the experiments in Chapters 4 to 6 involve about 60 independent runs).

7.4.9 PADO

PADO [Teller and Veloso, 1995c; Teller and Veloso, 1995d; Teller and Veloso, 1996; Teller and Veloso, 1995b; Teller, 1995a; Teller, 1995b; Teller and Veloso, 1995a; Teller, 1996] is a GP based learning architecture for object recognition and has been shown to be able to correctly classify real world images and sounds far better than random guessing (albeit with less than 100% accuracy). PADO is a complex system with many non-standard GP features. For example the classification system is built from a hierarchy of individual programs which may use libraries of evolving code as well as ADFs similar to Koza's, repeated execution of programs within a fixed execution time, programs are represented by a directed graph of execution nodes rather than as trees and the genetic operators used to create new program are themselves evolved, cf. Section 2.4.1. The programs it generates are large and their operation is poorly understood.

PADO was deliberately designed not to use domain knowledge and so only the simplest memory structure (indexed memory) is used. It has been applied to complex ill behaved problems where there is no obvious data structure. GP could in principle build problem specific structures on top of indexed memory which the complexity and size of the evolved programs might conceal, however there is no evidence that this is happening. The better than random performance of PADO may be due to its many other features rather than its simple memory structure.

7.5 SUMMARY

The experiments described in Sections 7.1 to 7.3 (which were reported in part in [Langdon, 1996c]) have shown GP can solve two new problems. In Section 7.2 we showed GP can induce programs which correctly classify test sentences as to whether they are in a Dyck language or not and in Section 7.3 we showed GP evolving code which evaluates Reverse Polish Notation (RPN) expressions. In Section 7.1 we showed GP can solve the nested bracket problem without requiring an intermediate step generating an abstract machine.

All three examples were solved by GP using the appropriate data structure for the problem. The two more complex examples (Dyck language and RPN) proved to be more difficult for GP when provided with indexed memory rather than when provided with a stack. Despite indexed memory being more powerful than stacks or simple scalars, none of the three problems has been solved using indexed memory.

Section 7.4 reviewed the current GP literature where problems have been solved using evolvable memory. It shows many cases where appropriate data structures have been used to solve problems. The principle counter example, where problem specific data structures have not been provided, is PADO, where better than random performance has been achieved on classification problems with no obvious structure.

It has often been argued, e.g. [Kinnear, Jr., 1994c, page 12], that functional primitives used with GP should be as powerful as possible, in these examples we have shown appropriate data structures are advantageous, that is GP can benefit from data abstraction.

These experiments have not provided evidence that existing GP can scale up and tackle larger problems. If they had shown GP solving problems by evolving the

Table 7.9.   Actions Performed by Terminals and Functions

Primitive	Purpose
DIV(x,y)	**if** $y \neq 0$ **return** x/y **else return** 1
SUBR(x,y) DIVR(x,y)	As SUB and DIV except yield $y-x$ and y/x, i.e. operands reversed.
max	constant 10 ($\geq$ max input size).
PROG2(t,u)	evaluate t; **return** u
ARG1, arg1, arg2	arguments of current operation or ADF
aux1	an auxiliary variable (i.e. in addition to indexed memory).
Set_Aux1(x)	aux1 = x; **return** aux1

forwhile(s,e,l)	**for** i0 = s; i0 $\leq e$; i0++
	   if timeout (128) **exit loop**
	   if l returns zero **exit loop**
	 return i0

i0	Yields value of loop control variable of most deeply nested loop or zero if not in a loop in current tree. NB loop control variable in one tree cannot be accessed in another (e.g. an ADF).
IFLTE($x,y,t1,t2$)	**if** $x \leq y$ **return** $t1$ **else return** $t2$
Ifeq($x,y,t1,t2$)	**if** $x = y$ **return** $t1$ **else return** $t2$

required data structures "on the fly" as it needed them this would have been powerful evidence. However this was not demonstrated. The failure of GP to solve the problems when provided with the more general (i.e. more powerful) directly addressable memory data structure shows that data structures should be chosen with care and it may not be sufficient to simply over provide, with more powerful structures than are needed.

Table 7.10.   Actions Performed by Terminals and Functions (cont)

ifopen(*x,t1,t2*)	**if** $x = 5, 13, 31$ or 43 **return** *t1* //i.e. opening symbol **else return** *t2*
ifmatch(*x,y,t1,t2*)	**if** $x = 5, 13, 31$ or 43 evaluate *y* //i.e. opening symbol **if** $(x,y) = (5,71), (13,103), (31,137)$ or $(43,167)$ **return** *t1* **else return** *t2* //*x* and *y* don't match **else return** *t2*

Makenull	clear stack; **return** 0
Empty	**if** stack is empty **return** 0; **else return** 1
Top	**if** stack is empty **return** 0; **else return** top of stack
Pop	**if** stack is empty **return** 0; **else** pop stack and **return** popped value
Push(*x*)	Evaluate *x*; **if** < 99 items on stack push *x*; **return** *x* **else return** 0

Indexed memory is held in store[$-l \ldots +l$], where $l = 63$, i.e. a total of 127 cells.

read(*x*)	**if** $|x| \le l$ **return** store[*x*] **else return** 0

write(*x,d*)	**if** $|x| \le l$ store[*x*] = *d*; **return** original contents of store[*x*] **else** evaluate *d*; **return** 0

swap(*x,y*)	**if** $|x| \le l$ **and** $|y| \le l$ exchange contents of store[*x*] and store[*y*] **if** $|x| > l$ **and** $|y| \le l$ store[*y*] = 0 **if** $|x| \le l$ **and** $|y| > l$ store[*x*] = 0 **return** 1

8 EVOLUTION OF GP POPULATIONS

In this chapter we investigate in detail what happens as GP populations evolve. We start in Section 8.1 by showing Price's covariance and selection theorem can be applied to artificial evolution. Following the proof of the theorem with experimental justification using the GP runs on the stack problem described in Chapter 4. Section 8.2 briefly describes Fisher's fundamental theorem of natural selection and shows in its *normal interpretation* it does not apply to genetic algorithms. The failure of most GP runs on the stack problem to find programs which pass the whole fitness test is explained in Section 8.3 by the presence of "deceptive" high scoring partial solutions in the population. These cause a negative correlation between necessary primitives and fitness. As Price's theorem predicts, their frequency falls, eventually leading to their extinction and so to the impossibility of finding solutions like those that are evolved in successful runs.

Section 8.4 investigates the evolution of variety in GP populations. While simple general models are developed they fail to predict in detail the evolution of variety in the stack populations and instead detailed measurements reveal loss of diversity causing crossover to produce offspring which are copies of their parents. Section 8.5 concludes with measurements that show in the stack population crossover readily produces improvements in performance initially but later no improvements at all are made by crossover.

8.1   PRICE'S SELECTION AND COVARIANCE THEOREM

Price's Covariance and Selection Theorem [Price, 1970] from population genetics relates the change in frequency of a gene in a population from one generation to the next, to the covariance of the gene's frequency in the original population with the number of offspring produced by individuals in that population (see Equation 8.1). The theorem holds "for a single gene or for any linear combination of genes at any number of loci, holds for any sort of dominance or epistasis (non-linear interaction between genes), for sexual or asexual reproduction, for random or non-random mating, for diploid, haploid or polyploid species, and even for imaginary species with more than two sexes" [Price, 1970]. In particular it applies to genetic algorithms (GAs) [Altenberg, 1994].

$$\Delta Q = \frac{\text{Cov}(z, q)}{\overline{z}} \qquad (8.1)$$

Q = Frequency of given gene (or linear combinations of genes) in the population
ΔQ = Change in Q from one generation to the next.
q_i = Frequency of gene in the individual i (more information is given in Section 8.1.1 below).
z_i = Number of offspring produced by individual i.
$\overline{z}$ = Mean number of children produced.
Cov = Covariance

8.1.1   Proof of Price's Theorem

In this section we follow the proof of Price's Theorem given in [Price, 1970] but recast it and simplify it for use with genetic programming. Firstly we define the additional symbols we shall use.

P_1 = Initial population.
P_2 = Population at next generation (for purposes of the proof generations are assumed to be separated).
N = Size of initial population.
g_i = Number of copies of gene in individual i.
q_i = g_i (We keep the term q_i for compatibility with [Price, 1970]).
$\overline{q}$ = Arithmetic mean of q_i in population P_1.
Q_1 = Frequency of given gene (or linear combinations of genes) in the population. I.e. number of copies of gene in population divided by the number of chromosomes it could occupy.
Q_2 = Frequency of gene in population P_2.
z_i = Number of offspring produced by individual i. (I.e. the number of individuals in the next population containing code fragments produced from i).
$\overline{z}$ = Mean number of children produced.

g_i' = Number of copies of the gene in all the code fragments in the next population produced by individual i.

q_i' = Frequency of gene in the offspring produced by individual i. Defined by

$$q_i' = \frac{g_i'}{z_i} \quad , \text{if } z_i \neq 0$$
$$= q_i \quad , \text{otherwise}$$

$\Delta q_i = q_i' - q_i$

We shall start with the frequency of the gene in the current population, Q_1. Then find the frequency in the subsequent generation, Q_2. Subtracting them yields the change in frequency, which we shall simplify to give Price's Theorem.

$$Q_1 = \frac{\sum g_i}{N}$$
$$= \frac{\sum q_i}{N}$$
$$= \bar{q}$$

Each individual in the new population is created by joining one or code fragments and the number of each gene in the individual is the sum of the number in each of the code fragments from which it was formed. Thus the number of genes in the new population is equal to the number in the code fragments produced by the previous generation.

$$Q_2 = \frac{\sum g_i'}{\sum z_i} \tag{8.2}$$
$$= \frac{\sum z_i q_i'}{\sum z_i}$$
$$= \frac{\sum z_i q_i'}{N\bar{z}} \tag{8.3}$$
$$= \frac{\sum z_i q_i}{N\bar{z}} + \frac{\sum z_i \Delta q_i}{N\bar{z}}$$
$$= \frac{\sum \left((z_i - \bar{z})(q_i - \bar{q}) + \bar{z}\, q_i + z_i \bar{q} - \bar{z}\,\bar{q} \right)}{N\bar{z}} + \frac{\sum z_i \Delta q_i}{N\bar{z}}$$
$$= \frac{\frac{1}{N}\sum(z_i - \bar{z})(q_i - \bar{q}) + \bar{z}\frac{1}{N}\sum q_i + \bar{q}\frac{1}{N}\sum z_i - \frac{1}{N}\sum \bar{z}\,\bar{q}}{\bar{z}} + \frac{\sum z_i \Delta q_i}{N\bar{z}}$$
$$= \frac{\frac{1}{N}\sum(z_i - \bar{z})(q_i - \bar{q}) + \bar{z}\,\bar{q} + \bar{q}\,\bar{z} - \bar{z}\,\bar{q}}{\bar{z}} + \frac{\sum z_i \Delta q_i}{N\bar{z}}$$
$$= \frac{\frac{1}{N}\sum(z_i - \bar{z})(q_i - \bar{q}) + \bar{q}\,\bar{z}}{\bar{z}} + \frac{\sum z_i \Delta q_i}{N\bar{z}}$$
$$= \frac{\text{Cov}(z, q)}{\bar{z}} + \bar{q} + \frac{\sum z_i \Delta q_i}{N\bar{z}}$$
$$\Delta Q = \frac{\text{Cov}(z, q)}{\bar{z}} + \frac{\sum z_i \Delta q_i}{N\bar{z}}$$

"If meiosis and fertilization are random with respect to the gene, the summation term at the right will be zero except for statistical sampling effects ('random drift'), and these will tend to average out to give equation 8.1." I.e. the expected value of $\sum z_i \Delta q_i$ is zero.

So while survival of an individual and the number of children it has may be related to whether it carries the gene, it is assumed that the production of crossover fragments and their fusing to form offspring is random. I.e. selection for reproduction is dependent upon fitness and in general dependent on the presence of specific genes but selection of crossover and mutation points is random and so independent of genes (Section 8.1.3 discusses this further for GPs).

8.1.2 Price's Theorem for Genetic Algorithms

Where the population size is unchanged, as is usually the case in GAs and GP (and two parents are required for each individual created by crossover), $\bar{z} = p_r + p_m + 2p_c$ (where p_r = copy rate, p_m = mutation rate and p_c is the crossover rate. Since $p_r + p_m + p_c = 1$, the mean number of children $\bar{z} = 1 + p_c$ and Equation 8.1 becomes:

$$\Delta Q = \frac{\text{Cov}(z, q)}{1 + p_c} \tag{8.4}$$

8.1.3 Applicability of Price's Theorem to GAs and GPs

The simplicity and wide scope of Price's Theorem has lead Altenberg to suggest that covariance between parental fitness and offspring fitness distribution is fundamental to the power of evolutionary algorithms. Indeed [Altenberg, 1995] shows Holland's schema theorem [Holland, 1973; Holland, 1992] can be derived from Price's Theorem. This and other analysis, leads [Altenberg, 1995, page 43] to conclude "the Schema Theorem has no implications for how well a GA is performing".

While the proof in [Price, 1970] assumes discrete generations the result "can be applied to species with overlapping, inter-breeding generations". Thus the theorem can be applied to steady state GAs [Syswerda, 1989; Syswerda, 1991b] such as we use in Chapters 4, 5, 6 and 7.

For the theorem to hold the genetic operations (crossover and mutation in GA terms) must be independent of the gene. That is on average there must be no relationship between them and the gene. In large populations random effects will be near zero on average but in smaller populations their effect may not be negligible. In GAs selection of crossover and mutation points is usually done independently of the contents of the chromosome and so Price's theorem will hold (except in small GA populations where random fluctuations may be significant). In GP populations are normally bigger (and the number of generations similar) so random effects, "genetic drift", are less important.

In standard GP it is intended that the genetic operators should also be independent, however in order to ensure the resultant offspring are syntactically correct and not too big, genetic operators must consider the chromosome's contents. This is normally limited to just its structure in terms of tree branching factor (i.e. the number of arguments a function has) and tree depth or size limits. That is, they ignore the actual meaning of a node in the tree (e.g. whether it is MUL or ADD) but do consider how many arguments it has. Thus a function with two arguments (e.g. MUL) and a terminal (e.g. max) may be treated differently.

It is common to bias the choice of crossover points in favour of internal nodes (e.g. in the GP experiments in this book internal points in program trees are deliberately chosen 30% of the time, the other 70% are randomly chosen through the whole tree, c.f. Section 3.7). This reduces the proportion of crossover fragments which contain only a single terminal. Once again the genetic operators ignore the meaning of nodes within the tree.

In a large diverse population these factors should have little effect and Price's Theorem should hold. However when many programs are near the maximum allowed size a function which has many arguments could be at a disadvantage since the potential offspring containing it have a higher chance of exceeding size limits. Therefore restrictions on program size may on average reduce the number of such functions in the next generation compared to the number predicted by considering only fitness (i.e. by Price's Theorem). [Altenberg, 1994, page 47] argues Price's theorem can be applied to genetic programming and we shall show experimental evidence for it based on genes composed of a single GP primitive. Further evidence is given in [Langdon and Poli, 1997a], which tests Price's theorem in a GP with separate generations.

8.1.4   Application of Price's Theorem to the GP Stack Problem

In this section we experimentally test Price's Theorem by comparing its predictions with what actually happened using GP populations from the 60 runs of the stack problem described in Chapter 4. Firstly we consider the change in numbers of a single primitive and then we examine the change in frequency versus fitness for all primitives in a typical and in a successful run.

In GAs the expected number of children each individual has is determined by its fitness. On average the expected number is equal to the actual number of offspring z (as used in Price's theorem, i.e. in Equations 8.1 and 8.4). For example when using roulette wheel selection the expected number of children is directly proportional to the parent's fitness. When using tournament selection (as in Chapters 4 to 7) the expected number of children is determined by the parent's rank within the population and the tournament size (see Section 8.4.2). The remainder of this section uses the expected number of offspring as predicted by the parents fitness ranking within the current population in place of z.

Price's theorem predicts the properties of the next generation. In a steady state population it can be used to predict the average rate of change. However in general subsequent changes to the population will change the predicted rate of change. For simplicity we assume that during one generation equivalent (i.e. the time taken to create as many new individuals as there are in the population, cf. Section 3.3) such effects are small and base the predicted properties of the new population on linear extrapolation using the predicted rate of change.

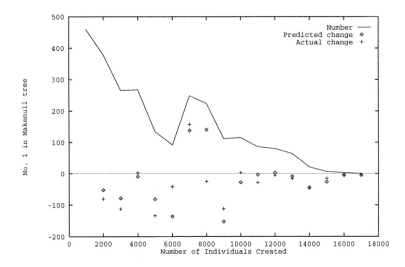

Figure 8.1.   Evolution of the number of the terminal "1" in the makenull tree plus predicted change and actual change in next generation, in typical stack (51) run.

The 60 runs of the stack problem use identical parameters and differ only in the initial seed used by the [Park and Miller, 1988] pseudo random number generator. For convenience individual runs are numbered (1) to (60).

The solid line in Figure 8.1 plots the evolution of the number of a particular primitive in a particular tree in the population for a typical run. (As there is no crossover between trees of different types, primitives of the same type but in different trees are genetically isolated from each other and so Equation 8.4 can be applied independently to each tree). The change from one generation equivalent to the next is plotted by crosses which show good agreement with the change predicted by linearly extrapolating the rate of change predicted by Price's theorem. Some discrepancy between the actual change and the predicted change is expected due to "noise". That is the number of children an individual has is a stochastic function of its fitness (see Figure 8.6). However non-random deviations from the prediction are to be expected as linear extrapolation assumes the rate of change will not change appreciably in the course of one generation equivalent (such as happens at generations 6 and 8).

Figures 8.2 to 8.5 plot the covariance of primitive frequency with normalised fitness against the change in the primitives frequency in the subsequent generation (equivalent). While these plots show significant differences from the straight line predicted by Equation 8.4, least squares regression yields best fit lines which pass very close to the origin but (depending upon run and primitive) have slopes significantly less than $1 + p_c = 1.9$ (they lie in the range 1.18 to 1.79, see Table 8.1).

Random deviations from the theory are expected but should have negligible effect when averaged by fitting the regression lines. The fact that regression coefficients differ from 1.9 is explained by the fact that we are recording changes over a generation, during this time it is possible for the population to change significantly. We would expect this

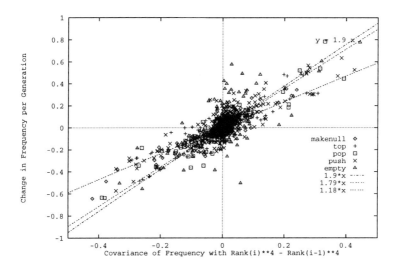

Figure 8.2. Covariance of Primitive frequency and $\left(\frac{R_i}{N}\right)^4 - \left(\frac{R_{i-1}}{N}\right)^4$ v. change in frequency in next generation, in typical stack (51) run. Data collected every generation equivalent.

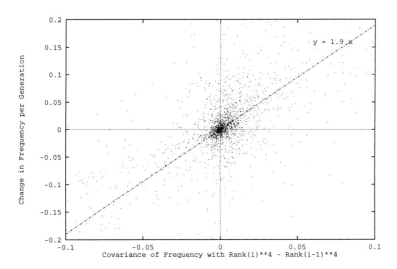

Figure 8.3. Covariance of Primitive frequency and $\left(\frac{R_i}{N}\right)^4 - \left(\frac{R_{i-1}}{N}\right)^4$ v. change in frequency in next generation, in typical stack (51) run. Only data near the origin shown.

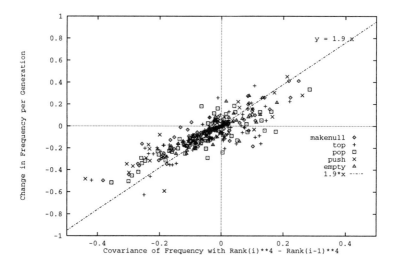

Figure 8.4. Covariance of Primitive frequency and $\left(\frac{R_i}{N}\right)^4 - \left(\frac{R_{i-1}}{N}\right)^4$ v. change in frequency in next generation, in successful stack (2) run. Data collected every generation equivalent.

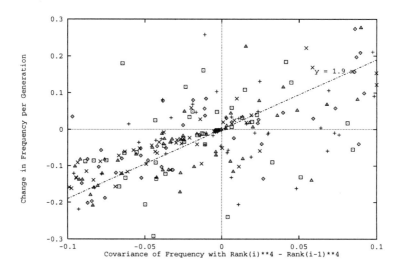

Figure 8.5. Covariance of Primitive frequency and $\left(\frac{R_i}{N}\right)^4 - \left(\frac{R_{i-1}}{N}\right)^4$ v. change in frequency in next generation, in successful stack (2) run. Data near origin.

Table 8.1. Least squares regression coefficients of covariance of primitive frequency and $\left(\frac{R_i}{N}\right)^4 - \left(\frac{R_{i-1}}{N}\right)^4$ with change in frequency in the next generation for a typical (51) stack run.

Primitive	makenull	top	pop	push	empty
		Δ Frequency – Intercept : Gradient			
ADD	-.026 : 1.26	-.007 : 1.39	-.007 : 1.33	.035 : 1.34	.010 : 1.78
SUB	-.017 : 1.21	-.016 : 1.44	.006 : 1.75	-.017 : 1.30	.006 : 1.83
0	-.001 : 1.35	.002 : 1.46	.011 : 1.50	.031 : 1.34	-.002 : 1.41
1	-.015 : 1.18	-.001 : 1.34	-.018 : 1.17	-.003 : 1.76	-.002 : 1.24
max	.001 : 1.52	-.017 : 1.34	-.008 : 1.44	.007 : 1.73	-.009 : 1.79
arg1	.000 : 1.50	-.008 : 1.60	.018 : 1.74	.012 : 1.39	.001 : 1.17
aux	-.025 : 1.20	.003 : 1.61	-.004 : 1.31	.004 : 1.37	-.024 : 1.29
inc_aux	.006 : 1.38	.004 : 1.67	-.002 : 1.49	-.011 : 1.50	-.012 : 1.19
dec_aux	-.002 : 1.51	-.001 : 1.40	-.005 : 1.72	.004 : 1.26	-.001 : 1.40
read	-.020 : 1.21	-.002 : 1.40	-.015 : 1.71	.009 : 1.38	-.037 : 1.54
write	-.003 : 1.42	-.002 : 1.30	.008 : 1.46	.015 : 1.30	-.038 : 1.54
write_Aux	-.001 : 1.30	-.011 : 1.20	-.011 : 1.58	.011 : 1.39	.049 : 1.33

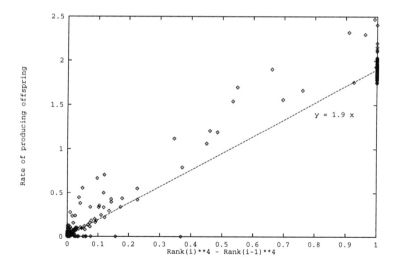

Figure 8.6. Rate of producing offspring v. $\left(\frac{R_i}{N}\right)^4 - \left(\frac{R_{i-1}}{N}\right)^4$ in typical stack (51) run. Data collected every generation equivalent.

effect to be most noticeable for primitives with a high rate of change since these affect the population! A high rate of change may not be sustainable for a whole generation and so the actual change will be less than predicted by extrapolating from its initial rate of change. However large changes have a large effect on least squares estimates so these outliers can be expected to reduce the slope of the regression line.

Regression coefficients can be calculated after excluding large values leaving only the smaller changes. However this makes the calculation dependent on small values with high noise. This may be exacerbated if the primitive quickly became extinct as there are few data points left. (When considering a typical run (51) of the stack problem and excluding covariances outside the range $-0.1 \ldots + 0.1$ regression coefficients were often effected by this noise and lie in the range $-0.96 \ldots 6.28$ for the twelve primitives in the empty tree).

In conclusion Price's Theorem gives quantitative predictions of the short term evolution of practical GP populations, however such predictions are affected by sampling noise in finite populations and may be biased if predictions are extrapolated too far in rapidly evolving populations. The theorem can also be used to explain the effects of fitness selection on GP populations.

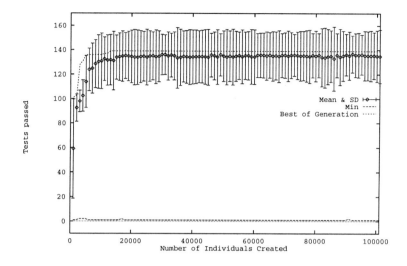

Figure 8.7.   Evolution of Fitness in a typical stack run (51)

8.2 FISHER'S FUNDAMENTAL THEOREM OF NATURAL SELECTION

Fisher's fundamental theorem of natural selection states "The rate of increase in fitness of any organism at any time is equal to its genetic variance in fitness at that time" [Fisher, 1958, page 37]. "Under the usual interpretation the theorem is believed to say that the rate of increase in the mean fitness of a population is equal to the population's additive variance for fitness". Since the variance can never be negative "natural selection causes a continual increase in mean fitness of a population. This interpretation of the theorem is only true when the population mates randomly and there is no dominance or epistasis" [Frank, 1995, page 382].

An example of this usage is given in [Tackett, 1995a, page 289] which claims "According to Fisher's fundamental *theory*" (emphasis added) "of natural selection the ability of a population to increase in fitness is proportional to the variance in fitness of the population members."

We would certainly expect epistasis (non-linear interaction between genes) to occur in most GAs and so would not expect this interpretation of the theorem to hold. Figure 8.7 shows the evolution of a stack population's fitness for one run. The error bars indicate a standard deviation either side of the mean population fitness. From Figure 8.7 we can see the standard deviation through out the bulk of the run is consistently close to 20, i.e. the variance of the population's fitness is near 400 (20×20). The usual interpretation of Fisher's theorem predicts the mean fitness will continually increase but obviously this is not the case as it remains fairly constant throughout the run and even falls occasionally.

We conclude that under the usual interpretation Fisher's theorem does not normally apply to GAs. This is important because this interpretation of Fisher's theorem has been used as an argument in favour of GA selection schemes which produce a high variance in population fitness [Tackett, 1995a, pages 272 and 290]. (There may be other reasons for preferring these selection methods. A high fitness variance may indicate a high degree of variation in the population, which might be beneficial).

[Price, 1972] makes the point that Fisher's publications on his fundamental theorem of natural selection "contains the most confusing published scientific writing I know of" [page 134] leading to "forty years of bewilderment about what he meant" [page 132]. [Price, 1972] and [Ewens, 1989; Ewens, 1992b; Ewens, 1992a] argue that the usual interpretation of Fisher's theorem is incorrect and his "fitness" should be considered as just the component of fitness which varies linearly with gene frequency. All other effects, such as "dominance, epistasis, population pressure, climate, and interactions with other species – he regarded as a matter of the environment" [Price, 1972, page 130]. Price and Ewens both give proofs for this interpretation of Fisher's theorem but conclude that it is "mathematically correct but less important than he thought it to be" [Price, 1972, page 140].

8.3   EVOLUTION OF STACK PROBLEM POPULATIONS

In this section we return to the stack problem of Chapter 4 and investigate why most runs failed to find a solution. Investigation of the evolved solutions shows which primitives are essential to the correct operation of all the evolved solutions and in most runs one or more of these becomes extinct, thus preventing the evolution of a solution like those found. The loss of these primitive is explained using Price's Theorem by the negative covariance of their frequency with their fitness. Similar covariances are found in successful runs and we conclude success requires a solution to be found quickly, before extinction of critical primitives occurs.

Table 8.2 contains an entry for each of the five program trees (which each trial stack data structure comprises) and the primitives that the tree can use (see Sections 4.2 and 4.3). Where the primitive is essential to the operation of one of the four stack solutions found, the entry contains the number(s) of the solutions. If the primitive is not essential to the correct operation of any of the four evolved solutions (in the particular tree) the entry is blank. Primitives ADD and max are omitted as they are always blank. (The essential primitives are shown within shaded boxes in Figures 4.4, 4.6, 4.8 and 4.10 (pages 71–73). NB in the stack problem each tree can use all of the primitives).

From Table 8.2 we can identify five primitives which are essential to the operation of all four evolved solutions and five pairs of primitives where one or other is required. These are shown in the two halves of Table 8.3 together with the number of runs where they were removed from the population by 21 generation equivalents (i.e. by the point where all four solutions had evolved).

After the equivalent of 21 generations in 43 of 60 runs, the number of one or more of the tree-primitives shown in the left hand side of Table 8.3 had fallen to zero. That is the population no longer contained one or more primitives required to evolve a solution (like the solutions that have been found). In 12 of the remaining 17 populations both

Table 8.2.   Primitives Essential to the Operation of Evolved Stack Programs

Tree/Primitive Essential to Evolved Stack Solutions										
Tree	SUB	0	1	arg1	aux	inc _aux	dec _aux	read	write	write _Aux
makenull	4	4	1 2 3 4							1 2 3 4
top					1 2 3			1 2 3 4		1 4
pop					1 2 4	1 2 3	4	3	1 2 4	3
push				1 2 3 4		4	1 2 3		1 2 3 4	
empty	4	4			1 3 4					2

Table 8.3.   Stack Primitives Essential to All Evolved Solutions

Tree	Primitive	Lost
makenul	1	14
makenul	write_Aux	7
top	read	21
push	arg1	6
push	write	29

Tree	Alternative Primitives			Both Lost
top	aux	or	write_Aux	12
pop	inc_aux	or	dec_aux	27
pop	read	or	write	15
push	inc_aux	or	dec_aux	40
empty	aux	or	write_Aux	9

of one or more of the pairs of primitives shown on the right hand side of Table 8.3 had been removed from the population. Thus by generation 21 in all but 5 of 60 runs, the population no longer contained primitives required to evolve solutions like those found. In four of these five cases solutions were evolved (in the remaining case one of the essential primitives was already at a low concentration, which fell to zero by the end of the run at generation 101).

Figure 8.8 shows the evolution of six typical stack populations (runs 00, 10, 20, 30, 40 and 51). For each run the first essential primitive (or pair or primitives) that becomes extinct is selected and its covariance of frequency with fitness in the population is plotted. Figure 8.8 shows the covariance is predominantly negative and thus Price's theorem predicts the primitives' frequencies will fall. Figure 8.10 confirms this. In most cases they become extinct by generation nine.

Figure 8.9 shows the evolution of frequency, fitness covariance for the same primitives in a successful run (1) (Figure 8.11 shows the evolution of their frequency). While two of the primitives (Push/arg1 and Push/dec_aux) have large positive covariances for part of the evolution the other four are much as the runs shown in Figure 8.8 where they were the first essential primitive to become extinct. That is, in terms of correlation between population fitness ranking and essential primitives, successful and unsuccessful runs are similar. It appears there is a race between finding high fitness partial solutions on which a complete solution can evolve and the removal of essential primitives from the population caused by fitness based selection. I.e. if finding a critical building block had been delayed, it might not have been found at all as one or more essential primitives might have become extinct in the meantime.

In successful stack run (1) by generation five, a solution in which top, pop and push effectively use aux, write_Aux, inc_aux and dec_aux to maintain aux as a stack pointer has been discovered (c.f. Figure 8.11). This is followed by the fitness of Pop/inc_aux increasing and whereas its frequency had been dropping it starts to increase preventing Pop/inc_aux from becoming extinct, which would have prevented a solution like the one found from evolving. This maintenance of aux as a stack pointer requires code in three trees to co-operate. An upper bound on the chance of this building block being disrupted in the offspring of the first program to contain it can be calculated by assuming any crossover in any of the three trees containing part of the building block will disrupt it. This yields an upper bound of $3p_c/5 = 54\%$. In other words on average at least $p_r + 2p_c/5 = 46\%$ of the offspring produced by programs containing this building block will also contain the building block and so it should spread rapidly through the population. With many individuals in the population containing functioning top, pop and push trees, evolution of working makenull and empty trees rapidly followed and a complete solution was found.

8.3.1   Discussion

The loss of some critical primitives in so many runs can be explained in many cases by the existence of high scoring partial solutions which achieve a relatively high score by saving only one item in aux. In such programs write_Aux, inc_aux and dec_aux may destroy the contents of aux and are likely to be detrimental (i.e. reduced fitness). As the number of such partial solutions increases write_Aux, inc_aux and dec_aux become more of a liability in the *current* population and are progressively removed from it. Thus trapping the population at the partial solution. This highlights the importance of the fitness function throughout the whole of the GP run. I.e. it must guide the evolution of the population toward the solution in the initial population, as well as later, when recognisable partial solutions have evolved.

Section 6.10 has described similar loss of primitives in the list problem and discussed potential solutions such as mutation, demes and fitness niches to allow multiple diverse partial solutions within the population and potentially slow down the impact of fitness selection on the population. Other approaches include: improving the fitness function (so it is no longer deceptive) e.g. by better design or using a dynamic fitness function which changes as the population evolves. A dynamic fitness function would aim to continually stretch the population, keeping a carrot dangling in front of it. (This is also known as the "Red Queen" [Carroll, 1871] approach where the population must continually improve itself). A dynamic fitness function could be pre-defined but dynamic GP fitness functions are often produced by co-evolution [Hillis, 1992; Angeline and Pollack, 1993; Angeline, 1993; Angeline and Pollack, 1994; Koza, 1991; Jannink, 1994; Reynolds, 1994a; Ryan, 1995; Davis, 1994]. Where it is felt certain characters will be required in the problem's solution the initial population and crossover can be controlled in order to ensure individuals within the population have these properties (Sections 5.10.3 and 6.4.2 have described ways in which this can be implemented).

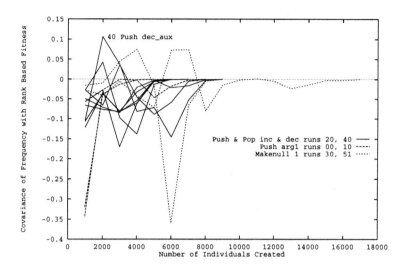

Figure 8.8. Evolution of the covariance of primitive frequency and $\left(\frac{R_i}{N}\right)^4 - \left(\frac{R_{i-1}}{N}\right)^4$ for the first critical primitive (or critical pair) to become extinct. Six typical stack runs.

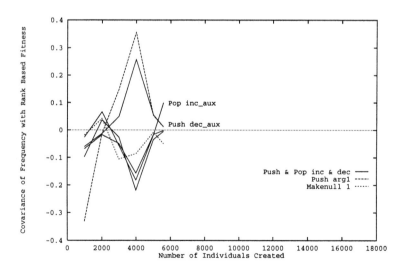

Figure 8.9. Evolution of the covariance of primitive frequency and $\left(\frac{R_i}{N}\right)^4 - \left(\frac{R_{i-1}}{N}\right)^4$ for critical primitives. Successful stack 1 run.

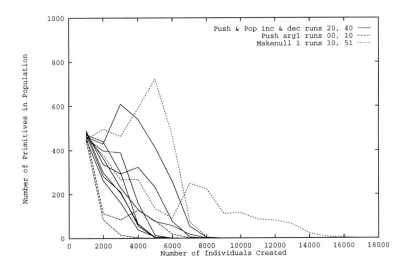

Figure 8.10. Evolution of number of primitives in the population for first critical primitive (or critical pair) to become extinct. Six typical stack runs.

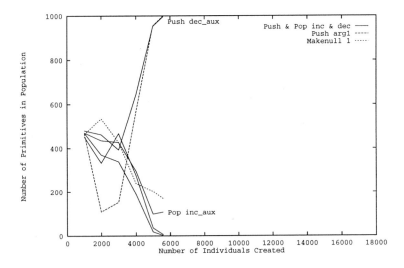

Figure 8.11. Evolution of number of primitives in the population for critical primitives. Successful stack 1 run.

An alternative approach is to avoid specialist high level primitives (particularly where they interlock, so one requires another) and use only a small number of general purpose primitives. Any partial solutions are likely to require all of them and so none will become extinct. This is contrary to established GP wisdom [Kinnear, Jr., 1994c, page 12], however recently (at the fall 1995 AAAI GP symposium) Koza advocated the use of small function sets containing only five functions ($+$, $-$, $\times$, $\div$ and a conditional branch).

8.4   LOSS OF VARIETY

We define variety as the number of unique individuals within the population. For example if a population contains three individuals A, B and C but A and B are identical (but different from C) then the variety of the population is 2 (A and B counting as one unique individual). ([Koza, 1992, page 93] defines variety as a ratio of the number of unique individuals to population size). These definitions have the advantage of simplicity but ignore several important issues:

- Individuals which are not identical may still be similar.

- Individuals which are not identical may be totally different, but *variety* makes no distinction between this and the first case.

- The differences between individuals may occur in "introns". That is in parts of the program tree which have no effect upon the program's behaviour, either because that part of the tree is never executed or because its effects are always overridden by other code in the program. For example, the value of a particular subtree may always be multiplied by zero which yields a result that is always zero no matter what value the subtree had calculated. Two such different programs have identical behaviour and fitness (but their offspring may not be the same, even on average).

- Behaviour of different program trees may be identical, either in general or in the specific test cases used to assign fitness. That is genetically diverse individuals may behave similarly, or even identically.

    As [Rosca, 1996] points out, in the absence of side effects, diverse programs with identical behaviour can be readily constructed if the function set contains functions that are associative or commutative by simple reordering of function arguments.

- Even if programs behave differently, in general or when evaluating the given test cases, the fitness function may assign them the same fitness value. E.g. the fitness function may be based upon the number of correct answers a program returns so two programs which pass different tests but the same number of tests will have the same fitness.

Faced with the above complexity we argue that variety has the advantage of simplicity and forms a useful upper bound to the diversity of the population. That is if the variety is low then any other measures of genetic, phenotypic or fitness diversity must also be low. The opposite does not hold when it is high. (Other definitions include fitness based population *entropy* [Rosca and Ballard, 1996, Section 9.5] and using the ratio of sum of the sizes of every program in the population to the number of distinct subtrees within the population [Keijzer, 1996]).

In this section we consider the variety of GP populations using the 60 runs on the stack problem as examples. Firstly (Section 8.4.1) we show how the number of unique individuals evolves and then in Section 8.4.2 we present simple but general models of the evolution of variety. While these give some explanation they don't predict some important features. Detailed measurements of the stack population are presented in Section 8.4.3. These are used to give better, but more problem specific, explanations of the populations' behaviour. The low variety of stack populations is shown to be primarily due to the high number of "clones" (i.e. offspring which are identical to their parents) produced by crossover, which is itself a reflection of the low variety. Thus low variety reinforces itself. In one run (23) variety collapses to near zero but in most cases it eventually hovers near 60% of the population size. This is low compared to reports of 80% to 95% in [Koza, 1992, pages 159, 609 and 614] and [Keijzer, 1996].

8.4.1   Loss of Variety in Stack Populations

Measurements show variety starts in the initial population at its maximum value with every member of the population being different. This is despite the fact there is no uniqueness check to guarantee this. Once evolution of the population starts variety falls rapidly, but in most cases rises later to oscillate chaotically near a mean value of about 60% (see Figures 8.12 to 8.15). However in one run (23) variety does not increase and the population eventually converges to a single genotype and four of its offspring (i.e. of the 1000 individuals in the population there are only five different chromosomes, with about 970 copies of the fittest of these five).

The number of duplicate individuals created by reproduction rises rapidly initially but then hovers in the region of 8.5% of the population size (see Figure 8.16 on page 192). This means initially most duplicate individuals are created by reproduction but this fraction falls rapidly as more duplicates are produced by crossover so after the seventh generation only about a quarter of duplicate individuals in the population were created by reproduction and the remaining three quarters are created by crossover (see Figure 8.12). In stack populations, crossover produces more duplicates shortly after each new improved solution is found (see Figure 8.17 on page 192).

8.4.2   Evolution of Variety in a Steady State GA

The GA used in the experiments in this book is GP-QUICK [Singleton, 1994], which implements a steady-state GA [Syswerda, 1989; Syswerda, 1991b]. In GP-QUICK crossover produces one offspring at a time rather than two which is immediately inserted into the population displacing another, rather than collecting offspring until a complete replacement population has been produced, i.e. the generation gap is one [De Jong and Sarma, 1993]. A separate tournament is held to decide which member of the population to remove.

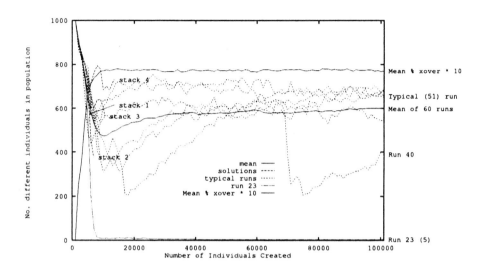

Figure 8.12.   Number of different individuals in stack populations and proportion of subsequent duplicates produced by crossover in stack selected runs.

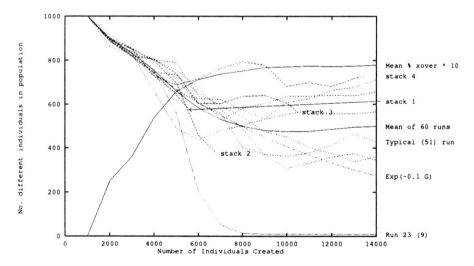

Figure 8.13.   Detail of above

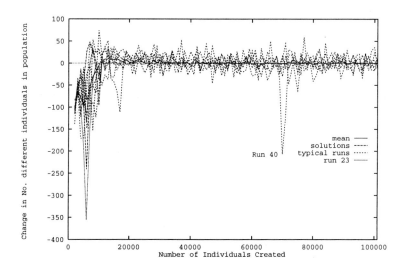

Figure 8.14.   Change in number of different individuals in stack populations.

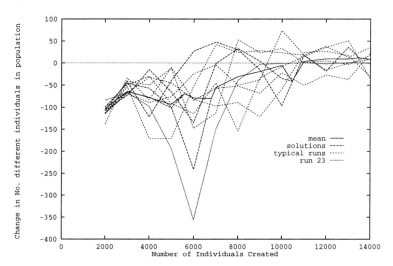

Figure 8.15.   Detail of above

Definitions.

N	= Population size
U_i	= A unique chrome in population
v	= Number of unique chromes in population
f_i	= Fitness of chrome U_i
C_i	= Number of copies of U_i in population
F_i	= Number of individuals in population with fitness f_i $(F_i \geq C_i)$
g	= Number of unique fitness values in population $(g \leq v)$
R_0	= 0
R_i	= Rank of U_i. Thus

$$R_1 = F_1$$
$$R_2 = F_1 + F_2$$
$$R_i = \sum_{j=1}^{i} F_j$$
$$R_g = \sum_{j=1}^{g} F_j = N$$

t	= Tournament size (4 in the experiments presented in Chapters 4 to 7).
k	= Kill tournament size (also 4)
p_r	= Proportion of offspring created by reproduction (0.1)
p_c	= Proportion of offspring created by crossover (0.9)

$p_r + p_c = 1$ (NB no mutation)

Tournament Selection in Steady State GA. The fitness distribution of individuals selected by tournament selection $(R_i/N)^t - (R_{i-1}/N)^t$ can be derived following [Blickle and Thiele, 1995, page 15]:

- The chance the winner of a tournament will have fitness $\leq f_i$ is the same as the chance all members of the tournament have fitness $\leq f_i$ (if any of them have a fitness greater than f_i then they would have won the tournament instead).

- The chance of selecting an individual with fitness $\leq f_i = R_i/N$.

- As each member of the tournament is selected at random and independently from the others, the chance they all have fitness $\leq f_i = (R_i/N)^t$.

- The chance the winner will have fitness $\leq f_{i-1} = (R_{i-1}/N)^t$.

- Thus the chance the winner will have fitness $f_i = (R_i/N)^t - (R_{i-1}/N)^t$.

For the kill tournament:

- the chance the loser of a tournament will have fitness $\geq f_i$ is the same as the chance all members of the tournament have fitness $\geq f_i$. The chance of selecting an individual with fitness $\geq f_i$ is the number of such individuals divided by the population size, i.e. $(N - R_{i-1})/N$.

- Thus the chance the loser of the kill tournament will have a fitness $\geq f_i = \left(\frac{N-R_{i-1}}{N}\right)^k$.

- The chance the loser will have fitness $\geq f_{i+1} = \left(\frac{N-R_i}{N}\right)^k$.

- Thus the chance the loser will have fitness $f_i = \left(\frac{N-R_{i-1}}{N}\right)^k - \left(\frac{N-R_i}{N}\right)^k$.

The extremes are interesting. Provided the number of individuals with the highest fitness value is small, i.e. $F_g \ll N$, the chance of selecting an individual with the best fitness is $1 - \left(\frac{N-F_g}{N}\right)^t \approx \frac{tF_g}{N}$ (i.e. $t \times$ random) and the chance of breeding from an individual with the worst fitness is $\left(\frac{F_1}{N}\right)^t$ (i.e. random^t). Similarly the chance of removing an individual with the worst fitness value (assuming $F_1 \ll N$) is $1 - \left(\frac{N-F_1}{N}\right)^k \approx \frac{kF_1}{N}$ (i.e. $k \times$ random) and the chance of removing an individual with the best fitness is $\left(\frac{N-R_{g-1}}{N}\right)^k = \left(\frac{F_g}{N}\right)^k$ (i.e. random^k). Similarly when the proportion of individuals with the same fitness is small, i.e. $F_i \ll R_i$ then (using the binomial expansion of $(R_i/N - F_i/N)^t$ and dropping terms in $(F_i/N)^2$ and above)

$$
\begin{aligned}
\left(\frac{R_i}{N}\right)^t - \left(\frac{R_{i-1}}{N}\right)^t &= \left(\frac{R_i}{N}\right)^t - \left(\frac{R_i - F_i}{N}\right)^t \\
&\approx \left(\frac{R_i}{N}\right)^t - \left(\frac{R_i}{N}\right)^t + t\left(\frac{F_i}{N}\right)\left(\frac{R_i}{N}\right)^{t-1} \\
&= t\left(\frac{F_i}{N}\right)\left(\frac{R_i}{N}\right)^{t-1}
\end{aligned}
$$

That is the chance the winner of a tournament will have fitness f_i is approximately (proportion of population with fitness f_i) $\times t \times \left(\frac{R_i}{N}\right)^{t-1}$. Similarly the chance the loser of the kill tournament will have a fitness f_i is approximately (the proportion of population with fitness f_i) $\times k \times \left(\frac{N-R_i}{N}\right)^{k-1}$.

Figure 8.6 on page 175 shows the actual rate of producing offspring (i.e. the number of children each individual has divided by its age) for a typical stack run. We see in most cases the actual rate lies close to the expected rate. (Data points are concentrated at either end of the possible range since due to the convergence of the population most individuals are either of the highest fitness or are of low rank. Raising the rank to the third power further concentrates low rank data points).

Loss of Variety. New individuals are created either by crossover or reproduction (mutation is not used in the experiments described in Chapters 4 to 7). In reproduction a new copy of an existing individual is created and inserted into the population. If the new individual replaces a copy of itself then the population is unchanged, if it replaces a non-unique individual (i.e. one for which the population contains copies) then the variety is unchanged. However if the deleted individual was unique then the variety falls by one. NB reproduction can never increase variety.

The offspring created by crossover can either be unique or they can be a copy of individuals in the population. If crossover produces a unique offspring but the individual it replaces is also unique then there is no change in the number of unique individuals in the population, i.e. the variety does not change. However if the population contains one or more copies of the deleted individual then its variety increases by one. If crossover produces an individual which is not unique then its effect is just as reproduction, i.e. it may reduce variety by one or leave it unchanged, depending upon whether the replaced individual was unique or not.

Loss of Variety – Due to reproduction.

$$\begin{array}{rl} \text{Expected} & \\ \text{change in} = & -p(\Delta v = -1) \\ \text{variety} & \\ = & -p(\text{deleted unique}) + p(\text{parent unique \& replace self}) \quad (8.5) \end{array}$$

In large populations (which are not separated into smaller demes) the chance of an individual being selected both as a parent and as the individual to be replaced will be small and so we can drop the second term. Initially there will be no relationship between the fitness of an individual and whether it is unique or not so

$$p(\text{delete unique}) = \frac{v}{N} \qquad (8.6)$$

As evolution proceeds we would expect the higher fitness individuals to have more copies and those of lower fitness, which are more likely to be replaced, to have fewer copies, i.e. have a higher chance of being unique. Thus Equation 8.6 should be an underestimate, even so it should be a reasonable estimate unless the population becomes very anisotropic (when v will be low).

$$p(\Delta v = -1) \approx p_r \frac{v}{N} \qquad (8.7)$$

I.e. the expected change in v is approximately $-p_r \frac{v}{N}$ where N is large this discrete case can be approximated by a differential equation which can be solved to yield expected $v = A \exp(-p_r G)$ where A is the variety in the initial population and G is the number of generation equivalents since the initial population was created. As Figure 8.13 shows this formula fits the measured variety well for a few generation. However it is necessary to consider crossover to explain later behaviour.

Change in Variety – Due to Crossover.   There are four distinct cases: the individual to be deleted is unique or not and the offspring created is unique or not (see Table 8.4). We define X_u to be the chance of crossover producing a unique offspring.

Once again we assume the chance of an offspring replacing one of its parents (which is unique) can be neglected so we can again ignore terms like the second one in Equation 8.5. In a typical population we would expect it to be reasonable to treat the uniqueness of the offspring and that of the individual it is to replace as independent of each other so we can approximate the probability of the two events occurring together with the product of each's probability (cf. Equations 8.8 and 8.9).

$$p(\Delta v = -1) \approx p_c(1 - X_u)\frac{v}{N} \qquad (8.8)$$

$$p(\Delta v = +1) \approx p_c X_u(1 - \frac{v}{N}) \qquad (8.9)$$

Table 8.4.   Change in Variety After Creating an Individual by Crossover

Offspring Unique		Deleted Individual Unique	
		no $(1 - \frac{v}{N})$	yes $\frac{v}{N}$
no	$1 - X_u$	0	-1
yes	X_u	$+1$	0

Combining 8.8 and 8.9 with 8.7 yields the expected change in variety

$$
\begin{aligned}
\Delta v &\approx p_c X_u(1 - \frac{v}{N}) - p_c(1 - X_u)\frac{v}{N} - p_r\frac{v}{N} \\
&= p_c X_u - p_c X_u \frac{v}{N} - p_c\frac{v}{N} + p_c X_u\frac{v}{N} - p_r\frac{v}{N} \\
&= p_c X_u + \frac{v}{N}(-p_c X_u - p_c + p_c X_u - p_r) \\
\Delta v &= p_c X_u - \frac{v}{N}
\end{aligned}
\tag{8.10}
$$

Constant Chance of Crossover Producing a Unique Offspring.   If we further assume that the chance of crossover producing a unique offspring is constant then we can integrate Equation 8.10 and it predicts variety will fall exponentially to an asymptotic value of $p_c X_u$ and further that should variety fall below this limit then it will rise exponentially to the same limit (see Equation 8.11).

While this crude model does predict some aspects of variety's behaviour it fails to predict the "overshoot" as variety initially falls below its long term value and its collapse in run (23). A slightly more sophisticated quadratic model is developed in the next section.

Let $x = p_c X_u - \frac{v}{N}$ then

$$
\Delta x = -\frac{1}{N}\Delta v = -\frac{1}{N}x
$$

For large N we can approximate this discrete case with a differential equation

$$
dx = -\frac{1}{N}x\, dg
$$

Whose solutions are of the form

$$
\begin{aligned}
x &= A\,e^{-\frac{g}{N}} \\
x &= p_c X_u - \frac{v}{N} \\
p_c X_u - \frac{v}{N} &= A\,e^{-\frac{g}{N}} \\
\frac{v}{N} &= p_c X_u - A\,e^{-\frac{g}{N}}
\end{aligned}
$$

For simplicity define $g = 0$ to be the start of the evolution of the population. From Figure 8.12 we have $v(0) = N$. So

$$
\begin{aligned}
1 &= p_c X_u - A \\
A &= p_c X_u - 1 \\
v &= N\left(p_c X_u - (p_c X_u - 1)\,e^{-\frac{g}{N}}\right)
\end{aligned}
\tag{8.11}
$$

It is obvious from Figure 8.12 that the assumption that X_u is constant is not valid for the stack populations. However the initial fall in variety can be reasonably be predicted by assuming $X_u \approx 1$, in which case $v = N(p_c + p_r e^{-\frac{g}{N}})$ and $dv/dg = -p_r/Ne^{-\frac{g}{N}}$ so initially $dv/dg = -p_r/N$. However variety does not behave in the predicted exponential decay but in many runs "overshoots" in the first five generations or so before recovering and climbing back up. Such overshooting also appears in [Koza, 1992, page 159] on the artificial ant and on the six-multiplexor problems [pages 609 and 614] and in a simple symbolic regression in [Keijzer, 1996, Figures 13.5 and 13.6] when hill climbing is used.

Quadratic Chance of Crossover Producing a Unique Offspring. As an alternative to assuming the chance of crossover producing a unique offspring is constant this subsection investigates solutions of Equation 8.10 assuming it depends upon the variety. As crossover uses two parents a quadratic model is tested.

Analytic solutions to Equation 8.10 are obtained which also predict asymptotic decay but there are now two asymptotes, i.e. the population can converge to two different stable variety levels. These solutions predict variety will evolve to whichever asymptote is closest to its current value. The quadratic assumption can thus model the behaviour of variety in run (23), where it converges to near zero, by choosing appropriate constants. However, like the constant model, the quadratic model fails to predict the "overshoot" where variety falls below its long term limit and then rises back towards it.

The failure of the two models is perhaps primarily because of their very simplicity which ignores the role of fitness in the evolution of the stack populations. As Figure 8.16 shows, apart from the first few generations, the number of duplicate individuals produced by the reproduction operator (copying) in stack populations remains fairly constant at slightly less than $p_r N$ so the major source of changes in variety is crossover. It appears that at critical points in the evolution of stack populations crossover produces far fewer different individuals which are fit enough to be retained in the population and then gradually the proportion of diverse high fitness individuals increases.

Typically (see Figure 8.17) finding a solution with a higher fitness is followed by a large fall in variety. However once the new solution has been spread, crossover produces diverse individuals with the same high fitness which are thus retained in the population and variety gradually rises again while the maximum fitness remains unchanged.

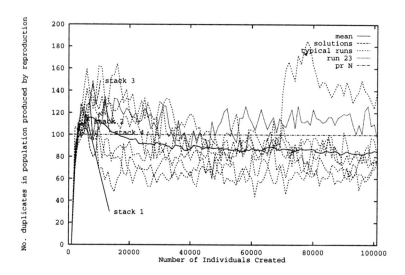

Figure 8.16. Number of duplicate individuals in stack populations that were produced by reproduction in selected runs.

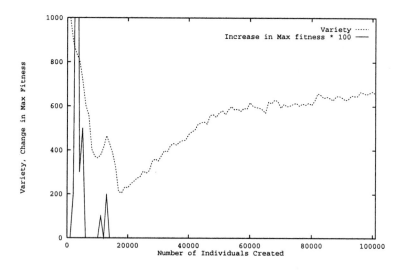

Figure 8.17. Number of different individuals in stack populations and change in maximum fitness in a typical stack run (51).

Let $y = \frac{v}{N}$ and $X_u = \frac{N}{P_c}\left(a + \left(b + \frac{1}{N}\right)y + cy^2\right)$ so using Equation 8.10:

$$
\begin{aligned}
\Delta y &= \frac{\Delta v}{N} \\
&= \frac{p_c \frac{N}{P_c}\left(a + \left(b + 1/N\right)y + cy^2\right) - y}{N} \\
&= \left(a + \left(b + 1/N\right)y + cy^2\right) - y/N \\
&= a + by + cy^2 \\
dy &= \left(a + by + cy^2\right) dg
\end{aligned}
\tag{8.12}
$$

Provided $b^2 \geq 4ac$ (i.e. there is at least one value of y at which $dy = 0$) then solutions to Equation 8.12 have the form

$$
y = \frac{-b \pm \sqrt{b^2 - 4ac}\tanh\pm\frac{(\sqrt{b^2 - 4ac})(-g - C_1)}{2}}{2c}
\tag{8.13}
$$

where C_1 is an integration constant fixed by the boundary conditions. Notice that Equation 8.13 gives two solutions for y. As $x \gg 1$ or $x \ll -1$ $\tanh x \to \pm 1$ so Equation 8.13 predicts y will converge to

$$
\lim_{g \to \infty} y = \frac{-b \pm \sqrt{b^2 - 4ac}}{2c}
\tag{8.14}
$$

If $a \approx 0$, i.e. when variety is very small most crossovers don't produce unique offspring, then 8.14 becomes

$$
\lim_{g \to \infty,\, a \to 0} y = \frac{-b}{c} \qquad \text{and}
$$

$$
\begin{aligned}
\lim_{g \to \infty,\, a \to 0} y &= \frac{-b + \sqrt{b^2(1 - \frac{4ac}{b^2})}}{2c} \\
&= \frac{-b + b\sqrt{(1 - \frac{4ac}{b^2})}}{2c} \\
&\approx \frac{-b + b(1 - \frac{2ac}{b^2})}{2c} \\
&= \frac{-a}{b}
\end{aligned}
$$

Now from Figure 8.12 we know v is initially N and v falls initially at a rate of about 0.1, i.e. $y(0) = 1$ and $y'(0) = -p_r/N$. Subsituting these values into Equation 8.12 gives Equation 8.15. Note Equation 8.15 is consistent with the observation that initially almost all crossovers produce different offspring, i.e. $X_u(1) = 1$. Figure 8.12 also shows that in most cases v tends towards 600 i.e. $\lim_{g \to \infty} y = 0.6$ (Equation 8.16).

Also should the variety fall to a very low rate we would expect it would prove more difficult for crossover to create different offspring thus we expect $a \geq 0$ but $a \approx 0$ (Equation 8.17).

$$a + b + c = -p_r/N \tag{8.15}$$
$$\frac{-b}{c} = 0.6 \tag{8.16}$$
$$-b = 0.6c$$
$$a = 0 \tag{8.17}$$
$$0 + -0.6c + c = -p_r/N$$
$$0.4c = -p_r/N$$
$$c = -p_r/0.4N$$
$$c = -2.5p_r/N \tag{8.18}$$
$$b = 1.5p_r/N \tag{8.19}$$

So Equation 8.13 becomes

$$y = \frac{-1.5p_r/N \pm \sqrt{2.56p_r^2/N^2 + 10ap_r/N} \tanh \pm \frac{(\sqrt{2.56p_r^2/N^2+10ap_r/N})(-g-C_1)}{2}}{-5p_r/N}$$

$$y = 0.3 \mp \sqrt{0.09 + 0.4aN/p_r} \tanh \pm \frac{(\sqrt{2.56p_r^2/N^2 + 10ap_r/N})(-g - C_1)}{2} \tag{8.20}$$

Equation 8.20 predicts v will converge to either $\approx 0.6N$ or $\approx$ zero with a time constant of $2(2.56p_r^2/N^2 + 10ap_r/N)^{-1/2} \approx 2(2.56p_r^2/N^2)^{-1/2} = 2(1.6p_r/N)^{-1} = 12.5N$.

If we include insisting that crossover does not introduce variety into the population once it has become homogeneous then $X_u(0) = 0$ and $a = 0$ and solutions to Equation 8.12 have the simpler form

$$y = \frac{be^{bg}}{-ce^{bg} + bC_2} \qquad \text{or}$$
$$y = 0$$

Using the same initial gradient and limit values as before implies b and c have the same values (i.e. as given by (8.18) and (8.19)) gives the following solutions

$$y = \frac{(1.5p_r/N)e^{1.5p_rg/N}}{(2.5p_r/N)e^{1.5p_rg/N} + C_3}$$

$$= \frac{1.5e^{1.5p_rg/N}}{2.5e^{1.5p_rg/N} + C_4}$$

$$= \frac{0.6e^{1.5p_rg/N}}{e^{1.5p_rg/N} + C_5} \quad \text{or} \tag{8.21}$$

$$y = 0$$

The integration constant C_5 can be fixed from the boundary conditions by defining $g = 0$ at the start of the evolution of the population when $V = N$, i.e. $y(0) = 1$. So $C_5 = -0.4$ and the solutions (8.21) become

$$y = \frac{0.6e^{1.5p_rg/N}}{e^{1.5p_rg/N} - 0.4} \quad \text{or} \tag{8.22}$$

$$y = 0$$

In Figure 8.18 the evolution of variety predicted by Equation (8.22) is superimposed on the actual variety for selected stack populations (cf. Figure 8.12).

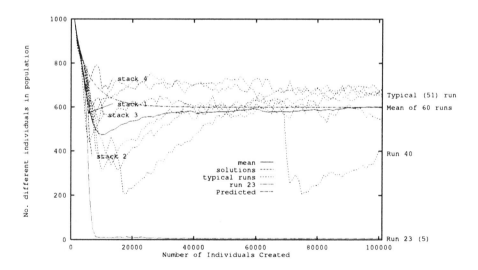

Figure 8.18. Variety predicted by quadratic crossover model and actual variety in selected stack runs.

8.4.3 Measurements of GP Crossover's Effect on Variety

The poor performance at intermediate points in the evolution of the stack populations of the general models described in the previous section leads to a detailed examination of the role of crossover in reducing variety in the stack populations. We discover there are two main causes; crossover which just involves swapping terminals and crossover which entails replacing whole trees. Where variety is low both lead to further production of clones of the first parent. Quantitative models of these two effects are in close agreement with measurements.

Figure 8.19 shows the proportion of cases where the offspring produced by crossover are identical to one or other of its parents. (In a typical stack run all offspring which are duplicates of other members of the population are identical to one or other parent). In a typical run of the stack problem about one third of crossovers produce offspring which are identical to their first parent. Table 8.5 gives the total number of offspring produced by crossover during the run that are clones for various size of crossover fragments.

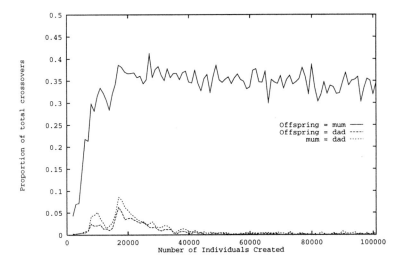

Figure 8.19.   Proportion of crossovers that yield offspring identical to one or other parents, typical stack (51) run (Also shows proportion where the two parents are identical).

For crossover to produce a clone of the first parent the fragment of code that is lost must be identical to that copied from the second parent. As crossover fragments which are taller are generally larger we would expect the chance of this happening to reduce rapidly with fragment height. Whilst Table 8.5 shows this is generally true, it is definitely not the case for fragment height 2.

In stack run 51 18,644 individuals are produced by crossover which are identical to their first parent and where the inserted subtree had a height of 2, i.e. fragments consisting of one function and its arguments which are all terminals. Of these 18,644, there were 16,536 individuals where the tree in which crossover occurred contained only one function and so crossover entailed replacing the whole tree with another from the other parent, which turned out to be identical to the first. In this regard the stack problem is atypical, normally trees or ADFs will have multiple functions and we would expect few clones to be produced by crossover of trees with a of height 2. In this run

Table 8.5.   Number of crossovers of each height of subtree inserted in a typical stack run (51) and number of these crossovers which produced a non-unique offspring.

Fragment height			Identical to				
	Total	%	mum	dad	both	either	%
1	28,783	32	9,513	38	128	9,679	32
2	28,277	31	18,644	60	305	19,009	62
3	15,360	17	1,060	79	28	1,167	4
4	3,884	4	303	42	6	351	1
5+	13,784	15	202	33	10	245	.8
Totals	90,088	100	29,722	252	477	30,451	100
		Percent	33	.3	.5	34	

of the stack problem most of the clones are produced by crossover in trees which are short (height of 2) and identical in both parents. Thus we see clones (which reduce variety) being caused by lack of diversity in the population.

Production of Clones by Crossover in Full Binary Trees.   In a full binary tree of height h there are $2^h - 1$ nodes of which 2^{h-1} are terminals and $2^{h-1} - 1$ are internal nodes. Consider crossover between two identical trees where each node is distinct. For crossover to produce an individual which is identical to its parents the crossover points selected in both parents must be the same. The chance of this happening would simply be $(2^h - 1)^{-1}$ if nodes were chosen at random. However the parameter pUnRestrictWt (cf. Section 3.7) means only 70% of crossover points are chosen totally at random. In the remaining 30% of cases the chosen point must be an internal tree node. From Equation 8.24 we see for large trees pUnRestrictWt's effect is to increase the chance of producing a clone by 9%. The probabilities for smaller trees are tabulated in Table 8.6.

$$
\begin{aligned}
\text{p(clone)} \;=\; & \text{p(Tree1 internal)} \times \text{p(Tree2 same internal)} + \\
& \text{p(Tree1 external)} \times \text{p(Tree2 same external)} \\
=\; & \left((1 - p_{any}) + p_{any} \frac{2^h - 1 - 2^{h-1}}{2^h - 1} \right) \times \text{p(Tree2 same internal)} + \\
& p_{any} \frac{2^{h-1}}{2^h - 1} \times \text{p(Tree2 same external)} \\
=\; & \left((1 - p_{any}) + p_{any} \frac{2^{h-1} - 1}{2^h - 1} \right) \times \text{p(Tree2 same internal)} + \\
& p_{any} \frac{2^{h-1}}{2^h - 1} \times \text{p(Tree2 same external)} \\
=\; & \frac{ \left((1 - p_{any}) + p_{any} \frac{2^{h-1}-1}{2^h-1} \right) \times \left((1 - p_{any}) + p_{any} \frac{2^{h-1}-1}{2^h-1} \right) }{ (2^{h-1} - 1) } +
\end{aligned}
$$

$$p_{any} \frac{2^{h-1}}{2^h - 1} \times p_{any} \frac{2^{h-1}}{2^h - 1} / 2^{h-1}$$

$$= \frac{\left((1 - p_{any}) + p_{any} \frac{2^{h-1}-1}{2^h-1}\right)^2}{(2^{h-1} - 1)} + \frac{\left(p_{any} \frac{2^{h-1}}{2^h-1}\right)^2}{2^{h-1}} \tag{8.23}$$

As h increases

$$p(clone) \approx \frac{(1 - p_{any}/2)^2}{(2^{h-1} - 1)} + \frac{p_{any}^2/4}{2^{h-1}}$$

$$\approx \frac{(1 - p_{any}/2)^2}{2^{h-1}} + \frac{p_{any}^2/4}{2^{h-1}}$$

$$= \frac{(1 - p_{any}/2)^2 + p_{any}^2/4}{2^{h-1}}$$

$$= \frac{1 - p_{any} + p_{any}^2/4 + p_{any}^2/4}{2^{h-1}}$$

$$= \frac{1 - p_{any} + p_{any}^2/2}{2^{h-1}}$$

Since $p_{any} = 0.7$ for large h

$$= 1.09 \, 2^{-h}$$

$$p(clone) \approx 1.09 \, (2^h - 1)^{-1} \tag{8.24}$$

Table 8.6. Chance of offspring being identical to parents when crossing two identical full binary trees

Tree height	Chance of clone		$p_{any} = 1$
1	1	1.000	1.000
2	$\left((1 - p_{any}) + p_{any}\frac{1}{3}\right)^2 + \frac{(p_{any}\frac{2}{3})^2}{2}$	0.393	.333
3	$\frac{((1-p_{any})+p_{any}\frac{3}{7})^2}{3} + \frac{(p_{any}\frac{4}{7})^2}{4}$	.160	.143
4	$\frac{((1-p_{any})+p_{any}\frac{7}{15})^2}{7} + \frac{(p_{any}\frac{8}{15})^2}{8}$	.074	.067
5	$\frac{\left((1-p_{any})+p_{any}\frac{15}{31}\right)^2}{15} + \frac{(p_{any}\frac{16}{31})^2}{16}$	.035	.032

The chance of producing a clone from two identical trees in a real GP population may not be exactly as given by Equation 8.23. This is because: the trees may not be full binary trees, i.e. they will be smaller if there are terminals closer to the root than the maximum height of the tree, or if functions have one argument rather than two. Conversely trees can be also be larger if functions have three or more arguments. Also the chance of producing a clone is increased if actual trees contain repeated subtrees.

In the case of two identical trees of height two and crossover fragments of height two the chance of producing a clone is equal to the chance of selecting the root in the

Table 8.7.   Chance of selecting a terminal as a crossover fragment in a full binary tree

Height		Both parents
1	100 %	100 %
2	47 %	22 %
3	40 %	16 %
4	37 %	14 %
∞	35 %	12.25 %

first tree which depends upon the number of arguments the tree has. For n arguments, the chance of producing a clone is $(1 - p_{any}) + p_{any}/(n+1) = 1 - n \, p_{any}/(n+1)$ which is 65%, 53%, 48% and 44% for $n = 1, 2, 3$ and 4. In other words given a population where the best solution found has a height of two and the inserted crossover fragment is also of height two and there is a high chance of selecting (copies of) the individual to be both parents we expect the offspring to be a clone between 53% and 65% of the time, which is consistent with the figure of 16,536 such clones produced in a typical stack run (cf. page 196).

Thus one of the major causes of the fall in variety in the stack populations can be traced to finding partial solutions early in the evolution of the population with relatively high fitness where trees within it are short. As the whole individual is composed of five trees, its total size need not be very small. Figure 4.16 (page 77) provides additional evidence for this as it shows on average stack individuals shrink early in the run to 23.3 at generation six. I.e. on average each tree contains 4.7 primitives and as there must be many trees shorter than this, many trees must have a height of two or less.

Production of Clones by Crossover Swapping Terminals.   The other major reason for crossover to produce clones in the stack runs is crossover fragments which contain a single terminal (cf. Table 8.5). The proportion of clones these crossovers produce can be readily related to lack of diversity. The proportion of crossover fragments which are a single terminal depends upon the depth and bushiness of the trees within the population, which in turn depends upon the number of arguments required by each function in the function set and how the distribution of functions evolves. The proportion of crossover fragments which are a single terminal is clearly problem dependent and changes with run and generation within the run, however as a first approximation in the stack problem it can be treated as a constant for each type of tree (cf. Figure 8.21).

For a full binary tree of height h the chance of selecting a terminal as a crossover fragment is $p_{any}2^{h-1}/(2^h - 1)$ and the chance of crossover swapping two terminals is $\left(p_{any}2^{h-1}/(2^h - 1)\right)^2$. Table 8.7 gives the numerical values for trees of different heights. Note the chance of selecting a terminal converges rapidly to 35% for large trees.

If parents were chosen at random the chance of selecting the same terminal in two trees would be simply the sum of the squares of their proportions in the population. Thus if the terminals are equally likely (as would be expected in the initial population)

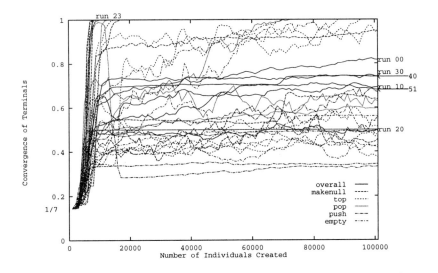

Figure 8.20.   Evolution of (Terminal Concentration)^2 in each operation tree, for six typical stack runs and run (23).

the chance of selecting two the same is just the reciprocal of the number of terminals and this rises as variety falls eventually reaching unity if all but one terminal are removed from the population. Figure 8.20 shows how this measure evolves for each tree in a sample of stack runs. Note in run (23) all five trees quickly converge on a single terminal. In many of the other runs the population concentrates on one or two terminals, so the chance of an offspring produced by changing a single terminal being a clone of one of its parents is much increased.

Typically 15.8% of crossovers replace one terminal with another terminal (cf. Table 8.8). This is near the proportion expected for full binary trees with a height of three or more. Table 8.8 shows reasonable agreement between the predicted number of clones produced by crossover inserting a single terminal and the actual number averaged over a typical run of the stack problem.

The second major source of crossover produced reduction in variety (cf. Table 8.5) is thus explained by the fall in terminal diversity, itself a product of the fall in variety. So again we see low variety being reinforced by crossover, i.e. the reversal of its expected role of creating new individuals.

8.5   MEASUREMENTS OF GP CROSSOVER'S EFFECTS

In this section we analyse how successful crossover is at finding new solutions with higher fitness and conclude in the case of the stack problem, crossover quickly tires and the rate of finding improvements slows rapidly so after generation eight very few are found and typically no improvements are found after generation 16. Note this includes all crossovers not just those that produce offspring that are better than anyone else in the population.

Table 8.8.   Number of clones produced by changing a terminal in run (51) of the stack problem

Tree	No. Crossovers	Terminal Only	$\sum(term\ conc)^2$	Predicted	Actual
makenull	18,020	3,326	.924424	3,074.6	3,075
top	17,914	3,022	.798273	2,412.4	2,684
pop	18,013	4,895	.565901	2,770.1	2,819
push	18,021	2,306	.318201	733.8	740
empty	18,120	668	.511968	342.0	339
Totals	90,088	14,217		9,334.9	9,657

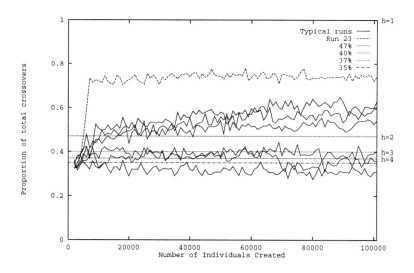

Figure 8.21.   Proportion of crossovers where a terminal is inserted for six typical stack runs and run (23) (averaged across all five trees within each individual).

Table 8.9. No. of Successful Crossovers, in Typical and Successful Stack Runs

Run	Crossover point in Tree					Total	Best Fitness
	Makenull	Top	Pop	Push	Empty		
23	33	32	54	18	46	183	130
00	22	34	57	43	20	176	108
10	27	34	85	29	24	199	108
20	36	41	31	13	59	180	128
30	22	25	44	21	44	156	131
51	38	31	48	16	30	163	139
40	63	75	50	26	90	304	150
27	72	67	47	18	53	257	160
32	69	56	42	25	77	269	160
09	42	63	54	22	75	256	160
53	33	55	44	38	25	195	160

Table 8.9 gives the number of crossovers which produced an offspring fitter than both its parents, for run (23), six typical runs and the four successful runs. The successful runs produce about 50% more successful crossovers than typical runs. The parents of successful crossovers and their offspring are plotted in Figures 8.22 and 8.23 for a typical and a successful run respectively. However the number of successful crossovers is more than the number of different fitness values, that is there are fitness values which have been "discovered" by multiple successful crossovers. Clusters of particularly popular fitness values that were "rediscovered" many times can be seen in Figures 8.22 and 8.23. E.g. fitness value 128 is discovered 22 times in run (51) (22 is 13% of all the successful crossovers).

The proportion of successful crossovers in six selected stack runs is shown in Figure 8.24. Note the number of crossovers that produce improved offspring is small and quickly falls so after generation 16 there are almost no crossovers that improve on both parents (or indeed improve on either).

Figure 8.25 shows the fitness of individuals selected to be crossover parents. This shows the convergence of the population with almost all parents having the maximum fitness value. (The asymmetry of the fitness function makes the mean fitness of the population lower than the fitness of the median individual).

8.6   DISCUSSION

Natural evolution of species requires variation within a population of individuals as well as selection for survival and reproduction. In the previous sections we have seen how, even on the most basic measure, variety in the stack populations falls to low levels primarily due to crossover producing copies of the first parent at high rates. Initially this is caused by the discovery of relatively high fitness partial solutions containing very small trees which dominate the population, reducing variety which causes feedback via crossover produced clones so keeping variety low, in one case causing it to collapse entirely. As we argued in Section 8.3, in most stack runs lack

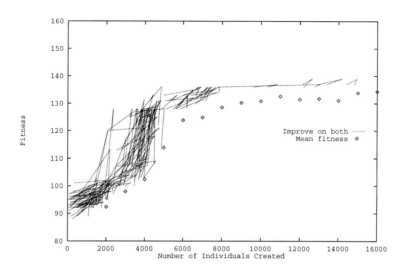

Figure 8.22.   All crossovers that produced offspring fitter than both parents, typical stack run (51).

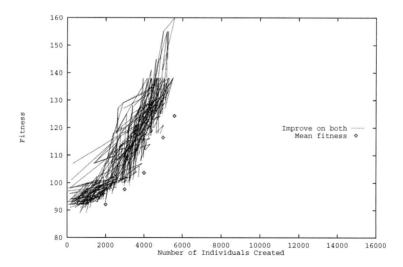

Figure 8.23.   All crossovers that produced offspring fitter than both parents, successful run (09).

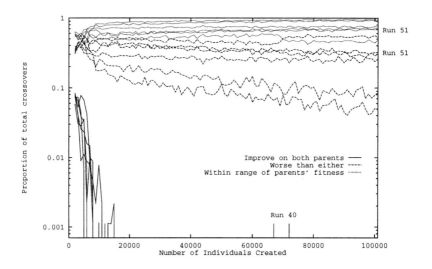

Figure 8.24. Proportion of crossovers that produced offspring fitter than both parents, worse than both or neither. Six typical stack runs.

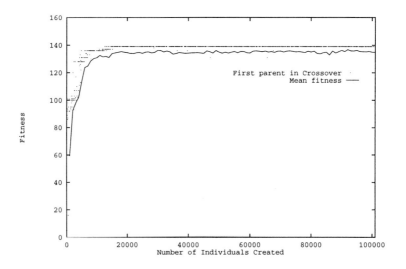

Figure 8.25. Fitness of parents selected for crossover in typical stack (51) run. (Extrema and 1% of data for first parent only are plotted).

of variety with corresponding extinctions of primitives prevents solutions like those found from evolving.

In any genetic search a balance between searching the whole search space for an optimum and concentrating the search in particular regions is required. Some convergence of the population is expected as the GA concentrates on particularly fruitful areas. In most stack runs partial solutions are found which act similarly to a stack of one item and so receive a high relative fitness and the population begins to converge to them. This would be fine apart from two problems: firstly the solutions contain short trees which causes rapid production of clones but more seriously there is no straightforward path from their implementation of a stack of one item to a general stack of many items. These two problems are to some extent specific to the stack problem, the five tree architecture and the terminal/function set used. A smaller terminal/function set without special primitives to manipulate "aux", having only general primitives and indexed memory, might avoid the trapping by "deceptive solutions" but partial solutions of any sort might then not evolve in a reasonable time. (Interestingly [Bruce, 1995] adopts a similar terminal/function set in his experiments on the evolution of stacks and other data structures). In the stack problem each terminal and function can appear in each of the five trees but crossover acts only between like trees so each tree is genetically isolated from each other. (This is known as *branch typing* and is commonly used with ADFs [Koza, 1994, page 86]. An alternative *point typing* allows crossover to move genetic material between trees). Branch typing means there are effectively $5 \times 12 = 60$ primitives in the stack problem. [Andre, 1996] also reports GP runs with similar numbers of primitives where one or more functions either evolved out of the population (i.e. became extinct) or became rare and suggests it was a factor in the decision to use mutation (albeit at a low rate). However he cautions that further experiments are required for confirmation.

The impact of deceptive partial solutions within the population might be reduced by partitioning the population into "demes" (c.f. Section 3.8), using fitness niches to ensure diverse solutions are retained (c.f. Section 3.6) or perhaps using co-evolution to reward solutions to parts of the test case which most of the population is unable to solve.

Mutation could also be used to increase population diversity (as discussed in Section 6.10) but a high mutation rate might be required to escape from a deceptive local optimum. This would increase the degree of randomness in the search but might introduce a beneficial element of "hill climbing".

While other GPs may not suffer from lack of variety, convergence of some sort is required if the GP is not to be random search. For example [Keijzer, 1996] shows convergence in terms of subtrees with GP populations reusing subtrees in many individuals. (GP may take advantage of this by reducing the space taken to store the population in memory [Keijzer, 1996] and on disk (by using file compression, see Section D.7). Where side-effects are controlled, retaining information on the evaluation of common subtrees within the population can also considerably reduce program execution time, c.f. Section D.5 and [Handley, 1994a]).

Existing GP systems could be modified to:

1. Increase variety by disabling the production of clones by the reproduction operator, e.g. by setting p_r to zero.

2. Detect when an offspring is identical to one of its parents. This information can be readily gathered and can be used either to:

(a) reduce GP run time or

(b) Increase variety.

In many problems (a) can be readily achieved by avoiding the fitness evaluation of the offspring and instead just copying the fitness value of its (identical) parent. Variety can be kept high (b) by preventing the duplicate offspring from entering the population. Typically this would prevent all duplicates produced by crossover. (It would also be feasible to *guarantee* every member of the population is unique by forbidding duplicates from entering the population. Using hashing techniques this can be done efficiently).

Given current GP populations sizes it would appear to be sensible to ensure variety remains high so the compromise between converging on good search location and exploring untried areas retains a high degree of exploration. Thus both changes 1. and 2.b) should be tried.

The use of $p_r = 0.1$ in this book stems from the decision to use parameters as similar to [Koza, 1992] as possible. It is also the supplied default value with GP-QUICK [Singleton, 1994]. However the use of reproduction is not universal, for example the CGPS [Nordin, 1994a; Nordin and Banzhaf, 1995; Francone et al., 1996] does not implement it. As far as is known, GP systems do not currently detect that crossover has produced a child which is identical to one of its parents for the purposes of either reducing run time (2.a) or increasing variety (2.b). [Koza, 1992, page 93] ensures every member of the initial population is unique but allows duplicates in subsequent generations. While hashing allows detection of duplicates in the whole population to be done quickly, in these experiments most duplicates were directly related to each other and so could be readily detected without comparison with the whole population.

It appears to be common practice for GP to "run out of steam" so after 20–30 generations no further improvement in the best fitness value in the population occurs or improvement occurs at a very low rate. Accordingly few GP runs are continued beyond generation 50. ([Iba et al., 1994c]'s STROGANOFF system provides a counter example with runs of 400 generations). It is suggested that failure of crossover to improve on the best individual in the population may, as we saw in Section 8.5, be accompanied by a general failure of crossover to make any improvement. This "death of crossover" means further evolution of the population is due to unequal production of individuals with the same (or worse) fitness as their parents, in fitness terms (and possible also phenotypically) at best they are copies of their parents. Typically this serves only to increase the convergence of the population.

An number of attempts to "scale up" GP have been made based upon imposing functional abstraction on individuals in the population [Koza, 1994; Angeline, 1993; Rosca, 1995]. These have had a degree of success. Another approach is to accept that complex problems will require many generations to solve and look to the various mechanisms described above and new techniques to allow long periods of GP evolution with controlled convergence of the GP population and means to retain and reuse (partial) solutions.

8.7   SUMMARY

In this chapter we discussed Price's selection and covariance theorem and showed it can be applied to genetic algorithms and applied it to genetic programming, where we used it to explain the evolution of the frequency of various critical primitives in stack populations including their rapid extinction in many cases. These extinctions are seen as the main reason why many runs of the stack problem (described in Chapter 4) failed. In Section 8.4 it was shown that the loss of these primitives was accompanied by a general loss in variety and general models were developed to try and explain this. While these predicted the initial as well as the final evolution of the stack populations, they were less successful at describing the middle portion. Quantitatively successful models based upon full binary trees of particular heights were developed. Section 8.5 concludes by looking at just the successful crossovers in the stack runs and concludes they are small in number, in many cases they "rediscover" solutions that have already been found and convergence of the population is accompanied by absence of crossovers that produce offspring fitter than their parents as well as none that are fitter than the best existing individuals in the population.

To some extent these problems are fundamental. Viewing GP as a search process there is necessarily a trade-off between concentrating the search in promising parts of the search space which increases the chance of finding local optima versus a wider ranging search which may therefore be unsuccessful but may also find a more remote but better global optimum. In GA terms a local search corresponds to a more converged population. The stack experiments indicate, after the fact, that the search was too focused too early and so the global optima were missed in many runs. There are many techniques that can be used to ensure population diversity remains high (and so the search is defocused) such as splitting the population into demes, fitness niches and mutation, some of which were used in Chapters 5, 6 and 7 and Appendix C. Techniques based on biased mate selection to preserve diversity are discussed in [Ryan, 1994].

Defocusing the search means the search is more random and will take longer, if indeed it succeeds. Other approaches to avoid getting trapped at local optima ("premature convergence") change the search space, for example by changing the representation by changing the primitives from which solutions are composed or changing the fitness function.

Changing the primitives can easily be done by hand. It would be interesting to discover to what extend the problems are due to provision of the auxiliary registers which allow the evolution of stacks but also allow ready formation of deceptive partial solutions. If these were not used, would stacks still evolve? It is interesting that [Bruce, 1995] uses very similar additional memory in his work. Alternatively perhaps cleverer genetic operations could avoid the trap by changing programs from using one type of memory to another in a consistent manner so new programs continue to work as before. While strongly typed GP can reduce the size of the search space [Montana, 1995], it may also transform it so that it is easier to search.

There are a number of techniques which automatically change the representation. The following three techniques co-evolve the representation as the population itself evolves; The Genetic Library Builder (GLiB) [Angeline, 1994], Automatically Defined Functions (ADFs) [Koza, 1994] and Adaptive Representations [Rosca, 1995]. [Koza,

1994, page 619] argues ADFs and other representations provide a different *lens* with which to view the solution space and that ADFs may help solve a problem by providing a better lens. ADFs were used in Chapters 5, 6 and 7.

The fitness function may be readily changed by hand. For example provision of an additional test case may "plug a gap" which GP populations are exploiting to achieve high fitness on the test case but at the expense of not generalising to the problem as a whole. Co-evolution can provide an automatic means of dynamically changing the fitness function [Siegel, 1994]. There is increasing interest in using co-evolution [Sen, 1996; Reynolds, 1994a; Ryan, 1995] and improved performance has been claimed [Hillis, 1992]. However a more dynamic framework makes analysis of population behaviour harder.

In GP runs the concentration of primitives and variety within the population should be monitored (both can be done with little overhead). Should a primitive fall to low concentration (such as close to the background level provided by mutation) or total extinction this should be taken as an indication of possible problems and so worthy of further investigation. Similarly if the number of unique individuals in the population falls below 90% this should also be investigated. [Keijzer, 1996] provides a means to measure the concentration of groups of primitives (sub trees) but the implementation is not straightforward for most existing GP systems and the interpretation of the results is more complex.

9 CONCLUSIONS

The key to successful human produced software is using abstraction to control the complexity of each task in hand. I.e. in each task, being able to use objects without considering in detail how they interact. The objects are abstractions of lower level code or data, which are in turn abstractions of still lower levels. Thus a programmer may use a file while knowing nothing about how to program the disk drive on which it is stored. Indeed the program can continue to work even if the file is moved to another disk drive, even if it is of a different type, even a type which had not been designed when the program was written.

Genetic programming, with its undirected random program creation, would appear to be the anathema of highly organised software engineering. It is an evolutionary technique, using only information in its current population. It does not plan ahead or use a global top-down design but we have already seen, via ADFs and other techniques, it too can gain considerable benefit from functional abstraction.

While GP work to date has concentrated on functional abstraction, we argue that techniques which allow GP to take advantage of data abstraction will be essential to enable it to scale up and tackle large real problems. Chapters 4, 5 and 6 show GP can produce structured data types (stacks, queues and lists). In Chapter 7 we demonstrate GP can use data abstraction, by solving three problems. For the two more complex examples we have shown a stack abstract data type is beneficial. While the first example does not require a stack, a general solution was evolved which used the appropriate data structure. The failure of indexed memory to solve the two more complex problems, is disappointing, but was expected. While it is anticipated that it is possible to evolve solutions to the two problems using indexed memory, e.g. if increased resources are available, the richness of interactions supported by indexed memory allows complex interactions to arise and these complicate the search space making it harder to search. This problem is a general one. The search effort increases rapidly with problem complexity. While other research has shown changes to the representation (e.g. ADFs and more powerful primitives) can help, this work has shown that reducing the complexity of evolved programs through use of data abstraction to control interactions within evolving programs can also be beneficial.

Appendix C has demonstrated that both the combination of a GA and hand coded heuristic, and a GP using the same heuristics as seeds in the initial population can produce low cost maintenance schedules for a real world electrical power transmission network.

In many of the problems in this book, general scalable solutions have been evolved. This is very encouraging. Perhaps general algorithms are easier for GP to find? It may be argued on the basis of the Minimum Description Length (MDL) principle or Occam's Razor that general programs tend to be shorter than programs which are specific to the test case and fail to generalise [Iba et al., 1994a; Zhang and Mühlenbein, 1995b]. Non-general program may "memorise" the tests and need to be longer and more complex to do this. Perhaps solutions occur more frequently in the search space of shorter programs or perhaps GP is less effective at searching for longer programs?

The idea that symbolic regression is compressing the training data into a program, can be inverted. If a required program's size can be estimated, then so too can its information content. This gives a lower bound on the information content of the training data and thus, a lower bound on the size of the training set. This indicates that the volume of training data will need to increase as we try and evolve more ambitious programs. If we continue to test all evolved programs on all the training set then GP machine resource usage will grow at least quadratically with task complexity. However techniques such as co-evolution [Angeline and Pollack, 1993], soft brood selection [Tackett, 1995a] and sparse training sets [Francone et al., 1996] indicate it may not be necessary to exhaustively test every evolved program.

9.1   RECOMMENDATIONS

A number of practical recommendations for GP work can be made. To a large extent the advice in [Kinnear, Jr., 1994c] and [Koza, 1992] remains sound, however a number of additional suggestions can be made:

1. GP populations should be closely studied as they evolve. There are several properties that can be easily measure which give indication of problems:

   (a) Frequency of primitives. Recognising when a primitive has been completely lost from the population (or its frequency has fallen to a low level, consistent with the mutation rate) may help to diagnose problems.

   (b) Population variety. If the variety falls below 90% of the population size, this indicates there may be a problem. However a high variety does not indicate all is well. Measuring phenotypic variation (i.e. diversity of behaviour) may also be useful.

2. Measures should be taken to encourage population diversity. Panmictic steady state populations with tournament selection and reproduction and crossover appear to converge too readily. The above metrics may indicate if this is happening in a particular case. Possible solutions include:

   (a) Removal of the reproduction operator.

   (b) Addition of one or more mutation operators.

   (c) Smaller tournament sizes and/or using uniform random selection to decide which individuals to remove from the population. NB the latter means the selection scheme is no longer elitist. It may be worthwhile forcing it to be elitist.

   (d) Splitting large populations, i.e. above 1000, into semi-isolated demes.

   (e) Using fitness sharing to encourage the formation of many fitness niches.

3. Use of fitness caches (either when executing an individual or between ancestors and children) can reduce run time and may repay the additional work involved with using them.

4. Where GP run time is long, periodically save the current state of the run. Should the system crash; the run can be restarted, from part way through rather than the at the start. Care should be taken to save the entire state, so restarting a run does not introduce any unknown variation.

   The bulk of the state to be saved is the current population. This can be compressed, e.g. using *gzip*. While compression can add a few percent to run time, reductions in disk space to less than one bit per primitive in the population have been achieved.

9.2   FUTURE WORK

There are many interesting questions raised by this work. There are a number of techniques that have been introduced or which are fairly new to GP which warrant further investigation to further explore their benefits or clarify the best circumstances in which to use them. Examples include:

- Multi-objective fitness functions.

- Pareto fitness.

- Fitness Niches.

- Fitness Sharing.

- Design of primitive sets and fitness functions (particularly concerning deceptive fitness functions and representations).

- Semantic and syntactic restrictions on evolving programs or parts of programs.

- Scoping rules.

- Reducing run time via caching or inheriting partial fitness information from ancestors.

However the failure of GP to evolve data structures "on the fly" is the most important. Aspects that could be investigated include: Is the failure specific to the problems tried, the primitive sets used or insufficient resources dedicated to the task? If the later how much extra resources are required? While these are possible explanations, it is felt that this failure is part of the general difficulty of scaling up GP to solve more complex problems and so its solution would have a direct bearing on the fundamental scaling problem for GP.

The addition of data structures greatly extends the power of genetic programming. GP plus data structures should be evaluated on such problems. The use of stack data structures with other context free languages is an obvious first step.

References

Abbott, R. J. (1991). Niches as a GA divide-and-conquer strategy. In Chapman, A. and Myers, L., editors, *Proceedings of the Second Annual AI Symposium for the California State University*. California State University.

Aho, A. V., Hopcroft, J. E., and Ullman, J. D. (1987). *Data Structures and Algorithms*. Addison-Wesley.

Aho, A. V. and Ullman, J. D. (1995). *Foundations of Computer Science*. Computer Science Press, C edition.

Alonso, L. and Schott, R. (1995). *Random Generation of Trees*. Kulwer Academic Publishers.

Altenberg, L. (1994). The evolution of evolvability in genetic programming. In Kinnear, Jr., K. E., editor, *Advances in Genetic Programming*, chapter 3, pages 47–74. MIT Press.

Altenberg, L. (1995). The Schema Theorem and Price's Theorem. In Whitley, L. D. and Vose, M. D., editors, *Foundations of Genetic Algorithms 3*, pages 23–49, Estes Park, Colorado, USA. Morgan Kaufmann.

Andre, D. (1994a). Automatically defined features: The simultaneous evolution of 2-dimensional feature detectors and an algorithm for using them. In Kinnear, Jr., K. E., editor, *Advances in Genetic Programming*, chapter 23, pages 477–494. MIT Press.

Andre, D. (1994b). Evolution of mapmaking ability: Strategies for the evolution of learning, planning, and memory using genetic programming. In *Proceedings of the 1994 IEEE World Congress on Computational Intelligence*, volume 1, pages 250–255, Orlando, Florida, USA. IEEE Press.

Andre, D. (1994c). Learning and upgrading rules for an OCR system using genetic programming. In *Proceedings of the 1994 IEEE World Congress on Computational Intelligence*, Orlando, Florida, USA. IEEE Press.

Andre, D. (1995a). The automatic programming of agents that learn mental models and create simple plans of action. In *IJCAI-95 Proceedings of the Fourteenth International Joint Conference on Artificial Intelligence*, volume 1, pages 741–747, Montreal, Quebec, Canada. Morgan Kaufmann.

Andre, D. (1995b). The evolution of agents that build mental models and create simple plans using genetic programming. In Eshelman, L., editor, *Genetic Algorithms:*

Proceedings of the Sixth International Conference (ICGA95), pages 248–255, Pittsburgh, PA, USA. Morgan Kaufmann.

Andre, D. (1996). Personal communication.

Andre, D. and Koza, J. R. (1995). Parallel genetic programming on a network of transputers. In Rosca, J. P., editor, *Proceedings of the Workshop on Genetic Programming: From Theory to Real-World Applications*, pages 111–120, Tahoe City, California, USA.

Andre, D. and Koza, J. R. (1996). Parallel genetic programming: A scalable implementation using the transputer network architecture. In Angeline, P. J. and Kinnear, Jr., K. E., editors, *Advances in Genetic Programming 2*, chapter 16, pages 317–338. MIT Press, Cambridge, MA, USA.

Andre, D. and Teller, A. (1996). A study in program response and the negative effects of introns in genetic programming. In Koza, J. R., Goldberg, D. E., Fogel, D. B., and Riolo, R. L., editors, *Genetic Programming 1996: Proceedings of the First Annual Conference*, pages 12–20, Stanford University, CA, USA. MIT Press.

Andrews, M. and Prager, R. (1994). Genetic programming for the acquisition of double auction market strategies. In Kinnear, Jr., K. E., editor, *Advances in Genetic Programming*, chapter 16, pages 355–368. MIT Press.

Angeline, P. J. (1993). *Evolutionary Algorithms and Emergent Intelligence*. PhD thesis, Ohio State University.

Angeline, P. J. (1994). Genetic programming and emergent intelligence. In Kinnear, Jr., K. E., editor, *Advances in Genetic Programming*, chapter 4, pages 75–98. MIT Press.

Angeline, P. J. (1996a). An investigation into the sensitivity of genetic programming to the frequency of leaf selection during subtree crossover. In Koza, J. R., Goldberg, D. E., Fogel, D. B., and Riolo, R. L., editors, *Genetic Programming 1996: Proceedings of the First Annual Conference*, pages 21–29, Stanford University, CA, USA. MIT Press.

Angeline, P. J. (1996b). Two self-adaptive crossover operators for genetic programming. In Angeline, P. J. and Kinnear, Jr., K. E., editors, *Advances in Genetic Programming 2*, chapter 5, pages 89–110. MIT Press, Cambridge, MA, USA.

Angeline, P. J. and Pollack, J. B. (1993). Competitive environments evolve better solutions for complex tasks. In Forrest, S., editor, *Proceedings of the 5th International Conference on Genetic Algorithms, ICGA-93*, pages 264–270, University of Illinois at Urbana-Champaign. Morgan Kaufmann.

Angeline, P. J. and Pollack, J. B. (1994). Coevolving high-level representations. In Langton, C. G., editor, *Artificial Life III*, volume XVII of *SFI Studies in the Sciences of Complexity*, pages 55–71, Sante Fe, New Mexico. Addison-Wesley.

Atlan, L., Bonnet, J., and Naillon, M. (1994). Learning distributed reactive strategies by genetic programming for the general job shop problem. In *Proceedings of the 7th annual Florida Artificial Intelligence Research Symposium*, Pensacola, Florida, USA. IEEE Press.

Back, T., Hoffmeister, F., and Schwefel, H.-P. (1991). A survey of evolution strategies. In Belew, R. K. and Booker, L. B., editors, *Proceedings of fourth International Conference on Genetic Algorithms*, pages 2–10, University of California - San Diego, La Jolla, CA, USA. Morgan Kaufmann.

Banzhaf, W. (1993). Genetic programming for pedestrians. In Forrest, S., editor, *Proceedings of the 5th International Conference on Genetic Algorithms, ICGA-93*, page 628, University of Illinois at Urbana-Champaign. Morgan Kaufmann.

Banzhaf, W., Frankone, F. D., and Nordin, P. (1996). The effect of extensive use of the mutation operator on generalization in genetic programming using sparse data sets. In Voigt, H.-M., Ebeling, W., Rechenberg, I., and Schwefel, H.-P., editors, *Parallel Problem Solving from Nature IV, Proceedings of the International Conference on Evolutionary Computation*, volume 1141 of *LNCS*, pages 300–309, Berlin, Germany. Springer Verlag.

Banzhaf, W., Nordin, P., Keller, R. E., and Francone, F. D. (1997a). *Genetic Programming – An Introduction On the Automatic Evolution of Computer Programs and its Applications*. Morgan Kaufmann, dpunkt.verlag.

Banzhaf, W., Nordin, P., and Olmer, M. (1997b). Generating adaptive behavior for a real robot using function regression within genetic programming. In Koza, J. R., Deb, K., Dorigo, M., Fogel, D. B., Garzon, M., Iba, H., and Riolo, R. L., editors, *Genetic Programming 1997: Proceedings of the Second Annual Conference*, pages 35–43, Stanford University, CA, USA. Morgan Kaufmann.

Beasley, D., Bull, D. R., and Martin, R. R. (1993a). Reducing epistasis in combinatorial problems by expansive coding. In Forrest, S., editor, *Proceedings of the 5th International Conference on Genetic Algorithms, ICGA-93*, pages 400–407, University of Illinois at Urbana-Champaign. Morgan Kaufmann.

Beasley, D., Bull, D. R., and Martin, R. R. (1993b). A sequential niche technique for multimodal function optimisation. *Evolutionary Computation*, 1(2):101–125.

Bettenhausen, K. D., Gehlen, S., Marenbach, P., and Tolle, H. (1995). BioX++ – New results and conceptions concerning the intelligent control of biotechnological processes. In Munack, A. and Schügerl, K., editors, *6th International Conference on Computer Applications in Biotechnology*, pages 324–327. Elsevier Science.

Beyer, H.-G. (1995). Towards a theory of evolution strategies: On the benefits of sex– the (u/u,l) theory. *Evolutionary Computation*, 3(1):81–111.

Bickel, A. S. and Bickel, R. W. (1987). Tree structured rules in genetic algorithms. In Grefenstette, J. J., editor, *Genetic Algorithms and their Applications: Proceedings of the second International Conference on Genetic Algorithms*, pages 77–81, MIT, Cambridge, MA, USA. Lawrence Erlbaum Associates.

Blickle, T. (1996). Evolving compact solutions in genetic programming: A case study. In Voigt, H.-M., Ebeling, W., Rechenberg, I., and Schwefel, H.-P., editors, *Parallel Problem Solving From Nature IV. Proceedings of the International Conference on Evolutionary Computation*, volume 1141 of *LNCS*, pages 564–573, Berlin, Germany. Springer-Verlag.

Blickle, T. and Thiele, L. (1994). Genetic programming and redundancy. In Hopf, J., editor, *Genetic Algorithms within the Framework of Evolutionary Computation (Workshop at KI-94, Saarbrücken)*, pages 33–38, Im Stadtwald, Building 44, D-66123 Saarbrücken, Germany. Max-Planck-Institut für Informatik (MPI-I-94-241).

Blickle, T. and Thiele, L. (1995). A comparison of selection schemes used in genetic algorithms. TIK-Report 11, TIK Institut fur Technische Informatik und Kommunikationsnetze, Computer Engineering and Networks Laboratory, ETH, Swiss Federal Institute of Technology, Gloriastrasse 35, 8092 Zurich, Switzerland.

Bohm, W. and Geyer-Schulz, A. (1996). Exact uniform initialization for genetic programming. In Belew, R. K. and Vose, M., editors, *Foundations of Genetic Algorithms IV*, University of San Diego, CA, USA. Morgan Kaufmann.

Brave, S. (1995). Using genetic programming to evolve mental models. In Louis, S., editor, *Fourth Golden West Conference on Intelligent Systems*, pages 91–96. International Society for Computers and their Applications - ISCA.

Brave, S. (1996a). The evolution of memory and mental models using genetic programming. In Koza, J. R., Goldberg, D. E., Fogel, D. B., and Riolo, R. L., editors, *Genetic Programming 1996: Proceedings of the First Annual Conference*, pages 261–266, Stanford University, CA, USA. MIT Press.

Brave, S. (1996b). Evolving deterministic finite automata using cellular encoding. In Koza, J. R., Goldberg, D. E., Fogel, D. B., and Riolo, R. L., editors, *Genetic Programming 1996: Proceedings of the First Annual Conference*, pages 39–44, Stanford University, CA, USA. MIT Press.

Brave, S. (1996c). Evolving recursive programs for tree search. In Angeline, P. J. and Kinnear, Jr., K. E., editors, *Advances in Genetic Programming 2*, chapter 10, pages 203–220. MIT Press, Cambridge, MA, USA.

Brooks, R. A. (1991). Intelligence without reason. Technical report, MIT AI Lab. AI Memo no 1293, *Prepared for Computers and Thought*.

Bruce, W. S. (1995). *The Application of Genetic Programming to the Automatic Generation of Object-Oriented Programs*. PhD thesis, School of Computer and Information Sciences, Nova Southeastern University, 3100 SW 9th Avenue, Fort Lauderdale, Florida 33315, USA.

Bruce, W. S. (1996). Automatic generation of object-oriented programs using genetic programming. In Koza, J. R., Goldberg, D. E., Fogel, D. B., and Riolo, R. L., editors, *Genetic Programming 1996: Proceedings of the First Annual Conference*, pages 267–272, Stanford University, CA, USA. MIT Press.

Carroll, L. (1871). *Through the Looking-Glass, and What Alice Found There*. Macmillan.

Cartwright, H. M. and Harris, S. P. (1993). Analysis of the distribution of airborne pollution using genetic algorithms. *Atmospheric Environment*, 27A(12):1783–1791.

Chellapilla, K. (1997). Evolutionary programming with tree mutations: Evolving computer programs without crossover. In Koza, J. R., Deb, K., Dorigo, M., Fogel, D. B., Garzon, M., Iba, H., and Riolo, R. L., editors, *Genetic Programming 1997: Proceedings of the Second Annual Conference*, pages 431–438, Stanford University, CA, USA. Morgan Kaufmann.

Chen, S.-H. and Yeh, C.-H. (1996). Genetic programming learning and the cobweb model. In Angeline, P. J. and Kinnear, Jr., K. E., editors, *Advances in Genetic Programming 2*, chapter 22, pages 443–466. MIT Press, Cambridge, MA, USA.

Chen, S.-H. and Yeh, C.-H. (1997). Using genetic programming to model volatility in financial time series. In Koza, J. R., Deb, K., Dorigo, M., Fogel, D. B., Garzon, M., Iba, H., and Riolo, R. L., editors, *Genetic Programming 1997: Proceedings of the Second Annual Conference*, pages 58–63, Stanford University, CA, USA. Morgan Kaufmann.

Clack, C. and Yu, T. (1997). Performance enhanced genetic programming. In Angeline, P. J., Reynolds, R. G., McDonnell, J. R., and Eberhart, R., editors, *Proceedings of the Sixth Conference on Evolutionary Programming*, volume 1213 of *Lecture Notes in Computer Science*, Indianapolis, Indiana, USA. Springer-Verlag.

Collins, R. J. (1992). *Studies in Artificial Evolution*. PhD thesis, UCLA, Artificial Life Laboratory, Department of Computer Science, University of California, Los Angeles, LA CA 90024, USA.

Cramer, N. L. (1985). A representation for the adaptive generation of simple sequential programs. In Grefenstette, J. J., editor, *Proceedings of an International Conference on Genetic Algorithms and the Applications*, pages 183–187, Carnegie-Mellon University, Pittsburgh, PA, USA.

Crepeau, R. L. (1995). Genetic evolution of machine language software. In Rosca, J. P., editor, *Proceedings of the Workshop on Genetic Programming: From Theory to Real-World Applications*, pages 121–134, Tahoe City, California, USA.

Daida, J. M., Bersano-Begey, T. F., Ross, S. J., and Vesecky, J. F. (1996). Computer-assisted design of image classification algorithms: Dynamic and static fitness evaluations in a scaffolded genetic programming environment. In Koza, J. R., Goldberg, D. E., Fogel, D. B., and Riolo, R. L., editors, *Genetic Programming 1996: Proceedings of the First Annual Conference*, pages 279–284, Stanford University, CA, USA. MIT Press.

Das, S., Franguidakis, T., Papka, M., DeFanti, T. A., and Sandin, D. J. (1994). A genetic programming application in virtual reality. In *Proceedings of the first IEEE Conference on Evolutionary Computation*, volume 1, pages 480–484, Orlando, Florida, USA. IEEE Press. Part of 1994 IEEE World Congress on Computational Intelligence, Orlando, Florida.

Davis, J. (1994). Single populations v. co-evolution. In Koza, J. R., editor, *Artificial Life at Stanford 1994*, pages 20–27. Stanford Bookstore, Stanford, California, 94305-3079 USA.

Davis, L., editor (1991). *Handbook of Genetic Algorithms*. Van Nostrand Reinhold, New York.

Dawkins, R. (1986). *The blind Watchmaker*. Harlow : Longman Scientific and Technical.

De Jong, K. (1987). On using genetic algorithms to search program spaces. In Grefenstette, J. J., editor, *Genetic Algorithms and their Applications: Proceedings of the second international conference on Genetic Algorithms*, pages 210–216, MIT, Cambridge, MA, USA. Lawrence Erlbaum Associates.

De Jong, K. A. and Sarma, J. (1993). Generation gaps revisited. In Whitley, L. D., editor, *Foundations of Genetic Algorithms 2*, Vail, Colorado, USA. Morgan Kaufmann.

Deakin, A. G. and Yates, D. F. (1996). Genetic programming tools available on the web: A first encounter. In Koza, J. R., Goldberg, D. E., Fogel, D. B., and Riolo, R. L., editors, *Genetic Programming 1996: Proceedings of the First Annual Conference*, page 420, Stanford University, CA, USA. MIT Press.

D'haeseleer, P. (1994). Context preserving crossover in genetic programming. In *Proceedings of the 1994 IEEE World Congress on Computational Intelligence*, volume 1, pages 256–261, Orlando, Florida, USA. IEEE Press.

D'haeseleer, P. and Bluming, J. (1994). Effects of locality in individual and population evolution. In Kinnear, Jr., K. E., editor, *Advances in Genetic Programming*, chapter 8, pages 177–198. MIT Press.

Dunay, B. D. and Petry, F. E. (1995). Solving complex problems with genetic algorithms. In Eshelman, L., editor, *Genetic Algorithms: Proceedings of the Sixth International Conference (ICGA95)*, pages 264–270, Pittsburgh, PA, USA. Morgan Kaufmann.

Dunay, B. D., Petry, F. E., and Buckles, W. P. (1994). Regular language induction with genetic programming. In *Proceedings of the 1994 IEEE World Congress on Computational Intelligence*, pages 396–400, Orlando, Florida, USA. IEEE Press.

Dunnett, R. M. (1993). A proposal to use a genetic algorithm for maintenance planning. PSBM note, National Grid, Technology and Science Laboratories. Private communication.

Dunning, T. E. and Davis, M. W. (1996). Evolutionary algorithms for natural language processing. In Koza, J. R., editor, *Late Breaking Papers at the Genetic Programming 1996 Conference Stanford University July 28-31, 1996*, pages 16–23, Stanford University, CA, USA. Stanford Bookstore.

Eiben, G. (1997). GP in leiden. electronic communication.

Esparcia-Alcazar, A. I. and Sharman, K. (1997). Evolving recurrent neural network architectures by genetic programming. In Koza, J. R., Deb, K., Dorigo, M., Fogel, D. B., Garzon, M., Iba, H., and Riolo, R. L., editors, *Genetic Programming 1997: Proceedings of the Second Annual Conference*, pages 89–94, Stanford University, CA, USA. Morgan Kaufmann.

Ewens, W. J. (1989). An interpretation and proof of the fundamental theorem of natural selection. *Theoretical Population Biology*, 36(2):167–180.

Ewens, W. J. (1992a). Addendum to "The fundamental theorem of natural selection in Ewens' sense (case of many loci)" by Catilloux and Lessard. *Theoretical Population Biology*, 48(3):316–317.

Ewens, W. J. (1992b). An optimizing principle of natural selection in evolutionary population genetics. *Theoretical Population Biology*, 42(3):333–346.

Falco, I. D., Conte, M., Cioppa, A. D., Tarantino, E., and Tautteur, G. (1997). Genetic programming estimates of kolmogorov complexity. In Goodman, E., editor, *Genetic Algorithms: Proceedings of the Seventh International Conference*, Michigan State University, East Lansing, MI, USA. Morgan Kaufmann.

Fang, H.-L., Ross, P., and Corne, D. (1993). A promising genetic algorithm approach to job-shop scheduling, rescheduling and open-shop scheduling problems. In Forrest, S., editor, *Proceedings of the 5th International Conference on Genetic Algorithms, ICGA-93*, pages 375–382, University of Illinois at Urbana-Champaign. Morgan Kaufmann.

Fang, H.-L., Ross, P., and Corne, D. (1994). A promising hybrid GA/heuristic approach for open-shop scheduling problems. In Cohn, A., editor, *ECAI 94 Proceedings of the 11th European Conference on Artificial Intelligence*, pages 590–594, Amsterdam, The Netherlands. John Wiley & Sons, Ltd.

Feldman, D. S. (1993). Fuzzy network synthesis with genetic algorithms. In Forrest, S., editor, *Proceedings of the 5th International Conference on Genetic Algorithms, ICGA-93*, pages 312–317, University of Illinois at Urbana-Champaign. Morgan Kaufmann.

Ferrer, G. J. and Martin, W. N. (1995). Using genetic programming to evolve board evaluation functions for a boardgame. In *1995 IEEE Conference on Evolutionary Computation*, volume 2, page 747, Perth, Australia. IEEE Press.

Fisher, R. A. (1958). *The Genetical Theory of Natural Selection*. Dover. Revision of first edition published 1930, OUP.

Fonseca, C. M. and Fleming, P. J. (1993). Genetic algorithms for multiobjective optimization: Formulation, discussion and generalization. In Forrest, S., editor, *Proceedings of the 5th International Conference on Genetic Algorithms, ICGA-93*, pages 416–423, University of Illinois at Urbana-Champaign. Morgan Kaufmann.

Fonseca, C. M. and Fleming, P. J. (1995). An overview of evolutionary algorithms in multiobjective optimization. *Evolutionary Computation*, 3(1):1–16.

Forsyth, R. (1981). BEAGLE A darwinian approach to pattern recognition. *Kybernetes*, 10:159–166.

Francone, F. D., Nordin, P., and Banzhaf, W. (1996). Benchmarking the generalization capabilities of a compiling genetic programming system using sparse data sets. In Koza, J. R., Goldberg, D. E., Fogel, D. B., and Riolo, R. L., editors, *Genetic Programming 1996: Proceedings of the First Annual Conference*, pages 72–80, Stanford University, CA, USA. MIT Press.

Frank, S. A. (1995). George Price's contributions to evolutionary genetics. *Journal of Theoretical Biology*, 175:373–388.

Fujiki, C. and Dickinson, J. (1987). Using the genetic algorithm to generate lisp source code to solve the prisoner's dilemma. In Grefenstette, J. J., editor, *Genetic Algorithms and their Applications: Proceedings of the second international conference on Genetic Algorithms*, pages 236–240, MIT, Cambridge, MA, USA. Lawrence Erlbaum Associates.

Fukunaga, A. S. and Kahng, A. B. (1995). Improving the performance of evolutionary optimization by dynamically scaling the evolution function. In *1995 IEEE Conference on Evolutionary Computation*, volume 1, pages 182–187, Perth, Australia. IEEE Press.

Gathercole, C. and Ross, P. (1994). Dynamic training subset selection for supervised learning in genetic programming. In Davidor, Y., Schwefel, H.-P., and Männer, R., editors, *Parallel Problem Solving from Nature III*, pages 312–321, Jerusalem. Springer-Verlag.

Gathercole, C. and Ross, P. (1996). An adverse interaction between crossover and restricted tree depth in genetic programming. In Koza, J. R., Goldberg, D. E., Fogel, D. B., and Riolo, R. L., editors, *Genetic Programming 1996: Proceedings of the First Annual Conference*, pages 291–296, Stanford University, CA, USA. MIT Press.

Gathercole, C. and Ross, P. (1997a). Small populations over many generations can beat large populations over few generations in genetic programming. In Koza, J. R., Deb, K., Dorigo, M., Fogel, D. B., Garzon, M., Iba, H., and Riolo, R. L., editors, *Genetic Programming 1997: Proceedings of the Second Annual Conference*, pages 111–118, Stanford University, CA, USA. Morgan Kaufmann.

Gathercole, C. and Ross, P. (1997b). Tackling the boolean even N parity problem with genetic programming and limited-error fitness. In Koza, J. R., Deb, K., Dorigo, M., Fogel, D. B., Garzon, M., Iba, H., and Riolo, R. L., editors, *Genetic Programming*

1997: Proceedings of the Second Annual Conference, pages 119–127, Stanford University, CA, USA. Morgan Kaufmann.

Goldberg, D. E. (1989). *Genetic Algorithms in Search Optimization and Machine Learning*. Addison-Wesley.

Goldberg, D. E. and Deb, K. (1991). A comparative analysis of selection schemes used in genetic algorithms. In Rawlins, G. J. E., editor, *Proceedings of the First Workshop on Foundations of Genetic Algorithms*, pages 69–93, San Mateo. Morgan Kaufmann.

Goldberg, D. E., Deb, K., and Clark, J. H. (1991). Genetic algorithms, noise and the sizing of populations. IlliGAL 91010, Department of General Engineering, University of Illinois, 117 Transportation Building, 104 South Mathews Avenue, Urbana, Illinois 61801, USA.

Goldberg, D. E., Deb, K., and Horn, J. (1992). Massive multimodality, deception and genetic algorithms. In Manner, R. and Manderick, B., editors, *Parallel Problem Solving from Nature 2*, pages 37–46, Brussels, Belgium. Elsevier Science.

Gordon, T. G. W. (1995). Schedule optimisation using genetic algorithms. Master's thesis, University College, London.

Grefenstette, J. J. (1993). Deception considered harmful. In Whitley, L. D., editor, *Foundations of Genetic Algorithms 2*, Vail, Colorado, USA. Morgan Kaufmann.

Grimes, C. A. (1995). Application of genetic techniques to the planning of railway track maintenance work. In Zalzala, A. M. S., editor, *First International Conference on Genetic Algorithms in Engineering Systems: Innovations and Applications, GALESIA*, volume 414, pages 467–472, Sheffield, UK. IEE.

Gritz, L. and Hahn, J. K. (1997). Genetic programming evolution of controllers for 3-D character animation. In Koza, J. R., Deb, K., Dorigo, M., Fogel, D. B., Garzon, M., Iba, H., and Riolo, R. L., editors, *Genetic Programming 1997: Proceedings of the Second Annual Conference*, pages 139–146, Stanford University, CA, USA. Morgan Kaufmann.

Gruau, F. (1993). Genetic synthesis of modular neural networks. In Forrest, S., editor, *Proceedings of the 5th International Conference on Genetic Algorithms, ICGA-93*, pages 318–325, University of Illinois at Urbana-Champaign. Morgan Kaufmann.

Gruau, F. (1996a). Modular genetic neural networks for six-legged locomotion. In Alliot, J.-M., Lutton, E., Ronald, E., Schoenauer, M., and Snyers, D., editors, *Artificial Evolution*, volume 1063 of *LNCS*, pages 201–219. Springer Verlag.

Gruau, F. (1996b). On using syntactic constraints with genetic programming. In Angeline, P. J. and Kinnear, Jr., K. E., editors, *Advances in Genetic Programming 2*, chapter 19, pages 377–394. MIT Press, Cambridge, MA, USA.

Gruau, F. and Quatramaran, K. (1996). Cellular encoding for interactive evolutionary robotics. Cognitive Science Research Paper 425, School of Cognitive and Computing Sciences, University of Sussex, Falmer, Brighton, Sussex, UK.

Hampo, R. J., Bryant, B. D., and Marko, K. A. (1994). IC engine misfire detection algorithm generation using genetic programming. In *EUFIT'94*, pages 1674–1678, Promenade 9, D-52076, Aachen, Germany. ELITE-Foundation.

Handley, S. (1993). Automatic learning of a detector for alpha-helices in protein sequences via genetic programming. In Forrest, S., editor, *Proceedings of the 5th*

International Conference on Genetic Algorithms, ICGA-93, pages 271–278, University of Illinois at Urbana-Champaign. Morgan Kaufmann.

Handley, S. (1994a). On the use of a directed acyclic graph to represent a population of computer programs. In *Proceedings of the 1994 IEEE World Congress on Computational Intelligence*, pages 154–159, Orlando, Florida, USA. IEEE Press.

Handley, S. G. (1994b). The automatic generations of plans for a mobile robot via genetic programming with automatically defined functions. In Kinnear, Jr., K. E., editor, *Advances in Genetic Programming*, chapter 18, pages 391–407. MIT Press.

Harries, K. and Smith, P. (1997). Exploring alternative operators and search strategies in genetic programming. In Koza, J. R., Deb, K., Dorigo, M., Fogel, D. B., Garzon, M., Iba, H., and Riolo, R. L., editors, *Genetic Programming 1997: Proceedings of the Second Annual Conference*, pages 147–155, Stanford University, CA, USA. Morgan Kaufmann.

Harvey, I. (1992). Species adaptation genetic algorithms: A basis for a continuing SAGA. In Varela, F. J. and Bourgine, P., editors, *Toward a Practice of Autonomous Systems, Proceeding of the first European Conference on Artificial Life (ECAL)*, pages 346–354. MIT Press.

Harvey, I., Husbands, P., and Cliff, D. (1993). Genetic convergence in a species of evolved robot control architectures. In Forrest, S., editor, *Proceedings of the 5th International Conference on Genetic Algorithms, ICGA-93*, page 636, University of Illinois at Urbana-Champaign. Morgan Kaufmann.

Haynes, T. (1996). Duplication of coding segments in genetic programming. In *Proceedings of the Thirteenth National Conference on Artificial Intelligence*, pages 344–349, Portland, OR.

Haynes, T., Sen, S., Schoenefeld, D., and Wainwright, R. (1995a). Evolving a team. In Siegel, E. V. and Koza, J. R., editors, *Working Notes for the AAAI Symposium on Genetic Programming*, pages 23–30, MIT, Cambridge, MA, USA. AAAI.

Haynes, T., Wainwright, R., Sen, S., and Schoenefeld, D. (1995b). Strongly typed genetic programming in evolving cooperation strategies. In Eshelman, L., editor, *Genetic Algorithms: Proceedings of the Sixth International Conference (ICGA95)*, pages 271–278, Pittsburgh, PA, USA. Morgan Kaufmann.

Haynes, T. D., Schoenefeld, D. A., and Wainwright, R. L. (1996). Type inheritance in strongly typed genetic programming. In Angeline, P. J. and Kinnear, Jr., K. E., editors, *Advances in Genetic Programming 2*, chapter 18, pages 359–376. MIT Press, Cambridge, MA, USA.

Haynes, T. D. and Wainwright, R. L. (1995). A simulation of adaptive agents in hostile environment. In George, K. M., Carroll, J. H., Deaton, E., Oppenheim, D., and Hightower, J., editors, *Proceedings of the 1995 ACM Symposium on Applied Computing*, pages 318–323, Nashville, USA. ACM Press.

Hillis, W. D. (1992). Co-evolving parasites improve simulated evolution as an optimization procedure. In Langton, C. G., Taylor, C., Farmer, J. D., and Rasmussen, S., editors, *Artificial Life II*, volume X of *Sante Fe Institute Studies in the Sciences of Complexity*, pages 313–324. Addison-Wesley, Santa Fe Institute, New Mexico, USA.

Holland, J. H. (1973). Genetic algorithms and the optimal allocation of trials. *SIAM Journal on Computation*, 2:88–105.

Holland, J. H. (1992). *Adaptation in Natural and Artificial Systems: An Introductory Analysis with Applications to Biology, Control and Artificial Intelligence.* MIT Press. First Published by University of Michigan Press 1975.

Holland, J. H., Holyoak, K. J., Nisbett, R. E., and Thagard, P. R. (1986). *Induction Processes of Inference, Learning, and Discovery.* MIT Press.

Hondo, N., Iba, H., and Kakazu, Y. (1996a). COAST: An approach to robustness and reusability in genetic programming. In Koza, J. R., Goldberg, D. E., Fogel, D. B., and Riolo, R. L., editors, *Genetic Programming 1996: Proceedings of the First Annual Conference*, page 429, Stanford University, CA, USA. MIT Press.

Hondo, N., Iba, H., and Kakazu, Y. (1996b). Sharing and refinement for reusable subroutines of genetic programming. In *Proceedings of the 1996 IEEE International Conference on Evolutionary Computation*, volume 1, pages 565–570, Nagoya, Japan.

Horn, J., Nafpliotis, N., and Goldberg, D. E. (1993). Multiobjective optimization using the niched pareto genetic algorithm. IlliGAL Report no. 93005, Illinois Genetic Algorithm Laboratory, University of Illinois at Urbana-Champaign, 117 Transportation Building, 104 South Mathews Avenue, Urbana, IL 61801-2296.

Huelsbergen, L. (1996). Toward simulated evolution of machine language iteration. In Koza, J. R., Goldberg, D. E., Fogel, D. B., and Riolo, R. L., editors, *Genetic Programming 1996: Proceedings of the First Annual Conference*, pages 315–320, Stanford University, CA, USA. MIT Press.

Iba, H. (1996a). Emergent cooperation for multiple agents using genetic programming. In Koza, J. R., editor, *Late Breaking Papers at the Genetic Programming 1996 Conference Stanford University July 28-31, 1996*, pages 66–74, Stanford University, CA, USA. Stanford Bookstore.

Iba, H. (1996b). Random tree generation of genetic programming. In Voigt, H.-M., Ebeling, W., Rechenberg, I., and Schwefel, H.-P., editors, *Parallel Problem Solving from Nature IV, Proceedings of the International Conference on Evolutionary Computation*, volume 1141 of *LNCS*, pages 144–153, Berlin, Germany. Springer Verlag.

Iba, H. and de Garis, H. (1996). Extending genetic programming with recombinative guidance. In Angeline, P. J. and Kinnear, Jr., K. E., editors, *Advances in Genetic Programming 2*, chapter 4, pages 69–88. MIT Press, Cambridge, MA, USA.

Iba, H., de Garis, H., and Sato, T. (1994a). Genetic programming using a minimum description length principle. In Kinnear, Jr., K. E., editor, *Advances in Genetic Programming*, chapter 12, pages 265–284. MIT Press.

Iba, H., de Garis, H., and Sato, T. (1994b). Genetic programming with local hill-climbing. In Davidor, Y., Schwefel, H.-P., and Männer, R., editors, *Parallel Problem Solving from Nature III*, pages 334–343, Jerusalem. Springer-Verlag.

Iba, H., de Garis, H., and Sato, T. (1995). Temporal data processing using genetic programming. In Eshelman, L., editor, *Genetic Algorithms: Proceedings of the Sixth International Conference (ICGA95)*, pages 279–286, Pittsburgh, PA, USA. Morgan Kaufmann.

Iba, H., Karita, T., de Garis, H., and Sato, T. (1993). System identification using structured genetic algorithms. In Forrest, S., editor, *Proceedings of the 5th International*

Conference on Genetic Algorithms, ICGA-93, pages 279–286, University of Illinois at Urbana-Champaign. Morgan Kaufmann.

Iba, H., Sato, T., and de Garis, H. (1994c). System identification approach to genetic programming. In *Proceedings of the 1994 IEEE World Congress on Computational Intelligence*, volume 1, pages 401–406, Orlando, Florida, USA. IEEE Press.

Ikram, I. M. (1996). An occam library for genetic programming on transputer networks. In Arabnia, H. R., editor, *Proceedings of the International Conference on Parallel and Distributed Processing Techniques and Applications*, pages 1186–1189, Sunnyvale, California. CSREA.

Jacob, C. (1997). *Principia Evolvica – Simulierte Evolution mit Mathematica*. dpunkt.verlag, Heidelberg, Germany.

Jannink, J. (1994). Cracking and co-evolving randomizers. In Kinnear, Jr., K. E., editor, *Advances in Genetic Programming*, chapter 20, pages 425–443. MIT Press.

Johnson, M. P., Maes, P., and Darrell, T. (1994). Evolving visual routines. In Brooks, R. A. and Maes, P., editors, *ARTIFICIAL LIFE IV, Proceedings of the fourth International Workshop on the Synthesis and Simulation of Living Systems*, pages 198–209, MIT, Cambridge, MA, USA. MIT Press.

Juille, H. and Pollack, J. B. (1995). Parallel genetic programming and fine-grained SIMD architecture. In Siegel, E. V. and Koza, J. R., editors, *Working Notes for the AAAI Symposium on Genetic Programming*, pages 31–37, MIT, Cambridge, MA, USA. AAAI.

Juille, H. and Pollack, J. B. (1996). Massively parallel genetic programming. In Angeline, P. J. and Kinnear, Jr., K. E., editors, *Advances in Genetic Programming 2*, chapter 17, pages 339–358. MIT Press, Cambridge, MA, USA.

Keijzer, M. (1996). Efficiently representing populations in genetic programming. In Angeline, P. J. and Kinnear, Jr., K. E., editors, *Advances in Genetic Programming 2*, chapter 13, pages 259–278. MIT Press, Cambridge, MA, USA.

Keith, M. J. and Martin, M. C. (1994). Genetic programming in C++: Implementation issues. In Kinnear, Jr., K. E., editor, *Advances in Genetic Programming*, chapter 13, pages 285–310. MIT Press.

Kernighan, B. W. and Ritchie, D. M. (1988). *The C Programming Language*. Prentice-Hall, Englewood Cliffs, NJ 07632, USA, second edition.

Kinnear, Jr., K. E. (1993a). Evolving a sort: Lessons in genetic programming. In *Proceedings of the 1993 International Conference on Neural Networks*, volume 2, San Francisco, USA. IEEE Press.

Kinnear, Jr., K. E. (1993b). Generality and difficulty in genetic programming: Evolving a sort. In Forrest, S., editor, *Proceedings of the 5th International Conference on Genetic Algorithms, ICGA-93*, pages 287–294, University of Illinois at Urbana-Champaign. Morgan Kaufmann.

Kinnear, Jr., K. E. (1994a). Alternatives in automatic function definition: A comparison of performance. In Kinnear, Jr., K. E., editor, *Advances in Genetic Programming*, chapter 6, pages 119–141. MIT Press.

Kinnear, Jr., K. E. (1994b). Fitness landscapes and difficulty in genetic programming. In *Proceedings of the 1994 IEEE World Conference on Computational Intelligence*, volume 1, pages 142–147, Orlando, Florida, USA. IEEE Press.

Kinnear, Jr., K. E. (1994c). A perspective on the work in this book. In Kinnear, Jr., K. E., editor, *Advances in Genetic Programming*, chapter 1, pages 3–19. MIT Press.

Kirkpatrick, S., Gelatt Jr., C. D., and Vecchi, M. P. (1983). Optimization by simulated annealing. *Science*, 220(4598):671–680.

Kodjabachian, J. and Meyer, J.-A. (1994). Development, learning and evolution in animats. In Gaussier, P. and Nicoud, J.-D., editors, *Perceptions to Action*, pages 96–109, Lausanne Switzerland. IEEE Computer Society Press.

Koza, J. R. (1991). Genetic evolution and co-evolution of computer programs. In Langton, C. T. C., Farmer, J. D., and Rasmussen, S., editors, *Artificial Life II*, volume X of *SFI Studies in the Sciences of Complexity*, pages 603–629. Addison-Wesley, Santa Fe Institute, New Mexico, USA.

Koza, J. R. (1992). *Genetic Programming: On the Programming of Computers by Natural Selection*. MIT Press, Cambridge, MA, USA.

Koza, J. R. (1994). *Genetic Programming II: Automatic Discovery of Reusable Programs*. MIT Press, Cambridge Massachusetts.

Koza, J. R. and Andre, D. (1995a). Evolution of both the architecture and the sequence of work-performing steps of a computer program using genetic programming with architecture-altering operations. In Siegel, E. V. and Koza, J. R., editors, *Working Notes for the AAAI Symposium on Genetic Programming*, pages 50–60, MIT, Cambridge, MA, USA. AAAI.

Koza, J. R. and Andre, D. (1995b). Parallel genetic programming on a network of transputers. Technical Report CS-TR-95-1542, Stanford University, Department of Computer Science.

Koza, J. R., Bennett III, F. H., Andre, D., and Keane, M. A. (1996a). Automated WYWIWYG design of both the topology and component values of electrical circuits using genetic programming. In Koza, J. R., Goldberg, D. E., Fogel, D. B., and Riolo, R. L., editors, *Genetic Programming 1996: Proceedings of the First Annual Conference*, pages 123–131, Stanford University, CA, USA. MIT Press.

Koza, J. R., Bennett III, F. H., Andre, D., and Keane, M. A. (1996b). Four problems for which a computer program evolved by genetic programming is competitive with human performance. In *Proceedings of the 1996 IEEE International Conference on Evolutionary Computation*, volume 1, pages 1–10. IEEE Press.

Koza, J. R., Bennett III, F. H., Andre, D., Keane, M. A., and Dunlap, F. (1997). Automated synthesis of analog electrical circuits by means of genetic programming. *IEEE Transactions on Evolutionary Computation*, 1(2):109–128.

Kraft, D. H., Petry, F. E., Buckles, W. P., and Sadasivan, T. (1994). The use of genetic programming to build queries for information retrieval. In *Proceedings of the 1994 IEEE World Congress on Computational Intelligence*, pages 468–473, Orlando, Florida, USA. IEEE Press.

Langdon, W. B. (1995a). Directed crossover within genetic programming. Research Note RN/95/71, University College London, Gower Street, London WC1E 6BT, UK.

Langdon, W. B. (1995b). Evolving data structures using genetic programming. In Eshelman, L., editor, *Genetic Algorithms: Proceedings of the Sixth International Conference (ICGA95)*, pages 295–302, Pittsburgh, PA, USA. Morgan Kaufmann.

Langdon, W. B. (1995c). Scheduling planned maintenance of the national grid. In Fogarty, T. C., editor, *Evolutionary Computing*, number 993 in Lecture Notes in Computer Science, pages 132–153. Springer-Verlag.

Langdon, W. B. (1996a). A bibliography for genetic programming. In Angeline, P. J. and Kinnear, Jr., K. E., editors, *Advances in Genetic Programming 2*, chapter B, pages 507–532. MIT Press, Cambridge, MA, USA.

Langdon, W. B. (1996b). Data structures and genetic programming. In Angeline, P. J. and Kinnear, Jr., K. E., editors, *Advances in Genetic Programming 2*, chapter 20, pages 395–414. MIT Press, Cambridge, MA, USA.

Langdon, W. B. (1996c). Using data structures within genetic programming. In Koza, J. R., Goldberg, D. E., Fogel, D. B., and Riolo, R. L., editors, *Genetic Programming 1996: Proceedings of the First Annual Conference*, pages 141–148, Stanford University, CA, USA. MIT Press.

Langdon, W. B. (1998). Program growth in simulated annealing, hill climbing and populations. In *1998 IEEE International Conference on Evolutionary Computation*, Anchorage, Alaska, USA. Forthcoming.

Langdon, W. B. and Poli, R. (1997a). An analysis of the MAX problem in genetic programming. In Koza, J. R., Deb, K., Dorigo, M., Fogel, D. B., Garzon, M., Iba, H., and Riolo, R. L., editors, *Genetic Programming 1997: Proceedings of the Second Annual Conference*, pages 222–230, Stanford University, CA, USA. Morgan Kaufmann.

Langdon, W. B. and Poli, R. (1997b). Fitness causes bloat. In Chawdhry, P. K., Roy, R., and Pan, R. K., editors, *Second On-line World Conference on Soft Computing in Engineering Design and Manufacturing*. Springer-Verlag London.

Langdon, W. B. and Treleaven, P. C. (1997). Scheduling maintenance of electrical power transmission networks using genetic programming. In Warwick, K., Ekwue, A., and Aggarwal, R., editors, *Artificial Intelligence Techniques in Power Systems*, chapter 10, pages 220–237. IEE.

Lankhorst, M. M. (1995). A genetic algorithm for the induction of pushdown automata. In *1995 IEEE Conference on Evolutionary Computation*, volume 2, pages 741–746, Perth, Australia. IEEE Press.

Lee, W.-P., Hallam, J., and Lund, H. H. (1997). Applying genetic programming to evolve behavior primitives and arbitrators for mobile robots. In *Proceedings of IEEE 4th International Conference on Evolutionary Computation*, volume 1. IEEE Press. to appear.

Levine, D. (1994). *A Parallel Genetic Algorithm for the Set Partitioning Problem*. PhD thesis, Illinois Institute of Technology, Mathematics and Computer Science Division, Argonne National Laboratory, 9700 South Cass Avenue, Argonne, IL 60439, USA.

Longshaw, T. (1997). Evolutionary learning of large grammars. In Koza, J. R., Deb, K., Dorigo, M., Fogel, D. B., Garzon, M., Iba, H., and Riolo, R. L., editors, *Genetic Programming 1997: Proceedings of the Second Annual Conference*, page 445, Stanford University, CA, USA. Morgan Kaufmann.

Louis, S. J. and Rawlins, G. J. E. (1993). Pareto optimality, GA-easiness and deception. In Forrest, S., editor, *Proceedings of the 5th International Conference on Genetic*

Algorithms, ICGA-93, pages 118–123, University of Illinois at Urbana-Champaign. Morgan Kaufmann.

Lucas, S. (1994). Structuring chromosomes for context-free grammar evolution. In *ICEC'94: Proceedings of The IEEE Conference on Evolutionary Computation, IEEE World Congress on Computational Intelligence*, volume 1, pages 130–135, Walt Disney World Dolphin Hotel, Orlando, Florida, USA. IEEE.

Luke, S., Hohn, C., Farris, J., Jackson, G., and Hendler, J. (1997). Co-evolving soccer softbot team coordination with genetic programming. In *Proceedings of the First International Workshop on RoboCup, at the International Joint Conference on Artificial Intelligence*, Nagoya, Japan.

Luke, S. and Spector, L. (1996). Evolving teamwork and coordination with genetic programming. In Koza, J. R., Goldberg, D. E., Fogel, D. B., and Riolo, R. L., editors, *Genetic Programming 1996: Proceedings of the First Annual Conference*, pages 150–156, Stanford University, CA, USA. MIT Press.

Luke, S. and Spector, L. (1997). A comparison of crossover and mutation in genetic programming. In Koza, J. R., Deb, K., Dorigo, M., Fogel, D. B., Garzon, M., Iba, H., and Riolo, R. L., editors, *Genetic Programming 1997: Proceedings of the Second Annual Conference*, pages 240–248, Stanford University, CA, USA. Morgan Kaufmann.

Maher, M. L. and Kundu, S. (1993). Adaptive design using a genetic algorithm. In Gero, J. S. and Sudweeks, F., editors, *Formal design methods for computer-aided design*, pages 211–228, University of Sydney, NSW, Australia. Key Center of Design Computing, University of Sydney.

Manela, M. (1993). *Contributions to the Theory and Applications of Genetic Algorithms*. PhD thesis, University College, London.

Masand, B. (1994). Optimising confidence of text classification by evolution of symbolic expressions. In Kinnear, Jr., K. E., editor, *Advances in Genetic Programming*, chapter 21, pages 445–458. MIT Press.

Maxwell, S. R. (1996). Why might some problems be difficult for genetic programming to find solutions? In Koza, J. R., editor, *Late Breaking Papers at the Genetic Programming 1996 Conference Stanford University July 28-31, 1996*, pages 125–128, Stanford University, CA, USA. Stanford Bookstore.

Maxwell III, S. R. (1994). Experiments with a coroutine model for genetic programming. In *Proceedings of the 1994 IEEE World Congress on Computational Intelligence, Orlando, Florida, USA*, volume 1, pages 413–417a, Orlando, Florida, USA. IEEE Press.

McKay, B., Willis, M. J., and Barton, G. W. (1995). Using a tree structured genetic algorithm to perform symbolic regression. In Zalzala, A. M. S., editor, *First International Conference on Genetic Algorithms in Engineering Systems: Innovations and Applications, GALESIA*, volume 414, pages 487–492, Sheffield, UK. IEE.

Michalewicz, Z. (1994). *Genetic Algorithms + Data Structures = Evolution Programs*. Springer-Verlag, Berlin, 2 edition.

Montana, D. J. (1993). Strongly typed genetic programming. BBN Technical Report #7866, Bolt Beranek and Newman, Inc., 10 Moulton Street, Cambridge, MA 02138, USA.

Montana, D. J. (1994). Strongly typed genetic programming. BBN Technical Report #7866, Bolt Beranek and Newman, Inc., 10 Moulton Street, Cambridge, MA 02138, USA.

Montana, D. J. (1995). Strongly typed genetic programming. *Evolutionary Computation*, 3(2):199–230.

Nachbar, R. B. (1995). Genetic programming. *The Mathematica Journal*, 5(3):44–55.

Nguyen, T. and Huang, T. (1994). Evolvable 3D modeling for model-based object recognition systems. In Kinnear, Jr., K. E., editor, *Advances in Genetic Programming*, chapter 22, pages 459–475. MIT Press.

Nordin, P. (1994a). A compiling genetic programming system that directly manipulates the machine code. In Kinnear, Jr., K. E., editor, *Advances in Genetic Programming*, chapter 14, pages 311–331. MIT Press.

Nordin, P. (1994b). Two stage genetic programming using prolog. Electronic Correspondence.

Nordin, P. and Banzhaf, W. (1995). Evolving turing-complete programs for a register machine with self-modifying code. In Eshelman, L., editor, *Genetic Algorithms: Proceedings of the Sixth International Conference (ICGA95)*, pages 318–325, Pittsburgh, PA, USA. Morgan Kaufmann.

Nordin, P. and Banzhaf, W. (1996). Programmatic compression of images and sound. In Koza, J. R., Goldberg, D. E., Fogel, D. B., and Riolo, R. L., editors, *Genetic Programming 1996: Proceedings of the First Annual Conference*, pages 345–350, Stanford University, CA, USA. MIT Press.

Nordin, P., Francone, F., and Banzhaf, W. (1995). Explicitly defined introns and destructive crossover in genetic programming. In Rosca, J. P., editor, *Proceedings of the Workshop on Genetic Programming: From Theory to Real-World Applications*, pages 6–22, Tahoe City, California, USA.

Nordin, P., Francone, F., and Banzhaf, W. (1996). Explicitly defined introns and destructive crossover in genetic programming. In Angeline, P. J. and Kinnear, Jr., K. E., editors, *Advances in Genetic Programming 2*, chapter 6, pages 111–134. MIT Press, Cambridge, MA, USA.

Oakley, H. (1994). Two scientific applications of genetic programming: Stack filters and non-linear equation fitting to chaotic data. In Kinnear, Jr., K. E., editor, *Advances in Genetic Programming*, chapter 17, pages 369–389. MIT Press.

Oei, C. K., Goldberg, D. E., and Chang, S.-J. (1991). Tournament selection, niching, and the preservation of diversity. IlliGAL Report No. 91011, University of Illinois at Urbana-Champaign, Urbana, Il 61801, USA.

Openshaw, S. and Turton, I. (1994). Building new spatial interaction models using genetic programming. In Fogarty, T. C., editor, *Evolutionary Computing*, Lecture Notes in Computer Science, Leeds, UK. Springer-Verlag.

O'Reilly, U.-M. (1995). *An Analysis of Genetic Programming*. PhD thesis, Carleton University, Ottawa-Carleton Institute for Computer Science, Ottawa, Ontario, Canada.

O'Reilly, U.-M. (1996). Investigating the generality of automatically defined functions. In Koza, J. R., Goldberg, D. E., Fogel, D. B., and Riolo, R. L., editors, *Genetic Programming 1996: Proceedings of the First Annual Conference*, pages 351–356, Stanford University, CA, USA. MIT Press.

O'Reilly, U.-M. and Oppacher, F. (1994). Program search with a hierarchical variable length representation: Genetic programming, simulated annealing and hill climbing. In Davidor, Y., Schwefel, H.-P., and Manner, R., editors, *Parallel Problem Solving from Nature – PPSN III*, number 866 in Lecture Notes in Computer Science, pages 397–406, Jerusalem. Springer-Verlag.

O'Reilly, U.-M. and Oppacher, F. (1995). The troubling aspects of a building block hypothesis for genetic programming. In Whitley, L. D. and Vose, M. D., editors, *Foundations of Genetic Algorithms 3*, pages 73–88, Estes Park, Colorado, USA. Morgan Kaufmann.

O'Reilly, U.-M. and Oppacher, F. (1996). A comparative analysis of GP. In Angeline, P. J. and Kinnear, Jr., K. E., editors, *Advances in Genetic Programming 2*, chapter 2, pages 23–44. MIT Press, Cambridge, MA, USA.

Oussaidene, M., Chopard, B., Pictet, O. V., and Tomassini, M. (1996). Parallel genetic programming: An application to trading models evolution. In Koza, J. R., Goldberg, D. E., Fogel, D. B., and Riolo, R. L., editors, *Genetic Programming 1996: Proceedings of the First Annual Conference*, pages 357–380, Stanford University, CA, USA. MIT Press.

Park, S. K. and Miller, K. W. (1988). Random number generators: Good ones are hard to find. *Communications of the ACM*, 32(10):1192–1201.

Perkis, T. (1994). Stack-based genetic programming. In *Proceedings of the 1994 IEEE World Congress on Computational Intelligence*, volume 1, pages 148–153, Orlando, Florida, USA. IEEE Press.

Perry, J. E. (1994). The effect of population enrichment in genetic programming. In *Proceedings of the 1994 IEEE World Congress on Computational Intelligence*, pages 456–461, Orlando, Florida, USA. IEEE Press.

Petry, F. E. and Dunay, B. D. (1995). Automatic programming and program maintenance with genetic programming. *International Journal of Software Engineering and Knowledge Engineering*, 5(2):165–177.

Polani, D. and Uthmann, T. (1993). Training kohonen feature maps in different topologies: an analysis using genetic algorithms. In Forrest, S., editor, *Proceedings of the 5th International Conference on Genetic Algorithms, ICGA-93*, pages 326–333, University of Illinois at Urbana-Champaign. Morgan Kaufmann.

Poli, R. (1996a). Evolution of recursive transistion networks for natural language recognition with parallel distributed genetic programming. Technical Report CSRP-96-19, School of Computer Science, University of Birmingham, B15 2TT, UK. Presented at AISB-97 workshop on Evolutionary Computation.

Poli, R. (1996b). Genetic programming for feature detection and image segmentation. In Fogarty, T. C., editor, *Evolutionary Computing*, number 1143 in Lecture Notes in Computer Science, pages 110–125. Springer-Verlag, University of Sussex, UK.

Poli, R. (1996c). Parallel distributed genetic programming. Technical Report CSRP-96-15, School of Computer Science, University of Birmingham, B15 2TT, UK. Submitted to Evolutionary Computation.

Poli, R. (1996d). Some steps towards a form of parallel distributed genetic programming. In *The 1st Online Workshop on Soft Computing (WSC1)*, http://www.bioele.nuee.nagoya-u.ac.jp/wsc1/. Nagoya University, Japan.

Poli, R. (1997a). Discovery of symbolic, neuro-symbolic and neural networks with parallel distributed genetic programming. In *3rd International Conference on Artificial Neural Networks and Genetic Algorithms, ICANNGA'97*, University of East Anglia, Norwich, UK.

Poli, R. (1997b). Evolution of graph-like programs with parallel distributed genetic programming. In Goodman, E., editor, *Genetic Algorithms: Proceedings of the Seventh International Conference*, Michigan State University, East Lansing, MI, USA. Morgan Kaufmann.

Poli, R. and Cagnoni, S. (1997). Genetic programming with user-driven selection: Experiments on the evolution of algorithms for image enhancement. In Koza, J. R., Deb, K., Dorigo, M., Fogel, D. B., Garzon, M., Iba, H., and Riolo, R. L., editors, *Genetic Programming 1997: Proceedings of the Second Annual Conference*, pages 269–277, Stanford University, CA, USA. Morgan Kaufmann.

Poli, R. and Langdon, W. B. (1997a). An experimental analysis of schema creation, propagation and disruption in genetic programming. In Goodman, E., editor, *Genetic Algorithms: Proceedings of the Seventh International Conference*, Michigan State University, East Lansing, MI, USA. Morgan Kaufmann.

Poli, R. and Langdon, W. B. (1997b). Genetic programming with one-point crossover. In Chawdhry, P. K., Roy, R., and Pant, R. K., editors, *Second On-line World Conference on Soft Computing in Engineering Design and Manufacturing*. Springer-Verlag London.

Poli, R. and Langdon, W. B. (1997c). A new schema theory for genetic programming with one-point crossover and point mutation. In Koza, J. R., Deb, K., Dorigo, M., Fogel, D. B., Garzon, M., Iba, H., and Riolo, R. L., editors, *Genetic Programming 1997: Proceedings of the Second Annual Conference*, pages 278–285, Stanford University, CA, USA. Morgan Kaufmann.

Price, G. R. (1970). Selection and covariance. *Nature*, 227, August 1:520–521.

Price, G. R. (1972). Fisher's 'fundamental theorem' made clear. *Annals of Human Genetics*, 36:129–140.

Qureshi, A. (1996). Evolving agents. In Koza, J. R., Goldberg, D. E., Fogel, D. B., and Riolo, R. L., editors, *Genetic Programming 1996: Proceedings of the First Annual Conference*, pages 369–374, Stanford University, CA, USA. MIT Press.

Raik, S. and Durnota, B. (1994). The evolution of sporting strategies. In Stonier, R. J. and Yu, X. H., editors, *Complex Systems: Mechanisms of Adaption*, pages 85–92. IOS Press.

Raik, S. E. and Browne, D. G. (1996). Implicit versus explicit: A comparison of state in genetic programming. In Koza, J. R., editor, *Late Breaking Papers at the Genetic Programming 1996 Conference Stanford University July 28-31, 1996*, pages 151–159, Stanford University, CA, USA. Stanford Bookstore.

Ray, T. S. (1991). Is it alive or is it GA. In Belew, R. K. and Booker, L. B., editors, *Proceedings of the Fourth International Conference on Genetic Algorithms*, pages 527–534, University of California - San Diego, La Jolla, CA, USA. Morgan Kaufmann.

Reynolds, C. (1996). Boids. WWW home page. http://reality.sgi.com/craig/boids.html.

Reynolds, C. W. (1992). An evolved, vision-based behavioral model of coordinated group motion. In Meyer and Wilson, editors, *From Animals to Animats (Proceedings of Simulation of Adaptive Behaviour)*. MIT Press.

Reynolds, C. W. (1994a). Competition, coevolution and the game of tag. In Brooks, R. A. and Maes, P., editors, *Proceedings of the Fourth International Workshop on the Synthesis and Simulation of Living Systems*, pages 59–69, MIT, Cambridge, MA, USA. MIT Press.

Reynolds, C. W. (1994b). Evolution of obstacle avoidance behaviour:using noise to promote robust solutions. In Kinnear, Jr., K. E., editor, *Advances in Genetic Programming*, chapter 10, pages 221–241. MIT Press.

Reynolds, C. W. (1994c). An evolved, vision-based behavioral model of obstacle avoidance behaviour. In Langton, C. G., editor, *Artificial Life III*, volume XVII of *SFI Studies in the Sciences of Complexity*, pages 327–346. Addison-Wesley, Santa Fe Institute, New Mexico, USA.

Ribeiro Filho, J. L. and Treleaven, P. (1994). GAME: A framework for programming genetic algorithms applications. In *Proceedings of the First IEEE Conference on Evolutionary Computing – Proceedings of the 1994 IEEE World Congress on Computational Intelligence*, volume 2, pages 840–845, Orlando, USA. IEEE Press.

Ribeiro Filho, J. L., Treleaven, P. C., and Alippi, C. (1994). Genetic-algorithm programming environments. *Computer*, 27(6):28.

Romaniak, S. G. (1993). Evolutionary growth perceptrons. In Forrest, S., editor, *Proceedings of the 5th International Conference on Genetic Algorithms, ICGA-93*, pages 334–341, University of Illinois at Urbana-Champaign. Morgan Kaufmann.

Rosca, J. (1996). GP population variety. GP electronic mailing list.

Rosca, J. P. (1995). Genetic programming exploratory power and the discovery of functions. In McDonnell, J. R., Reynolds, R. G., and Fogel, D. B., editors, *Evolutionary Programming IV Proceedings of the Fourth Annual Conference on Evolutionary Programming*, pages 719–736, San Diego, CA, USA. MIT Press.

Rosca, J. P. and Ballard, D. H. (1996). Discovery of subroutines in genetic programming. In Angeline, P. J. and Kinnear, Jr., K. E., editors, *Advances in Genetic Programming 2*, chapter 9, pages 177–202. MIT Press, Cambridge, MA, USA.

Ross, P. (1994). *About PGA 2.8*. Available via ftp `ftp.dai.ed.ac.uk` directory `pub/pga-2.8`.

Ryan, C. (1994). Pygmies and civil servants. In Kinnear, Jr., K. E., editor, *Advances in Genetic Programming*, chapter 11, pages 243–263. MIT Press.

Ryan, C. (1995). GPRobots and GPTeams - competition, co-evolution and co-operation in genetic programming. In Siegel, E. V. and Koza, J. R., editors, *Working Notes for the AAAI Symposium on Genetic Programming*, pages 86–93, MIT, Cambridge, MA, USA. AAAI.

Salustowicz, R. P. and Schmidhuber, J. (1997). Probabilistic incremental program evolution. *Evolutionary Computation*, 5(2):123–141.

Schoenauer, M., Lamy, B., and Jouve, F. (1995). Identification of mechanical behaviour by genetic programming part II: Energy formulation. Technical report, Ecole Polytechnique, 91128 Palaiseau, France.

Schoenauer, M., Sebag, M., Jouve, F., Lamy, B., and Maitournam, H. (1996). Evolutionary identification of macro-mechanical models. In Angeline, P. J. and Kinnear,

Jr., K. E., editors, *Advances in Genetic Programming 2*, chapter 23, pages 467–488. MIT Press, Cambridge, MA, USA.

Self, S. (1992). On the origin of effective procedures by means of artificial selection. Master's thesis, Birkbeck College, University of London, UK.

Sen, S. (1996). Adaptation, coevolution and learning in multiagent systems. Technical Report SS-96-01, AAAI Press, Stanford, CA.

Shannon, C. E. and Weaver, W. (1964). *The Mathematical Theory of Communication*. The University of Illinois Press, Urbana.

Sharman, K. C. and Esparcia-Alcazar, A. I. (1993). Genetic evolution of symbolic signal models. In *Proceedings of the Second International Conference on Natural Algorithms in Signal Processing, NASP'93*, Essex University, UK.

Sharman, K. C., Esparcia Alcazar, A. I., and Li, Y. (1995). Evolving signal processing algorithms by genetic programming. In Zalzala, A. M. S., editor, *First International Conference on Genetic Algorithms in Engineering Systems: Innovations and Applications, GALESIA*, volume 414, pages 473–480, Sheffield, UK. IEE.

Shaw, J. (1994). References on the application of genetic algorithms to production scheduling. Available via anonymous ftp site cs.ucl.ac.uk file genetic/biblio/ga-js-shed-bibliography.txt.

Siegel, E. V. (1994). Competitively evolving decision trees against fixed training cases for natural language processing. In Kinnear, Jr., K. E., editor, *Advances in Genetic Programming*, chapter 19, pages 409–423. MIT Press.

Sims, K. (1991). panspermia. In Langton, C. G., editor, *Artificial Life II Video Proceedings*. Addison-Wesley, Sante Fe Institute, New Mexico, USA.

Sims, K. (1994). Evolving 3D morphology and behaviour by competition. In Brooks, R. and Maes, P., editors, *Artificial Life IV Proceedings*, pages 28–39, MIT, Cambridge, MA, USA. MIT Press.

Singleton, A. (1993). Meta GA, desktop supercomputing and object-orientated GP. Notes from Genetic Programming Workshop at ICGA-93.

Singleton, A. (1994). Genetic programming with C++. *BYTE*, pages 171–176.

Slavov, V. and Nikolaev, N. I. (1997). Inductive genetic programming and superposition of fitness landscapes. In Goodman, E., editor, *Genetic Algorithms: Proceedings of the Seventh International Conference*, Michigan State University, East Lansing, MI, USA. Morgan Kaufmann.

Spector, L. (1995). Evolving control structures with automatically defined macros. In Siegel, E. V. and Koza, J. R., editors, *Working Notes for the AAAI Symposium on Genetic Programming*, pages 99–105, MIT, Cambridge, MA, USA. AAAI.

Spector, L. and Alpern, A. (1994). Criticism, culture, and the automatic generation of artworks. In *Proceedings of Twelfth National Conference on Artificial Intelligence*, pages 3–8, Seattle, Washington, USA. AAAI Press/MIT Press.

Spector, L. and Alpern, A. (1995). Induction and recapitulation of deep musical structure. In *Proceedings of International Joint Conference on Artificial Intelligence, IJCAI'95 Workshop on Music and AI*, Montreal, Quebec, Canada.

Spector, L. and Luke, S. (1996). Cultural transmission of information in genetic programming. In Koza, J. R., Goldberg, D. E., Fogel, D. B., and Riolo, R. L., editors, *Genetic Programming 1996: Proceedings of the First Annual Conference*, pages 209–214, Stanford University, CA, USA. MIT Press.

Spencer, G. F. (1994). Automatic generation of programs for crawling and walking. In Kinnear, Jr., K. E., editor, *Advances in Genetic Programming*, chapter 15, pages 335–353. MIT Press.

Starkweather, T., McDaniel, S., Mathias, K., Whitley, D., and Whitley, C. (1991). A comparison of genetic sequencing operators. In Belew, R. K. and Booker, L. B., editors, *Proceedings of the fourth international conference on Genetic Algorithms*, pages 69–76, University of California - San Diego, La Jolla, CA, USA. Morgan Kaufmann.

Stender, J., editor (1993). *Parallel Genetic Algorithms: Theory and Applications*. IOS press.

Stoffel, K. and Spector, L. (1996). High-performance, parallel, stack-based genetic programming. In Koza, J. R., Goldberg, D. E., Fogel, D. B., and Riolo, R. L., editors, *Genetic Programming 1996: Proceedings of the First Annual Conference*, pages 224–229, Stanford University, CA, USA. MIT Press.

Sun, G. Z., Chen, H. H., Giles, C. L., Lee, Y. C., and Chen, D. (1990). Connectionist pushdown automata that learn context-free grammars. In *Proceedings of the International Joint Conference on Neural Networks 1990*, volume I, pages 577–580, Washington, DC, USA. Lawrence Erlbaum.

Syswerda, G. (1989). Uniform crossover in genetic algorithms. In Schaffer, J. D., editor, *Proceedings of the third international conference on Genetic Algorithms*, pages 2–9, George Mason University. Morgan Kaufmann.

Syswerda, G. (1991a). Schedule optimization using genetic algorithms. In Davis, L., editor, *Handbook of Genetic Algorithms*, pages 332–349. Van Nostrand Reinhold, New York.

Syswerda, G. (1991b). A study of reproduction in generational and steady state genetic algorithms. In Rawlings, G. J. E., editor, *Foundations of genetic algorithms*, pages 94–101. Morgan Kaufmann, Indiana University.

Tackett, W. A. (1993). Genetic programming for feature discovery and image discrimination. In Forrest, S., editor, *Proceedings of the 5th International Conference on Genetic Algorithms, ICGA-93*, pages 303–309, University of Illinois at Urbana-Champaign. Morgan Kaufmann.

Tackett, W. A. (1994). *Recombination, Selection, and the Genetic Construction of Computer Programs*. PhD thesis, University of Southern California, Department of Electrical Engineering Systems.

Tackett, W. A. (1995a). Greedy recombination and genetic search on the space of computer programs. In Whitley, L. D. and Vose, M. D., editors, *Foundations of Genetic Algorithms 3*, pages 271–297, Estes Park, Colorado, USA. Morgan Kaufmann.

Tackett, W. A. (1995b). Mining the genetic program. *IEEE Expert*, 10(3):28–38.

Tackett, W. A. and Carmi, A. (1994). The donut problem: Scalability and generalization in genetic programming. In Kinnear, Jr., K. E., editor, *Advances in Genetic Programming*, chapter 7, pages 143–176. MIT Press.

Taylor, S. N. (1995). Evolution by genetic programming of a spatial robot juggling control algorithm. In Rosca, J. P., editor, *Proceedings of the Workshop on Genetic Programming: From Theory to Real-World Applications*, pages 104–110, Tahoe City, California, USA.

Teller, A. (1993). Learning mental models. In *Proceedings of the Fifth Workshop on Neural Networks: An International Conference on Computational Intelligence: Neural Networks, Fuzzy Systems, Evolutionary Programming, and Virtual Reality.*

Teller, A. (1994a). The evolution of mental models. In Kinnear, Jr., K. E., editor, *Advances in Genetic Programming*, chapter 9, pages 199–219. MIT Press.

Teller, A. (1994b). Genetic programming, indexed memory, the halting problem, and other curiosities. In *Proceedings of the 7th annual Florida Artificial Intelligence Research Symposium*, pages 270–274, Pensacola, Florida, USA. IEEE Press.

Teller, A. (1994c). Turing completeness in the language of genetic programming with indexed memory. In *Proceedings of the 1994 IEEE World Congress on Computational Intelligence*, volume 1, pages 136–141, Orlando, Florida, USA. IEEE Press.

Teller, A. (1995a). The discovery of algorithms for automatic database retrieval. In Rosca, J. P., editor, *Proceedings of the Workshop on Genetic Programming: From Theory to Real-World Applications*, pages 76–88, Tahoe City, California, USA.

Teller, A. (1995b). Language representation progression in genetic programming. In Siegel, E. V. and Koza, J. R., editors, *Working Notes for the AAAI Symposium on Genetic Programming*, pages 106–113, MIT, Cambridge, MA, USA. AAAI.

Teller, A. (1996). Evolving programmers: The co-evolution of intelligent recombination operators. In Angeline, P. J. and Kinnear, Jr., K. E., editors, *Advances in Genetic Programming 2*, chapter 3, pages 45–68. MIT Press, Cambridge, MA, USA.

Teller, A. and Andre, D. (1997). Automatically choosing the number of fitness cases: The rational allocation of trials. In Koza, J. R., Deb, K., Dorigo, M., Fogel, D. B., Garzon, M., Iba, H., and Riolo, R. L., editors, *Genetic Programming 1997: Proceedings of the Second Annual Conference*, pages 321–328, Stanford University, CA, USA. Morgan Kaufmann.

Teller, A. and Veloso, M. (1995a). Algorithm evolution for face recognition: What makes a picture difficult. In *International Conference on Evolutionary Computation*, pages 608–613, Perth, Australia. IEEE Press.

Teller, A. and Veloso, M. (1995b). A controlled experiment: Evolution for learning difficult image classification. In *Seventh Portuguese Conference On Artificial Intelligence*, volume 990 of *Lecture Notes in Computer Science*, pages 165–176, Funchal, Madeira Island, Portugal. Springer-Verlag.

Teller, A. and Veloso, M. (1995c). PADO: Learning tree structured algorithms for orchestration into an object recognition system. Technical Report CMU-CS-95-101, Department of Computer Science, Carnegie Mellon University, Pittsburgh, PA, USA.

Teller, A. and Veloso, M. (1995d). Program evolution for data mining. *The International Journal of Expert Systems*, 8(3):216–236.

Teller, A. and Veloso, M. (1996). PADO: A new learning architecture for object recognition. In Ikeuchi, K. and Veloso, M., editors, *Symbolic Visual Learning*, pages 81–116. Oxford University Press.

Tettamanzi, A. G. B. (1996). Genetic programming without fitness. In Koza, J. R., editor, *Late Breaking Papers at the Genetic Programming 1996 Conference Stanford University July 28-31, 1996*, pages 193–195, Stanford University, CA, USA. Stanford Bookstore.

Tufts, P. (1996). Genetic programming resources on the world-wide web. In Angeline, P. J. and Kinnear, Jr., K. E., editors, *Advances in Genetic Programming 2*, chapter A, pages 499–506. MIT Press, Cambridge, MA, USA.

Turton, Openshaw, and Diplock (1996). Some geographic applications of genetic programming on the cray T3D supercomputer. In Jesshope and Shafarenko, editors, *UK Parallel'96*. Springer.

Uiterwijk, J. W. H. M., van den Herik, H. J., and Allis, L. V. (1989). A knowledge-based approach to connect-four. In Levy, D. and Beals, D., editors, *Heuristic Programming in Artificial Intelligence: The First Computer Olympiad*, pages 113–133. Ellis Harwood; John Wiley.

Valenzuela, C. L. and Jones, A. J. (1993). Evolutionary divide and conquer (I): novel genetic approach to the TSP. *Evolutionary Computation*, 1(4):313–333.

Whigham, P. A. (1995a). Grammatically-based genetic programming. In Rosca, J. P., editor, *Proceedings of the Workshop on Genetic Programming: From Theory to Real-World Applications*, pages 33–41, Tahoe City, California, USA.

Whigham, P. A. (1995b). Inductive bias and genetic programming. In Zalzala, A. M. S., editor, *First International Conference on Genetic Algorithms in Engineering Systems: Innovations and Applications, GALESIA*, volume 414, pages 461–466, Sheffield, UK. IEE.

Whigham, P. A. (1996). Search bias, language bias, and genetic programming. In Koza, J. R., Goldberg, D. E., Fogel, D. B., and Riolo, R. L., editors, *Genetic Programming 1996: Proceedings of the First Annual Conference*, pages 230–237, Stanford University, CA, USA. MIT Press.

Whigham, P. A. and Crapper, P. F. (1997). Applying genetic programming to model rainfall-runoff. CSIRO Land and Water, Canberra, Australia.

Whigham, P. A. and McKay, R. I. (1995). Genetic approaches to learning recursive relations. In Yao, X., editor, *Progress in Evolutionary Computation*, volume 956 of *Lecture Notes in Artificial Intelligence*, pages 17–27. Springer-Verlag.

Whitley, L. D. (1991). Fundamental principles of deception in genetic search. In Rawlings, G. J. E., editor, *Foundations of genetic algorithms*, pages 221–241. Morgan Kaufmann, Indiana University.

Willis, M., Hiden, H., Hinchliffe, M., McKay, B., and Barton, G. W. (1997). Systems modelling using genetic programming. *Computers in Chemical Engineering*, 21:S1161–1166. Supplemental.

Wineberg, M. and Oppacher, F. (1994). A representation scheme to perform program induction in a canonical genetic algorithm. In Davidor, Y., Schwefel, H.-P., and Männer, R., editors, *Parallel Problem Solving from Nature III*, pages 292–301, Jerusalem. Springer-Verlag.

Wineberg, M. and Oppacher, F. (1996). The benefits of computing with introns. In Koza, J. R., Goldberg, D. E., Fogel, D. B., and Riolo, R. L., editors, *Genetic Programming 1996: Proceedings of the First Annual Conference*, pages 410–415, Stanford University, CA, USA. MIT Press.

Wirth, N. (1975). *Algorithms + Data Structures = Programs*. Prentice-Hall.

Wolpert, D. H. and Macready, W. G. (1997). No free lunch theorems for optimization. *IEEE Transactions on Evolutionary Computation*, 1(1):67–82.

Wong, M. L. and Leung, K. S. (1995). Applying logic grammars to induce sub-functions in genetic programming. In *1995 IEEE Conference on Evolutionary Computation*, volume 2, pages 737–740, Perth, Australia. IEEE Press.

Wong, M. L. and Leung, K. S. (1996). Evolving recursive functions for the even-parity problem using genetic programming. In Angeline, P. J. and Kinnear, Jr., K. E., editors, *Advances in Genetic Programming 2*, chapter 11, pages 221–240. MIT Press, Cambridge, MA, USA.

Wyard, P. (1991). Context free grammar induction using genetic algorithms. In Belew, R. K. and Booker, L. B., editors, *Procceedings of the Fourth International Conference on Genetic Algorithms*, pages 514–518, University of California - San Diego, La Jolla, CA, USA. Morgan Kaufmann.

Wyard, P. (1994). Representational issues for context free grammar induction using genetic algorithms. In Carrasco, R. C. and Oncina, J., editors, *Grammatical Inference and Applications. Second International Colloquium, ICGI-94*, volume 862 of *Lecture Notes in Artificial Intelligence*, pages 222–235, Pueblo Acantilado, Alicante, Spain. Springer-Verlag.

Yamada, T. and Nakano, R. (1992). A genetic algorithm applicable to large-scale job-shop problems. In Manner, R. and Manderick, B., editors, *Parallel Problem Solving from Nature 2*, pages 281–290, Brussels, Belgium. Elsevier Science.

Yang, D. and Flockton, S. J. (1995). An evolutionary algorithm for parametric array signal processing. In Fogarty, T. C., editor, *Evolutionary Computing*, number 993 in Lecture Notes in Computer Science, pages 191–199. Springer-Verlag.

Zhang, B.-T., Kwak, J.-H., and Lee, C.-H. (1996). Building software agents for information filtering on the internet: A genetic programming approach. In Koza, J. R., editor, *Late Breaking Papers at the Genetic Programming 1996 Conference Stanford University July 28-31, 1996*, page 196, Stanford University, CA, USA. Stanford Bookstore.

Zhang, B.-T. and Mühlenbein, H. (1993a). Evolving optimal neural networks using genetic algorithms with Occam's razor. *Complex Systems*, 7:199–220.

Zhang, B.-T. and Mühlenbein, H. (1993b). Genetic programming of minimal neural nets using Occam's razor. In Forrest, S., editor, *Proceedings of the 5th International Conference on Genetic Algorithms, ICGA-93*, pages 342–349, University of Illinois at Urbana-Champaign. Morgan Kaufmann.

Zhang, B.-T. and Mühlenbein, H. (1995a). Balancing accuracy and parsimony in genetic programming. *Evolutionary Computation*, 3(1):17–38.

Zhang, B.-T. and Mühlenbein, H. (1995b). Bayesian inference, minimum description length principle, and learning by genetic programming. In Rosca, J. P., editor, *Proceedings of the Workshop on Genetic Programming: From Theory to Real-World Applications*, pages 1–5, Tahoe City, California, USA.

Zomorodian, A. (1995). Context-free language induction by evolution of deterministic push-down automata using genetic programming. In Siegel, E. V. and Koza, J. R., editors, *Working Notes for the AAAI Symposium on Genetic Programming*, pages 127–133, MIT, Cambridge, MA, USA. AAAI.

Appendix A
Number of Fitness Evaluations Required

Table A.1 summarises the estimated effort, in terms of the number of trial solutions evaluated, required to solve (with at least 99% assurance) the problems presented in this book. Where problems were not solved a lower bound has been calculated based on assuming the very next run would have succeeded by generation 25.

The number of program executions required (for 99% probability of solving the problem) is estimated by multiplying the number of trial solutions by the mean number of times each was run during its fitness testing. Where the mean number of program executions per program tested is not available, the maximum is used to give an estimated upper bound. Run time reductions via: ancestor fitness re-use (cf. Section D.5), ADF caching (cf. Section D.6) and avoiding fitness evaluation of individuals produced by reproduction, are excluded.

Table A.1. Number of trial programs that must be generated to solve problems (with ≥ 99% assurance) and the corresponding total number of program executions

| Problem Name | Parameters | | Effort | Runs/Eval | | Executions |
	Table	Page	$(\times 10^3)$	Max	Mean	$(\times 10^6)$
Stack	4.2	66	938	160	–	150
Queue: shuffler	5.5	95	383,680	320	–	123,000
Given MInc	5.7	99	3,360	320	320	1,075
Evolving MInc	5.10	108	86,000	320	320	27,520
List	6.3	127	254,000	538	173	44,000
List in two parts	6.3	127	2,580	538	406	1,050
Nested Brackets	7.1	145	190	1,403	1,403	266
Dyck Language (stack given)	7.3	150	230	1,756	729	167
(indexed memory)	7.3	150	$\geq 18,000$	1,756	788	$\geq 14,000$
Reverse Polish (stack given)	7.5	156	2,530	970	900	2,300
(indexed memory)	7.5	156	$\geq 68,750$	970	822	$\geq 57,000$

Appendix B
Glossary

Building Block A pattern of genes in a contiguous section of a chromosome which, if present, confers a high fitness to the individual. According to the building block hypothesis, a complete solution can be constructed by crossover joining together in a single individual many building blocks which where originally spread throughout the population.

Cellular Automata A regular array of identical finite state automata whose next state is determined solely by their current state and the state of their neighbours. The most widely seen is the game of *Life* in which complex patterns emerge from a (supposedly infinite) square lattice of simple two state (living and dead) automata whose next state is determined solely by the current states of its four closes neighbours and itself.

Classifiers An extension of genetic algorithms in which the population consists of a co-operating set of rules (i.e. a rulebase) which are to learn to solve a problem given a number of test cases. Between each generation the population as a whole is evaluated and a fitness is assigned to each rule using the bucket-brigade algorithm or other credit sharing scheme (e.g. the Pitt scheme). These schemes aims to reward or punish rules which contribute to a test case according to how good the total solution is by adjusting the individual rules fitness.

At the end of the test data a new generation is created using a genetic algorithm as if each rule were independent using its own fitness (measures may be taken are taken to ensure a given rule only appears once in the new population).

Coevolution Two or more populations are evolved at the same time. Often the separate populations compete against each other.

Convergence Tendency of members of the population to be the same. May be used to mean either their representation or behaviour are identical. Loosely a genetic algorithm solution has been reached.

Chromosome Normally, in genetic algorithms the bit string which represents the individual. In genetic programming the individual and its representation are usually the same, both being the program parse tree. In nature many species store their genetic information on more than one chromosome.

Crossover Creating a new individual's representation from parts of its parents' representations.

Deme A separately evolving subset of the whole population. The subsets may be evolved on a different computers. Emigration between subset may be used (see Panmixia).

Elitist An elitist genetic algorithm is one that always retains in the population the best individual found so far.

Epistasis A term from biology used to denote that the fitness of an individual depends upon the interaction of a number of their genes. In genetic algorithms this would be indicated by the fitness containing a non-linear combination of components of the string.

Evolution Programming A population containing a number of trial solutions each of which is evaluated to yield an error. Typically, at the end of each generation, the best half of the population is retained and a new solution is produced from each survivor. The process is continued with the aim that the population should evolve to contain an acceptable solution.

Evolutionary programming like Evolution Strategy produces new children by mutating at random from a single parent solution. The analogue components (e.g. the connection weights when applied to artificial neural networks) are changed by a gaussian function whose standard deviation is given by a function of the parent's error called its temperature. Digital components (e.g. presence of a hidden node) are created and destroyed at random.

Evolution Strategy *or Evolutionsstrategie* A search technique first developed in Berlin. Each point in the search space is represented by a vector of real values. In the original Evolution Strategy, $(1 + 1)$-ES, the next point to search is given by adding gaussian random noise to the current search point. The new point is evaluated and if better the search continues from it. If not the search continues from the original point. The level of noise is automatically adjusted as the search proceeds.

Evolutionary Strategies can be thought of as like an analogue version of genetic algorithms. In $(1 + 1)$-ES, 1 parent is used to create 1 offspring. In $(\mu + \lambda)$-ES and (μ, λ)-ES μ parents are used to create λ children (perhaps using crossover).

Finite State Automaton (FSA) *or Finite State Machine (FSM)* A machine which can be totally described by a finite set of states, it being in one these at any one time, plus a set of rules which determine when it moves from one state to another.

Fitness Function A process which evaluates a member of a population and gives it a score or fitness. In most cases the goal is to find an individual with the maximum (or minimum) fitness.

Function Set The set of operators used in a genetic program, e.g. $+ - \times \div$. These act as the branch points in the parse tree, linking other functions or terminals. See also non-terminals.

Generation When the children of one population replace their parents in that population. Where some part of the original population is retained, as in steady state GAs, generation typically refers to the interval during which the number of new individuals created is equal to the population size.

Generation Equivalent In a steady state GA, the time taken to create as many new individuals as there are in the population.

Genetic Algorithm A population containing a number of trial solutions each of which is evaluated (to yield a fitness) and a new generation is created from the better of them. The process is continued through a number of generations with the aim that the population should evolve to contain an acceptable solution.

GAs are characterised by representing the solution as an (often fixed length) string of digital symbols, selecting parents from the current population in proportion to their fitness (or some approximation of this) and the use of crossover as the dominate means of creating new members of the population. The initial population may be created at random or from some known starting point.

GA Deceptive A gene pattern which confers high fitness but is not present in the optimal solution is said to be deceptive; in that it may lead the genetic algorithm away from the global optimum solution.

Genetic Operator An operator in a genetic algorithm or genetic programming, which acts upon the chromosome to produce a new individual. Example operators are mutation and crossover.

Genetic Program A program produced by genetic programming.

Genetic Programming A subset of genetic algorithms. The members of the populations are the parse trees of computer programs whose fitness is evaluated by running them. The reproduction operators (e.g. crossover) are refined to ensure that the child is syntactically correct (some protection may be given against semantic errors too). This is achieved by acting upon subtrees.

Genetic programming is most easily implemented where the computer language is tree structured so there is no need to explicitly evaluated its parse tree. This is one of the reasons why Lisp is often used for genetic programming.

This is the common usage of the term *genetic programming* however it has also been used to refer to the programming of cellular automata and neural networks using a genetic algorithm.

Hits The number of hits an individual scores is the number of test cases for which it returns the correct answer (or close enough to it). This may or may not be a component of the fitness function. When an individual gains the maximum number of hits this may terminate the run.

Infix Notation Notation in which the operator separates its operands. E.g. $(a + b) \times c$. Infix notation requires the use of brackets to specify the order of evaluation, unlike either prefix or postfix notations.

Non-Terminal Functions used to link parse tree together. This name may be used to avoid confusion with functions with no parameters which can only act as end points of the parse tree (i.e. leafs) and so are part of the terminal set.

Mutation Arbitrary change to representation, often at random. In genetic programming, a subtree is replaced by another, some or all of which is created at random.

Panmixia When a population is split into a number of separately evolving populations (demes) but the level of emigration is sufficiently high that they continue to evolve as if a single population.

Parsimony Brevity. In GP, this is measured by counting the nodes in the tree. The smaller the program, the smaller the tree, the lower the count and the more parsimonious it is.

Postfix Notation *Reverse Polish Notation or Suffix Notation* Notation in which the operator follows its operands. E.g. $a + b \times c$ represented as $abc \times +$.

Prefix Notation *Polish Notation* Notation in which the operator comes before its operands. E.g. $a + b$ represented as $+ab$.

Premature Convergence When a genetic algorithm's population converges to something which is not the solution you wanted.

Recombination as crossover.

Reproduction Production of new member of population from existing members. May be used to mean an exact copy of the original member.

Simulated Annealing Search technique where a single trial solution is modified at random. An *energy* is defined which represents how good the solution is. The goal is to find the best solution by minimising the energy. Changes which lead to a lower energy are always accepted; an increase is probabilistically accepted. The probability is given by $\exp(-\Delta E/k_B T)$. Where ΔE is the change in energy, k_B is a constant and T is the *Temperature*. Initially the temperature is high corresponding to a liquid or molten state where large changes are possible and it is progressively reduced using a *cooling schedule* so allowing smaller changes until the system *solidifies* at a low energy solution.

Stochastic Random or probabilistic but with some direction. For example the arrival of people at a post office might be random but average properties (such as the queue length) can be predicted.

Terminal Set A set from which all end (leaf) nodes in the parse trees representing the programs must be drawn. A terminal might be a variable, a constant or a function with no arguments.

Tournament Selection A mechanism for choosing individuals from a population. A group (typically between 2 and 7 individuals) are selected at random from the population and the best (normally only one, but possibly more) is chosen.

Appendix C
Scheduling Planned Maintenance of the National Grid

C.1   INTRODUCTION

In England and Wales electrical power is transmitted by a high voltage electricity transmission network which is highly interconnected and carries large power flows (in the region of $4 \ 10^{10}$ Watts). It is owned and operated by The National Grid Company plc. (NGC) who maintain it and wish to ensure its maintenance is performed at least cost, consistent with plant safety and security of supply.

There are many components in the cost of planned maintenance. The largest is the cost of replacement electricity generation, which occurs when maintenance of the network prevents a cheap generator from running so requiring a more expensive generator to be run in its place.

The task of planning maintenance is a complex constrained optimisation scheduling problem. The schedule is constrained to ensure that all plant remains within its capacity and the cost of replacement generation, throughout the duration of the plan is minimised. At present maintenance schedules are initially produced manually by NGC's Planning Engineers (who use computerised viability checks and optimisation on the schedule after it has been produced). This chapter describes work by NGC's Technology and Science Laboratories and University College London which investigates the feasibility of generating practical and economic maintenance schedules using genetic algorithms (GAs) [Holland, 1992].

Earlier work [Langdon, 1995c] investigated creating electrical network maintenance plans using Genetic Algorithms on a demonstration four node test problem devised by NGC [Dunnett, 1993]. [Langdon, 1995c] showed the combination of a Genetic Algorithm using an order or permutation chromosome combined with hand coded "Greedy" schedulers can readily produce an optimal schedule for this problem.

In this chapter we report (1) the combination of GAs and greedy schedulers and (2) genetic programming (GP), automatically generating maintenance schedules for the South Wales region of the NGC network.

In Sections C.2 and C.3 we describe the British power transmission network and the South Wales region within it, Sections C.4 and C.5 describe the fitness function, while Sections C.6 and C.7 describe the GA used and the motivations behind its choice. Sections C.8, C.9 and C.10 describe three approaches which have produced low cost schedules, firstly without the network resilience requirement and secondly using a GP and finally when including fault tolerance requirements. Our conclusions (Section C.11) are followed by discussion of the problems in applying these techniques to the complete NGC network (Section C.12). Details of the GA parameters used are given in Section C.13.

C.2   THE ELECTRICITY TRANSMISSION NETWORK IN GREAT BRITAIN

The complete high voltage electricity transmission network is show in Figure C.1. The bulk of it (shown below the dark diagonal line) is owned and operated by The National Grid Company plc (NGC). For maintenance planning purposes the NGC

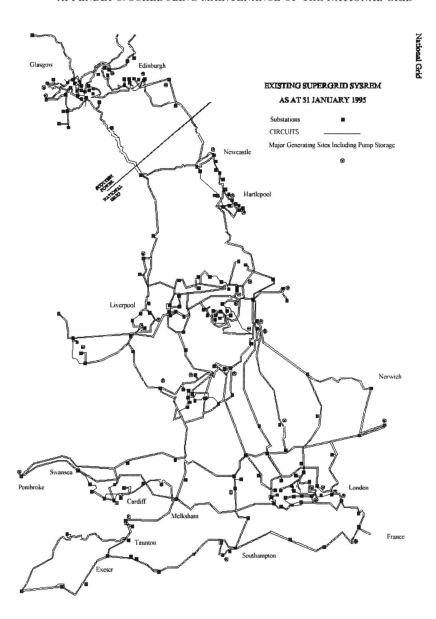

Figure C.1.   British High Voltage Electrical Power Transmission Network

network can be considered as comprising about 300 nodes connected by about 400 lines. We consider the yearly maintenance plan which contains 52 weeks. The South Wales region is the region in the lower middle left hand side. It is connected to the remainder of the network at only two points. This makes it an easy example to study but at the same time allowing us to use a real network.

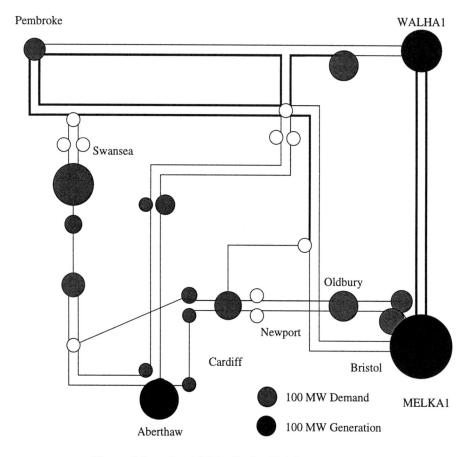

Pembroke

WALHA1

Swansea

Oldbury

Newport

Cardiff

Bristol

● 100 MW Demand

MELKA1

Aberthaw

● 100 MW Generation

Figure C.2. South Wales Region High Voltage Network

C.3   THE SOUTH WALES REGION OF THE UK ELECTRICITY NETWORK

The South Wales region of the UK electricity network carries power at 275K Volts and 400K Volts between electricity generators and regional electricity distribution companies and major industrial consumers. The region covers the major cites of Swansea, Cardiff, Newport and Bristol, steel works and the surrounding towns and rural areas (see Figure C.2). The major sources of electricity are infeeds (2) from the English Midlands, coal fired generation at Aberthaw, nuclear generation at Oldbury and oil fired generation at Pembroke. Both demand for electricity and generation change significantly through the year (See Figures C.3 and C.4).

The representation of the electricity network used in these experiments is based upon the engineering data available for the physical network; however a number of simplifications have to be made. Firstly the regional network has been treated as an isolated network; its connections to the rest of the network have been modelled by two sources of generation connected by a pair of low impedance high capacity conductors.

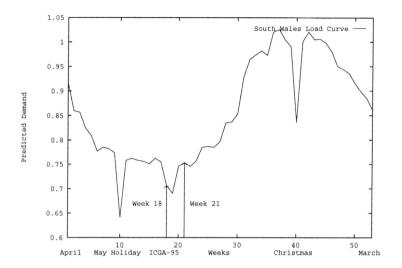

Figure C.3.   Predicted Demand in South Wales Region

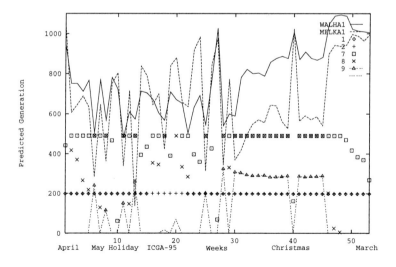

Figure C.4.   Predicted Generation in South Wales Region

Secondly the physical network contains short spurs run to localised load points such as steel works. These "T" points have been simplified (e.g. by inserting nodes into the simulation) so all conductors connect two nodes. The industry standard DC load flow approximation is used to calculate power flows through the network.

In the experiments reported in this chapter the maintenance planning problem for the South Wales region has been made deliberately more difficult than the true requirement. In these experiments:

- All lines must be maintained during the 53 week plan (1995 had 53 weeks rather than 52). Typically about one third of the lines are maintained in any one year.

- All maintenance takes four weeks. Typically scheduled outage of a line is between a week and $1\frac{1}{2}$ months.

- We consider two versions of the problem. In the first the requirement that the network must remain secure against faults in the network was ignored. To compensate for this, the problem was artificially increased in difficulty by reducing the capacity of all lines by 50%. When satisfactory solutions to this version of the problem have been evolved, we then considered evolving maintenance plans which contain a degree of network resilience (cf. Section C.10). In this second problem the true conductor rating were used.

Considering potential network faults is highly CPU intensive and so the genetic programming approach described in Section C.9 does not attempt to solve the second version of the South Wales problem.

C.4   APPROXIMATING REPLACEMENT GENERATION COSTS

NGC use computer tools for costing maintenance schedules, however because of their computational complexity, it was felt that these were unsuitable for providing the fitness function. Instead our fitness function is partially based upon estimating the replacement generation costs that would occur if a given maintenance plan were to be used. The estimate is made by calculating the electrical power flows assuming the maintenance will not force a change in generation. In practice alternative generators must be run to reduce the power flow through over loaded lines in the network. The cost of the alternative generators is modelled by setting the amount of replacement generation equal to the excess power flow and assuming alternative generators will be a fixed amount more expensive than the generators they replace.

As a first approximation issues concerning security of supply following a fault are not covered. We plan to increase the realism of the GA as we progress. Other costs (e.g. maintenance workers' overtime, travel) are not considered.

C.5   THE FITNESS FUNCTION

All optimisation techniques require an objective function to judge the quality of the solutions they produce. In genetic algorithms (GAs) this has become known as the fitness function and is used to guide the evolution of the population of solutions.

The fitness function used by both GA and genetic programming (GP) approaches to scheduling maintenance in the South Wales region is based on that used in the four node problem. To summarise;

- The demand for electricity for the coming year is predicted (cf. Figure C.3).

- The cheapest electrical generators are scheduled to meet this demand (cf. Figure C.4).

  To optimise costs across the whole network, these two steps are performed nationally. Imbalances between demand and generation in each region result in power transfers between regions and in the case of the South Wales region for this year, large inward power flows were planned (cf. the top two curves in Figure C.4).

- The fitness function includes a maintenance benefit for each maintenance task completed (i.e. for each line maintained for at least four consecutive weeks).

- If maintenance were to cause power flows to be redistributed in such a way as to overload part of the network it would be necessary to re-arrange the network to avoid this. In practice this may entail changes to the pattern of electricity generation. As we started with the cheapest generators, this will be more expensive. In practice this is the major cost of planned network maintenance. The fitness function models this cost with a penalty given by the amount each line is overloaded.

- Large penalties are also included to punish schedules which isolate nodes which directly supply demand or generation. When nodes are isolated or the network is split, the penalty for each node in the disconnected part of the network are summed and then the usual loadflow and fitness calculations are performed on the remaining connected network (i.e. the connected network containing the most nodes). In the South Wales problem there is no separate penalty for splitting the network.

$$
\begin{aligned}
\text{cost} = \ &\sum_{\text{target}} K \times (1 - \text{maintenance\_scheduled}) \\[2ex]
&+ \sum_{\text{weeks}} \left(+ \begin{array}{l} S \times \displaystyle\sum_{\text{isolated\_nodes}} |\,\text{demand} \vee \text{generation}\,| \\[2ex] \displaystyle\sum_{\text{remaining\_lines}} \begin{array}{l}\textbf{If } |\text{flow}| > \text{rating } \textbf{then} \\ |\text{flow}| - \text{rating}\end{array} \end{array} \right)
\end{aligned} \qquad \text{(C.1)}
$$

Equation C.1 gives the fitness function used in Sections C.8 and C.9, i.e. excluding consideration of contingencies (network faults). In Equation C.1 the first summation is over all target maintenance (n.b. the trial plan's cost is increased by K if the corresponding maintenance is not scheduled). The second outer summation being over each week of the maintenance plan; the first inner one, being over all isolated nodes, and the second, over all lines in the network.

Where contingencies are to be considered (as in Section C.10), the second part of Equation C.1 is extended to include a penalty for each contingency which is calculated as if the contingency had occurred but weighted by an arbitrary scaling factor based upon the severity of the contingency (cf. Equation C.2). During the contingency part of the fitness calculation the post fault rating on all the conductors is used. This is about 17% higher for each conductor than the corresponding rating used in the first part.

$$
\begin{aligned}
\text{cost} = \quad & \sum_{\text{target}} K \times (1 - \text{maintenance\_scheduled}) \\[2ex]
+ \quad & \sum_{\text{weeks}} \left(
\begin{array}{l}
S \times \displaystyle\sum_{\text{isolated\_nodes}} |\,\text{demand} \vee \text{generation}\,| \\[2ex]
+ \\[1ex]
\displaystyle\sum_{\text{remaining\_lines}} \begin{array}{l} \textbf{If } |\text{flow}| > \text{rating } \textbf{then} \\ |\text{flow}| - \text{rating} \end{array}
\end{array}
\right) \\[4ex]
+ \quad & \sum_{\text{contingency}} \text{scaling} \times \sum_{\text{weeks}} \left(
\begin{array}{l}
S \times \displaystyle\sum_{\text{isolated\_nodes}} |\,\text{demand} \vee \text{generation}\,| \\[2ex]
+ \\[1ex]
\displaystyle\sum_{\text{remaining\_lines}} \begin{array}{l} \textbf{If } |\text{flow}| > \text{rating}_{+17\%} \textbf{then} \\ |\text{flow}| - \text{rating}_{+17\%} \end{array}
\end{array}
\right)
\end{aligned}
$$

$$\text{(C.2)}$$

The constants of proportional, K and S need to be chosen so that the maintenance benefit dominates. For the four node problem this was done by calculating the line costs associated with many feasible schedules [Langdon, 1995c, page 140]. This gave the highest feasible line cost as being 3870MW weeks. K was set to 4,000 MW weeks, so that any schedule which failed to maintain even one line would have a higher cost that the worst "reasonable" schedule which maintains them all.

S was chosen so that isolating any node would have a high cost. In the four node problem the lowest demand/generation on a node is 800 MW. Setting S to five ensures that any schedule which isolates any node will have a cost higher the worst "reasonable" schedule (800MW × 5weeks = 4,000MW weeks).

For the South Wales problem the same values of K and S as the four node system where used. I.e. K is 4,000 MW and $S = 5$. In general the balance between the costs of maintenance and the (typically unknown) costs of not maintaining a plant item is complex. Such choices are beyond the scope of this work, however [Gordon, 1995] verified the values used for the four node problem are applicable to the South Wales region.

C.6 THE CHROMOSOME

Various ways of representing schedules within the GA, were considered. When choosing one, we looked at the complete transmission network which contains about 300 nodes and about 400 transmission lines of which about 130 are schedules to be maintained during a 52 week plan. Table C.1 summarises the GA representations investigated ([Shaw, 1994] gives a bibliography of GAs used on many scheduling problems).

Table C.1.   Possible chromosomes for the maintenance scheduling problem

Organization	Size	Gene	Expected Benefit	Disadvantages Selected References
Linear	7,000	bit	Simple	Crossover disruptive, Too long, No structure, Sparse [Goldberg, 1989]
2D	130 by 52	bit	Simple, Obvious temporal structure	Crossover disruptive, Still very big, No grid structure, Sparse [Cartwright and Harris, 1993] [Valenzuela and Jones, 1993] [Andre, 1994a]
Graph	130 by 52	bit	Realistic	Crossover disruptive, Complex, Little preceding work, Sparse [Maher and Kundu, 1993]
TSP	7,000	link	Widely studied	"By edge" costs, Sparse [Starkweather et al., 1991] [Valenzuela and Jones, 1993]
GP		S-expression		Complex, Little preceding work [Atlan et al., 1994]
Expansive Coding	$7,000 \times n$	complex	Crossover friendly	Complex, Little preceding work [Beasley et al., 1993a]
"Greedy Optimization"	130	line id	Good crossover, Compact, Widely studied	Fitness evaluation expensive [Syswerda, 1991a] [Fang et al., 1993] [Fang et al., 1994]

In the linear, 2D and TSP structures every attempt should be made to keep electrically close lines close to each other in the representation. The graph representation has the advantage that this can be naturally built into the chromosome.

With a simple linear chromosome, Holland or multi-point crossover [Goldberg, 1989], would appear to be too disruptive to solve the problem. A simple example illustrates this. Suppose lines L_1 and L_2 are close together. It will often be the case that good solutions maintain one or the other but neither at the same time. But crossover of solutions maintaining L_1 but not L_2 with those maintaining L_2 but not L_1 will either make no change to L_1 and L_2 or not maintain either or maintain both. The first makes no change to the fitness whilst the second and third make it worse. That is, we would expect crossover to have difficulty assembling better solutions from good "building blocks" [Goldberg, 1989]. The same problem appears in the temporal dimension and so affects the first three representations given in Table C.1. This coupled with the sparseness of the chromosome (about 1 bit in 50 set) and other difficulties, has led to the decision to try a "greedy optimisation" representation. ([Gordon, 1995] used a linear chromosome with non-binary alleles [Ross, 1994] to solve the four node problem but was less successful on the South Wales problem).

C.7 GREEDY OPTIMISERS

The approach taken so far to solving the power transmission network maintenance scheduling problem has been to split the problem in two; a GA and a "greedy optimiser". The greedy optimiser is presented with a list of work to be done (i.e. lines to be maintained) by the GA. It schedules those lines one at a time, in the order presented by the GA, using some problem dependent heuristic. Figure C.5 shows this schematically, whilst the dotted line on Figure C.6 shows an *order* in which lines are considered.

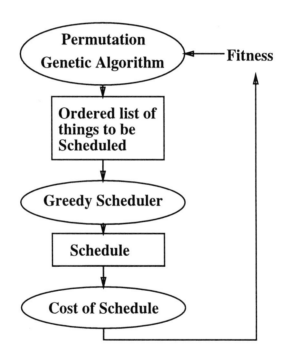

Figure C.5.   Hybrid GA and "greedy optimiser"

This approach of hybridising a GA with a problem specific heuristic has been widely studied. [Davis, 1991] for example firmly advocates using hybrid GAs when attempting to solve difficult real world problems. Hybrid GAs, of various sorts, have been used on a number of scheduling problems (e.g. flight crew scheduling [Levine, 1994], task scheduling [Syswerda, 1991a] and job-shop and open-shop scheduling [Fang et al., 1993; Fang et al., 1994; Yamada and Nakano, 1992]).

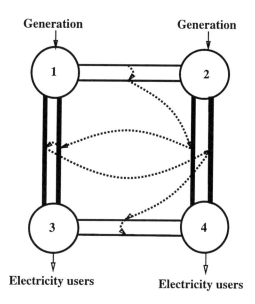

Figure C.6. Example order (dotted) in which lines are considered by a "greedy optimiser"

C.8 SOUTH WALES PROBLEM WITHOUT CONTINGENCIES

C.8.1 Greedy Scheduler

The greedy scheduler used is based upon the minimum increase cost greedy scheduler that solved the four node problem (Heuristic 4 in [Langdon, 1995c]) but modified to take into account maintenance takes four weeks rather than one. Briefly the greedy scheduler (cf. Figure C.5) is presented with each line in the order determined by the GA chromosome. For each line it determines which four weeks will cause the overall cost of the schedule to increase the least (or decrease the most). The line is then scheduled in those four weeks and the next line is processed. If there is a tie, the earliest weeks are used. NB this optimiser makes its choice by studying the effect each maintenance outage would have on the network, rather than using only at the existing network information. I.e. it performs a limited look ahead.

C.8.2 Results

Figure C.7 contains the least cost schedule produced using the minimum increase cost greedy scheduler using the same GA that was used to solve the four node problem with the same population size (cf. Section C.13).

Not only is this a low cost schedule (it has a cost of 616MW weeks) but it is a good one in that it contains several "sensible" decisions, for example performing maintenance on lines and the transformers which supply them simultaneously. For example line "Swansea L9" and transformer "Swansea T9" which supply Swansea, are both maintained in weeks 4–7.

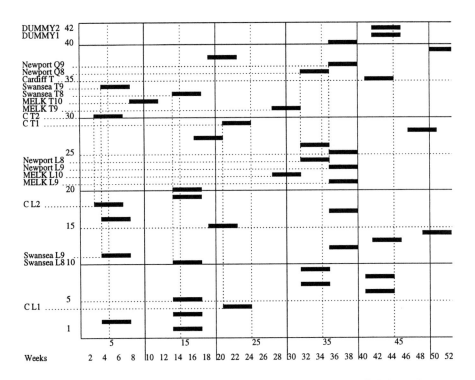

Figure C.7.   GA produced Schedule for South Wales without Contingencies

C.8.3   Discussion

While still better performance could be obtained using modified greedy schedulers, these results were sufficiently encouraging as to warrant including the fault resilience requirements by explicitly including contingencies. This is described in Section C.10.

It is encouraging that reasonable results have been obtained using essentially the same technique as was used on the four node problem, despite this problem's search space being $2.1 \; 10^{60}$ fold larger.

Another heuristic, which produced improved results, replaced the line overloading component of the minimum increase in cost greedy scheduler with the square of the powerflow. It is felt this produced improved performance because in the case of the South Wales network, unlike the four node problem, many conductors are not near their ratings and so the minimum increase in cost heuristic is relatively independent of changes to their powerflows. By using power flow squared, the greedy scheduler becomes more sensitive to changes but particularly to changes in lines near their capacities.

C.9   SOUTH WALES AND GENETIC PROGRAMMING

The requirement that the network should be fault resistant during maintenance is only considered in Section C.10 and not in the GP work in this section. This is because consideration of potential network faults is highly CPU intensive.

A number of different GP approaches have been tried on these problems. A "pure" GP approach can find the optimal solution to the four node problem without the need for hand coded heuristics. On the South Wales problem, possibly due to insufficient resources, a "pure" GP has not been able to do as well as the best solution produced by the GA and "greedy optimiser" combination, described in Section C.8. The remainder of this section describes the evolution of lower cost schedules using a GP population which is "seeded" with two heuristics.

C.9.1   Architecture

Each individual in the GP population is an executable program represented as a tree. This program is called once for each line that is to be maintained, its return value is converted from floating point to an integer which is treated as the first week in which to schedule maintenance of that line. If this is outside the legal range 1 ... 50 then that line is not maintained.

The lines are processed in fixed but arbitrary order given by NGC when the network was constructed. Thus the GP approach concentrates upon evolving the scheduling heuristic whereas in the GA approach this is given and the GA searches for the best order in which to ask the heuristic to process the lines.

C.9.2   Choice of Primitives

The functions, terminals and parameters used are given in Table C.3. The function and terminal sets include indexed memory, loops and network data.

Indexed memory was deliberately generously sized to avoid restricting the GP's use of it. It consists of 4,001 memory cells each containing a single precision floating point value. They had addresses in the range $-2000 \ldots +2000$. Memory primitives (read, set, swap) had defined behaviour which allows the GP to continue on addressing errors. All stored data within the program is initialised to zero before the trial program is executed for the first line. It is not initialised between runs of the same trial program.

The for primitive takes three arguments, an initial value for the loop control variable, the end value and a subtree to be repeatedly executed. It returns the last value of the loop control variable. A run time check prevents loops being nested more than four deep and terminates execution of any loop when more than 10,000 iteration in total have been executed in any one program call. I.e. execution of different loops contribute to the same shared limit. The current value of the innermost for loop control variable is given by the terminal i0, that of the next outer loop by i1, the control variable of the next outer loop by terminal i2 and so on. When not in a loop nested to depth n, in is zero.

The network primitives return information about the network as it was just before the test program was called. Each time a change to the maintenance schedule is made, power flows and other affected data are recalculated before the GP tree is executed again to schedule maintenance of the next line. The network primitives are those available to the C programmer who programmed the GA heuristics and the fitness function (see Table C.2). Where these primitives take arguments, they are checked to see if they are within the legal range. If not the primitive normally evaluates to 0.0

C.9.3   Mutation

Approximately 90% of new individuals are created by crossover between two parents using GP crossover (as [Koza, 1992] except only one individuals is created at a time). The remainder are created by mutating a copy of a single parent. Two forms of mutation are used with equal likelihood. In subtree mutation [Koza, 1992] a single node within the program is chosen at random. This is the root of a subtree which is removed and replaced with a randomly generated new subtree. The other form or mutation selects nodes at random (with a frequency of 10/1024) and replaces them with a randomly selected function (or terminal) which takes the same number of arguments. Thus the tree shape is unchanged but a Poissonly distributed number of node are changed within it. Notice the expected number of changes rises linearly with the size of the tree.

C.9.4   Constructing the Initial Population

The initial population was created from two "seed" individuals. These are the GA heuristics described in Section C.8.1 and [Langdon, 1995c, page 141], re-written as GP individuals using the primitives described in Section C.9.2 and modified for the South Wales region (see Figures C.8 and C.9). Half the remaining population is created from each seed by making a copy of it and then mutating the copy. The same mutation operators are used to create the initial population as to create mutants during the main part of the GP run. I.e. there is equal chance to mutate a subtree as to create mutants by random change to nodes with the tree.

Table C.2.   Network Primitives

Primitive	Meaning
max	10.0
ARG1	Index number of current line, 1.0 ... 42.0
nn	Number of nodes in network, 28.0
nl	Number of lines in network, 42.0
nw	Number of weeks in plan, 53.0
nm_weeks	Length of maintenance outage, 4.0
$P(n)$	Power injected at node n in 100MW. Negative values indicate demand.
NNLK(l)	Node connected to first end of line l.
NNLJ(l)	Node connected to 2nd end of line l
XL(l)	Impedance of line l Ω.
LINERATING	Power carrying capacity of line l in MW.
MAINT(w, l)	1.0 if line l is scheduled for maintenance in week w, otherwise 0.0
splnod(w, n)	1.0 if node n is isolated in week w of the maintenance plan, 0.0 otherwise.
FLOW(w, n)	Power flow in line l from first end to second in week w, negative if flow is reversed MW.
shed(w, l)	Demand or generation at isolated nodes in week w if line l is maintained in that week in addition to current scheduled maintenance MW.
loadflow(w, l, a)	Performs a load flow calculation for week w assuming line l is maintained during the week in addition to the currently scheduled maintenance. Returns cost of schedule for week w. If a is valid also sets memory locations a ... $a + nl - 1$ to the power flows through the network MW.
fit(w)	Returns the current cost of week w of the schedule.

Table C.3.   South Wales Problem

Objective	Find a program that yields a good maintenance schedule when presented with maintenance tasks in network order
Architecture	One result producing branch
Primitives	ADD, SUB, MUL, DIV, ABS, mod, int, PROG2, IFLTE, Ifeq, Iflt, 0, 1, 2, max, ARG1, read, set, swap, for, i0, i1, i2, i3, i4, nn, nl, nw, nm_weeks, P, NNLK, NNLJ, XL, LINERATING, MAINT, splnod, FLOW, shed, loadflow fit
Max prog size	200
Fitness case	All 42 lines to be maintained
Selection	Pareto Tournament group size of 4 (with niche sample size 81) used for both parent selection and selecting programs to be removed from the population. Pareto components: Schedule cost, CPU penalty above 100,000 per line, schedule novelty. Steady state panmictic population. Elitism used on schedule cost.
Wrapper	Convert to integer. If ≥ 1 and ≤ 50, treat as week to schedule start of maintenance of current line, otherwise the current line is not maintained.
Parameters	Pop = 1000, G = 50, no aborts. $p_c = 0.9$, $p_{subtree\ mutation} = 0.05$, $p_{node\ mutation} = 0.05$. Node mutation rate = 10/1024.
Success predicate	Schedule cost ≤ 616

```
week = (PROG2 (set (SUB 0 1) (SUB (SUB 0 max) nw))
       (PROG2 (for 1 nw (set ((ADD i0 (read (SUB 0 1))))
                              (ABS (FLOW i0 ARG1))))
       (PROG2 (set (SUB 0 (ADD 1 1))
                   (SUB (read (SUB 0 1)) nw))
       (PROG2 (for 1 (SUB nw (SUB nm_weeks 1))
               (PROG2 (set 0 0)
               (PROG2
                (for i0 (ADD i0 (SUB nm_weeks 1) )
                 (set 0 (ADD (read 0)
                             (read (ADD i0 (read (SUB 0 1)
                                                 )))
                         )))
                (set ((ADD i0 (read (SUB 0 (ADD 1 1)))))
                     (read 0)))))
       (PROG2 (set 0 (MUL max (MUL max (MUL max max)))))
       (PROG2 (set 1 0)
       (PROG2
         (for 1 (SUB nw (SUB nm_weeks 1))
           (Iflt
             (read ((ADD i0 (read (SUB 0 (ADD 1 1)
                                        )))))
             (read 0)
             (PROG2
               (set 1 i0)
               (set 0 (read ((ADD i0 (read (SUB 0 (ADD 1 1)
                                                 )))))))
             0))
         (read 1)))))))))
```

Figure C.8. Seed 1 : Minimum Power flow Heuristic. Length 133, Cost of schedule 9830.19

```
%[-2,-1,0]=working areas
week = (PROG2 (set (SUB 0 1) (SUB (SUB 0 max) nw))
       (PROG2 (for 1 nw (set ((ADD i0 (read (SUB 0 1))))
                        %store answer   %discard flow info
                              (loadflow i0 ARG1 (ADD 2 2))
                        ))
       (PROG2 (set (SUB 0 (ADD 1 1))
                   (SUB (read (SUB 0 1)) nw))
           %work2 = sum over 4 weeks
       (PROG2 (for 1 (SUB nw (SUB nm_weeks 1))
              (PROG2 (set 0 0)                      %[0]=temp
              (PROG2
                (for i0 (ADD i0 (SUB nm_weeks 1) )
                 (set 0 (ADD (read 0)
                            (read (ADD i0 (read (SUB 0 1)
              ))))))
              (set ((ADD i0 (read (SUB 0 (ADD 1 1)))))
                   (read 0)))))
       (PROG2 (set 0 (MUL max (MUL max (MUL max max))))
       (PROG2 (set 1 0)

              %find min increase in cost
       (PROG2
         (for 1 (SUB nw (SUB nm_weeks 1))
           (Iflt
            (SUB       %calculate increase in cost
              (read ((ADD i0 (read (SUB 0 (ADD 1 1))))))
              (PROG2 (PROG2
                      (set 2 0)
                      (for i0 (ADD i0 (SUB nm_weeks 1))
                        (set 2 (ADD (read 2) (fit i0)))
                      ))
                    (read 2)))
           (read 0)
           (PROG2
             (set 1 i0)
             (set 0 (SUB
                    (read (ADD i0 (read (SUB 0 (ADD 1 1)
                                  ))))
                    (read 2))))
           0))
           (read 1))))))))
```

Figure C.9.   Seed 2 : Minimum Increase in Cost Heuristic. Length 160, Cost 1120.13

C.9.5   Fitness Function

The fitness of each individual is comprised of three independent components; the fitness (cost) of the schedule it produces (as described in Section C.5), a CPU penalty and a novelty reward for scheduling a line in a week which is unusual. These components are not combined instead selection for reproduction and replacement uses Pareto tournaments and fitness niches [Goldberg, 1989]. The cost and CPU penalty are determined when the individual is created but the novelty reward is dynamic and may change whilst the individual is within the population.

The CPU penalty is the mean number of primitives evaluated per line. However if this below the threshold of 100,000 then the penalty is zero. Both seeds are comfortably below the threshold. (The minimum power flow seed executes 206,374 primitives ($206,374/42 \approx 4914$) and the minimum increase in cost seed executes 301,975 primitives ($301,975/42 \approx 7190$)).

The novelty reward is 1.0 if the program constructs a schedule where the start of any line's scheduled maintenance is in a week when less than 100 other schedules schedule the start of the same line in the same week. Otherwise it is 0.0.

C.9.6   Results

In one GP run the cost of the best schedule in the population is 1120.05 initially. This is the cost of schedule produced by seed 2. Notice this is worse than the best schedule found by the GA using this seed because the heuristic is being run with an arbitrary ordering of the tasks and not the best order found by the GA. By generation 4 a better schedule of cost 676.217 was found. By generation 19 a schedule better than that found by the GA was found. At the end of the run (generation 50) the best schedule found had a cost of 388.349 (see Figure C.10). The program that produced it is shown in Figure C.11.

The best program differs from the best seed in eight subtrees and has expanded almost to the maximum allowed size. At first sight some of the changes appear trivial and unlikely to affect the result but in fact only two changes can be reversed with out worsening the schedule. However all but one of the other changes can be reversed (one at a time) and yield a legal schedule with a cost far better than the population average, in some cases better than the initial seeds.

C.9.7   Other GP Approaches

Genetic Programming has been used in other scheduling problems, notably Job Shop Scheduling [Atlan et al., 1994] and scheduling maintenance of railway track [Grimes, 1995].

An approach based on [Atlan et al., 1994] which used a chromosome with a separate tree per task (i.e. line) to be maintained was tried. However unlike [Atlan et al., 1994] there was no central coordinating heuristic to ensure "the system's coherence" and each tree was free to schedule its line independent of the others. The fitness function guiding the co-evolution of these trees. This was able to solve the four node problem, where there are eight tasks, but good solutions were not found (within the available

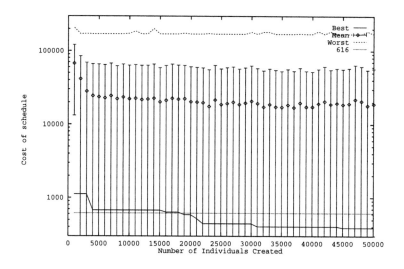

Figure C.10.   Evolution of GP Produced Schedule Costs

machine resources) when this architecture was used on the South Wales problem, where it required 42 trees within the chromosome.

Another architecture extended the problem asking the GP to simultaneously evolve a program to determine the order in which the "greedy" scheduler should process the tasks and evolve the greedy scheduler itself. Each program is represented by a separate tree in the same chromosome. Access to Automatically Defined Functions (ADFs) was also provided.

The most recent approach is to retain the fixed network ordering of processing the tasks but allow the scheduler to change its mind and reschedule lines. This is allowed by repeatedly calling the evolved program, so having processed all 42 tasks it called again for the first, and then the second, and the third and so on. Processing continues until a fixed CPU limit is exceeded (cf. PADO [Teller and Veloso, 1995d]). These alternative techniques were able to produce maintenance schedules but they had higher costs than those described in Sections C.8 and C.9.6.

C.9.8   Discussion

The permutation GA approach has a significant advantage over the GP approach in that the system is constrained by the supplied heuristic to produce only legal schedules. This greatly limits the size of the search space but if the portion of the search space selected by the heuristic does not contain the optimal solution, then all schedules produced will be suboptimal. In the GP approach described the schedules are not constrained and most schedules produced are poor (see Figure C.10) but the potential for producing better schedules is also there.

During development of the GA approach several "greedy" schedulers were coded by hand, i.e. they evolved manually. The GP approach described further evolves the

```
week = (PROG2 (set (SUB 0 1) (SUB (SUB 0 max) nw))
       (PROG2 (for i0 nw (set ((ADD i0 (read (SUB 0 1))))
                               (loadflow i0 ARG1 (ADD 2 i2))
                         ))
       (PROG2 (set (SUB 0 (ADD 1 ARG1))
                      (set (SUB (read (ADD i0 (read (SUB 0
(ADD 1 1))))) (read 2)) (SUB (read (SUB (read (MUL 0 (ADD 1 1))) 1)) i0)))
              (PROG2 (for 1 (SUB nw (SUB nm_weeks (swap i0 (NNLK 1))))
                     (PROG2 (set 0 (XL 1))
                     (PROG2
                      (for i0 (ADD i0 (SUB nm_weeks 1) )
                       (set 0 (ADD (read 0)
                                   (read (ADD i0 (read (SUB 0 1)
                      ))))))
                     (set ((ADD i0 (read (SUB 0 (ADD 1 1)))))
                          (read 0)))))

              (PROG2 (set 0 (MUL max
                                 (SUB nw (SUB 1 (swap (XL 1) (read 0)))))) )
              (PROG2 (set
(PROG2 (fit nw) (set nw (ADD (read 2) (ADD i0 (read (SUB 0 1)))))) 0)
              (PROG2
                (for 1 (SUB nw (SUB nm_weeks 1))
                  (Iflt
                    (SUB
                      (read ((ADD i0 (read (SUB 0 (ADD 1 1))))))
                      (PROG2 (PROG2
                                (set 2 0)
                                (for i0 (ADD i0 (SUB nm_weeks 1))
                                  (set 2 (ADD (read 2) (fit i0)))
                                ))
                              (read 2)))
                  (read 0)
                  (PROG2
                    (set 1 i0)
                    (set 0 (SUB
                              (read (ADD i0 (read (SUB 0 (ADD 1 1)
                                                          ))))
                              (read 2))))
                  0))
                (read 1)))))))))
```

Figure C.11.   Evolved Heuristic. Length 199, Cost of schedule 388.349, CPU 306,438

best of these. It would be possible to start the GP run not only with the best hand coded "greedy" scheduler but also the best task ordering found by the GA. This would ensure the GP started from the best schedule found by previous approaches.

The run time of the GA is dominated by the time taken to perform loadflow calculations and the best approaches perform many of these. A possible future approach is to hybridise the GA and GP, using the GP to evolve the "greedy scheduler" looking not only for the optimal schedule (which is a task shared with the GA) but also a good compromise between this and program run time. Here GP can evaluate many candidate programs and so have an advantage over manual production of schedulers. This would require a more realistic calculation of CPU time with loadflow and shed functions being realistically weighted in the calculation rather than (as now) being treated as equal to the other primitives.

When comparing these two approaches the larger machine resources consumed by the GP approach must be taken into consideration (population of 1000 and 50 generation versus population of 20 and 100 generations).

C.10   SOUTH WALES PROBLEM WITH CONTINGENCIES

In the experiments reported in this section all 52 contingencies (i.e. potential faults which prevent a line carrying power) were included. This greatly increases run time. The 52 contingencies comprise; 42 single fault contingencies (one for each line in the network and twelve double fault contingencies (for cases where lines run physically close together, often supported by the same towers). The scaling factors for the single fault contingencies were 0.1, with 0.25 for the double fault contingencies, except the most severe where it was 1.0.

C.10.1   Greedy Scheduler

A number of "Greedy Schedulers" were tried with the permutation GA (described in Section C.13). Satisfactory schedules where obtained when considering all 52 contingencies, using the following two stage heuristic.

The choice of which four weeks to schedule a line's maintenance in is performed in two stages. In the first stage, we start with the maintenance schedule constructed so far and calculate the effect on network connectivity of scheduling the line in each of the 53 available weeks if each of the possible contingencies occurred simultaneously with the line's maintenance. (NB one contingency at a time). To reduce computational load, at this stage we only consider if the result would cause disconnections, i.e. we ignore line loadings. In many cases none of the contingencies would isolate nodes with demand or generation attached to them and all weeks are passed onto the second stage. However as the maintenance schedule becomes more complete there will be cases where one or more contingencies would cause disconnection in one or more weeks. Here the sum over all contingencies, of the load disconnected, weighted by the each contingency's' scaling factor, is calculated and only those weeks where it is a minimum are passed to the second stage.

In the second stage the modified version of the minimum increase in line cost heuristic, used in Section C.8.1, is used to select the weeks in which to perform maintenance. NB the second stage can only choose from weeks passed to it by the

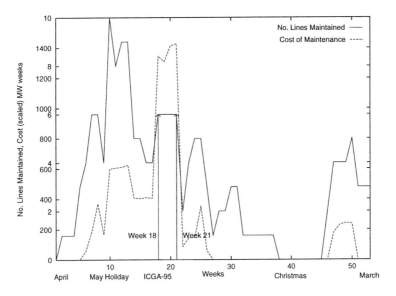

Figure C.12.   South Wales with Contingencies Maintenance Schedule

contingency pre-pass. By considering contingencies only in the first stage, run time is
kept manageable.

C.10.2   Results

The least cost schedule found in generation 18 after 78 minutes of one run of QGAME
on a 50 MHz SUN server 690MP is shown in Figure C.12. The cost of the schedule
is dominated by the contingency costs incurred in weeks 18–21. Four of the six lines
maintained during these four weeks will always incur contingency costs, because once
taken out of service nearby demand nodes are only connected to the remaining network
by a single line (see Figure C.13). By placing these in weeks 18–21 their contingency
costs have been minimised as these weeks correspond to minimum demand.

C.10.3   Discussion

While the schedules found do represent low cost solutions to the problem presented
to the GA, unlike in the four node problem, they may not be optimal. With problems
of this complexity, low cost solutions are all that can reasonably be expected. Computer generated schedules have been presented to NGC's planning engineers, while
expressing some concerns, they confirm they are reasonable.

The two principle concerns were; firstly the GA appears to have been concerned
to optimise the contingency costs associated with small demand nodes with only two
connections. Since contingency costs associated with them are inevitable, currently
planning engineers do not concentrate on minor improvements to them.

The greedy scheduler approach, schedules each line one at a time. There is a
concern that there may be circumstances where the optimal solution requires two lines

Pembroke

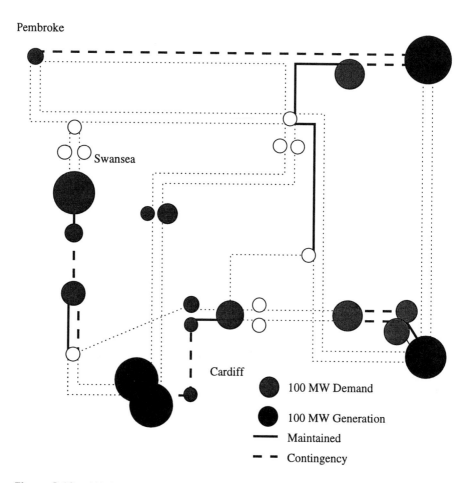

Swansea

Cardiff

● 100 MW Demand

● 100 MW Generation

— Maintained

– – Contingency

Figure C.13.   Weeks 18–21 of South Wales with Contingencies Maintenance Schedule

to be maintained at times which do not correspond to the local best for either of them. For example suppose it is planned that a generator will be run at half power for eight weeks and that it is connected by several lines, two of which are to be maintained. It would make sense to maintain them one after the other but the greedy scheduler could decide the best time to schedule one of them (looking just at the best for that line) was in the second of these eight weeks, so preventing the optimal schedule from being found. This circumstance does not arise in the South Wales problem, investigations of the complete network are required to see if it occurs elsewhere and how serious a problem it is. We feel that the greedy scheduler approach is sufficiently flexible that it could, it if necessary, be readily extended to include consideration of such special cases. However the approach is deliberately general purpose with a view to discovering novel schedules which an approach constrained by existing engineering wisdom might miss.

Since this work began NGC's manual methods have been augmented by a computerised single pass hill climbing technique, which has produced considerable financial savings by optimising manually generated schedules.

C.11   CONCLUSIONS

In this appendix, which was published in part in [Langdon, 1995c] and [Langdon and Treleaven, 1997], we have described the complex real world problem of scheduling preventive maintenance of a very large electricity transmission network. The combination of a GA and hand coded heuristic has been shown to produce acceptable schedules for a real regional power network when including consideration of network robustness to single and double failures.

C.12   FUTURE WORK

Having evolved satisfactory fault tolerant schedules for the preventive maintenance of the South Wales high voltage regional electricity transmission network. (Indeed we have tackled a version of the problem which schedules maintenance for many more plant items than are typically required). We now consider how this technique will scale up to larger problems, such as the NGC network. Currently the problem is solved by (1) manually decomposing the network in to regions (such as South Wales), (2) manually producing schedules for them, (3) assembling the complete schedule from them and finally (4) manually reconciling them all. (An automatic single pass optimiser can now be run to optimise critically components of the manually produced schedule). This chapter has already demonstrated the feasibility of using genetic algorithms to automate step (2). In this section we discuss using our GA on the complete NGC network.

The NGC network contains about ten times as many nodes and lines as the South Wales network and requires approximately three times as many maintenance activities to be scheduled than we considered in this chapter. In this chapter we considered all possible single and double fault contingencies. In practice run time consideration mean a study of the complete network is unlikely to consider all possible contingencies.

There are two aspects to scaling up; how difficult it is to search the larger search space and how the run time taken by the schedule builder and fitness evaluation scales.

A large component of run time is the DC load flow calculation, which assuming the number of nodes ≈ number of lines, is $O(n^3)$. In practice we expect to do rather better because:

- $O(n^3)$ reflects scaling for large problems, i.e. the time taken by low order terms will fall as a proportion of the total as the problem grows,

- We expect to use sparse matrix such as SDRS2 and other techniques such as "rank one modification" to speed up the DC load flow calculation,

- The may be considerable scope for the uses of caches of previously calculated partial results which can be reused on different members of the GA populations,

- The code has not been optimised as yet.

But even so, considerable growth in the fitness evaluation time must be anticipated, as the size of the problem is increased and parallel execution on multiple CPUs is anticipated.

We can also calculate how the size of the search space grows with problem size but assessing how difficult it will be to search is more problematic. The size of the complete search space grows exponentially with both the number of lines to be maintained and the duration of the plan, being $2^{\text{maintenance} \times \text{weeks}}$. However this includes many solutions that we are not interested in, e.g. we are not interested in solutions which take a line out of service when all its maintenance has already been done.

If we are prepared to consider only solutions which maintain each line in a single operation for exactly the required time then the number of such solutions is:

$$(1 + \text{weeks} - \text{weeks to do maintenance})^{\text{maintenance}} . \qquad (C.3)$$

Although a big number this is considerably less than $2^{\text{maintenance} \times \text{weeks}}$. For the South Wales problem the ratio between them is $1.3 \ 10^{-586}$ and this difference grows expo-nentially as the problem increases in size to $1.3 \ 10^{-1812}$ for the NGC problem.

The greedy optimisers use their problem specific knowledge to further reduce the search space. They consider at most (maintenance)! points in the smaller search space referred to in (C.3). Once again this is a considerable reduction. For the South Wales problem it is a $2.8 \ 10^{-21}$ fold reduction and this difference grows rapidly as the problem increases in size. However there is a danger in all such heuristics that by considering some solutions rather than all, the optimum solution may be missed.

There is no guarantee that NGC problem's fitness landscapes will be similar to that of the regional network. However we can gain some reassurance from the fact that the GA which optimally solved the four node problem also produced good solutions to the bigger regional problem. This give us some comfort as we increase the problem size again.

C.13   USING QGAME

QGAME [Ribeiro Filho and Treleaven, 1994] was used in all the GA experiments on grid scheduling problems. In every case the genetic algorithm contain a single population of 20 individuals, each contained a chromosome which consisted of a permutation of the lines to be scheduled. Permutation crossover and default parameters were used (see Table C.4).

Table C.4.   QGAME genetic algorithm parameters

Name	Value	Meaning
Problem_type	Combin-atorial	Combinatorial crossover and mutation operators are used on the chromosome, which holds a permutation of the lines to be scheduled
GeneType	G_INT	Line identification number
POPULATION	20	Size of population
CHROM_LEN	42	Forty two genes (lines) per chromosome
OptimiseType	Minimise	Search for lowest fitness value
PCROSS	0.6	On average each generation $0.6 \times$ POPULATION/2 pairs of individuals are replaced by two new ones created by crossing them over
PMUT	0.03	On average each generation $0.03 \times$ POPULATION individuals are mutated by swapping two genes
Selection	Truncated	The best TRUNCATION $\times$ POPULATION of the population are passed directly to the next generation. The remainder are selected using normalised fitness proportionate (roulette wheel) selection. Fitness is linearly rescaled so the best in the population has a normalised fitness of 1.0 and the worst zero
TRUNCATION	0.5	The best 50% passed directly to the next generation
POOLS	1	Single population
CHROMS	1	Individuals use single chromosome
MAX_GEN	100	Run for 100 generations

The four_node problem definition and QGAME are available via anonymous ftp and a graphical demonstration of the problem can be run via the Internet. Section D.9 gives the network addresses.

Appendix D
Implementation

D.1 GP-QUICK

For reasons of convenience of use, support and speed, our experiments were primarily coded in C++. The GP-QUICK package written by Andy Singleton [Singleton, 1994] was chosen as a basis because:

- It was written in C++.

- It was freely available, for non-commercial use.

- It was stable.

- There was some limited bug fixing support.

- There were early problems with the alternative C++ GP package, GPCPlus.

- It implements (via the FASTEVAL macro) linear prefix jump tables ([Keith and Martin, 1994, page 300] describes these as the best of the options they considered).

- GP-QUICK stores GP individuals in fixed length arrays. This is believed to considerably simplify the dynamic memory allocation/deallocation problem and avoid fragmenting the heap; however it means wasting some memory where individuals are less than the maximum length.

Some disadvantages to GP-QUICK have been encountered. For example, GP-QUICK accesses the population at random. This can cause severe performance problems if part of the population is swapped out of main memory.

D.2   CODING CHANGES TO GP-QUICK-2.1

Over the course of this work numerous changes have been made to GP-QUICK. The following list contains some of the more important:

- Support for multiple trees within one individual.

- Support for Automatically Defined Functions (ADFs).

- Reduction in space to store population to one byte per primitive.

- Run parameters set by control file and/or command line.

- Separate file of test cases.

- Check pointing (so long runs can be restarted after a workstation reboots).

D.3   DEFAULT PARAMETERS

The default values for GP-QUICK parameters used are given in Table D.1. They are the same as those used by [Koza, 1994, page 655] except, the following GP-QUICK parameters have also been used:

- GP-QUICK implements a steady state, rather than a generational, population.

- The GP-QUICK default tournament size is 4, rather than 7. Additionally selecting individuals for removal from the population is performed using tournament selection (again with a tournament size of 4).

- A maximum total program length limit is used rather than a maximum program depth limit of 17. In addition to the total length restriction, some experiments impose a limit, when the initial population is created, of 50 nodes on individual trees within the program.

- A single child is produced by each crossover. (If the potential offspring exceeds the maximum program size then the roles of the two parents are swapped, given both parents are of legal length this second offspring cannot be too big).

Table D.1.   Default GP-QUICK Parameters

pPopSize	: 10000	pMuteWt	: 0
pGenerateLimit	: 1000000	pAnnealMuteWt	: 0
pPopSeed	: 0	pAnnealCrossWt	: 0
pTestSeed	: 1	pCopyWt	: 10
pTrace	: 0	pSelectMethod	: 4
pMaxExpr	: 250	pTournSize	: 4
pInitExpr	: 6	pGaussRegion	: 0
pMuteRate	: 0	pRepeatEval	: 0
pCrossSelf	: 1	pKillTourn	: 4
pUnRestrictWt	: 70	pMaxAge	: 0
pCrossWt	: 90	pParsimony	: 0

D.4   NETWORK RUNNING

All the experiments were carried out on the UCL Computer Science department's heterogeneous network of SUN workstations. The runs being independent of each other. Using the queue problem as an example, with a population of 10,000, each job occupies about 13 Megabytes of RAM within the workstation. However the elapse time of each job varies considerably depending upon the load on the workstation (most runs were done out of hours), the speed of the workstation and the details of the GP run. To perform a million fitness evaluations (each of which requires the program under test to be run 320 times) takes all day on the faster workstations and cannot be completed in a day on the slower ones.

D.5   REUSING ANCESTORS FITNESS INFORMATION

This section briefly describes an implementation which has achieved reductions in run time by a factor of two. It can be applied to multi-tree programs whose primitives have side effects and is implemented using a conventional representation for the population. (Section 2.4.1 describes DAG based caches which can be used where there are no side-effects).

When tests are independent of each other, unless a particular test causes code which is different in a child from its parent to be run, the child's result on that test must be the same as that of its parent on the same test. Since the only difference between the child's code and the parent's is produced by crossover (or mutation), it can be readily determined if the child's result on a particular test could be different from its parent. Only those tests where the result could be different need be run. For the others, the result can be taken from the parent. The complete fitness of the child is assembled from the individual test results. NB result values can be inherited indefinitely, i.e. not only directly from the child's mother but also from its grandmother, great grandmother etc.

Our implementation considers changes only at the tree level. If crossover changes a tree which is not executed in a particular test then the new program's behaviour on that test must be identical to its parent's. I.e. its score must be identical and therefore the child's score on that test is inherited, and that test is not executed. The savings produced are dependent upon the test sequences, GP parameters and other time saving techniques (cf. Section D.6), nonetheless run time was halved in some cases. Since results for each test in the test case must be stored, as well as the overall fitness value, the technique increases execution speed at the expense of greater use of memory.

The technique could be extended to cover other cases where a child's score must be identical to that of one of its parents. For example children produced by crossovers which occur within introns, must behave identically to their parent and so have identical fitness.

D.6   CACHES

Handley's [Handley, 1994a] combination of caches and directed acyclic graphs, requires all the primitives to be free of side effects. read, write and other primitives *do* have side effects, nevertheless caching can be used when parts of the program (such as trees or ADFs) are known to be free of side effects. In the case of some runs of the list problem, cache hit ratios of between 70% and 97% were obtained with caches on End (1000 words), First (200), Next (1000) and Previous (200). This reduced run time by about 50%.

D.7   COMPRESSING THE CHECK POINT FILE

As mentioned in Section D.4, GP runs may take a long time. Under these circumstances a check point file can be used to restart a run from the last check point, rather than from the beginning. The check point file can also be used to extend particularly interesting runs.

The bulk of the check point file is occupied by the GP population. If written as plain text the population consumes too much disk space, particularly if more than one GP run is active at the same time. Therefore the population is written in a coded form, which occupies one byte per program primitive. As the GP run continues and the population converges, considerable reductions in disk space can be achieved by using *gzip* to compress the check point file. Compression ratios as high as 25 fold can occur but compression to about one bit per program primitive is common. (The high compression achieved indicates low diversity within the GP population). A balance needs to be struck between the time taken to process the check point file and the potential time saved should the check point file be used. Typically it takes about a minute to compress the check point file. Therefore check points are written about once an hour.

D.8   BENCHMARKS

A number of CPU and memory usage measurements were made using the MAX problem [Langdon and Poli, 1997a] running on a 400 MHz Digital Alphastation 500/400 with a 2MB cache and a SUN SPARCstation 2 fitted with an 80MHz CPU Weitek PowerUP CPU and floating point processor giving a performance of about 1.6 × that of a standard SPARCstation 2.

Table D.2.   GP-QUICK MAX Problem μS CPU

Total time	SPARC	Alpha
per individual	680	92
per primitive	6.3	0.8
Evaluation only		
individual	37	4.8
primitive	0.3	0.042

D.8.1 Memory

In GP-QUICK the memory occupied by the GP process is normally dominated by the space required to store the population. When run as a steady state GA there is a single population but when run as a generational GA the new population is created separately from the current one and so (in this implementation) twice as much memory is required. (With a little code re-organisation the double memory overhead could be removed).

GP-QUICK uses fixed length objects to store the population. The memory required for each GP individual is one byte times the maximum allowed program length plus a fixed overhead. The overhead is 182 bytes on the SUN and 304 bytes on the Alpha. To estimate the total memory, the number of bytes per GP individual is multiplied by the size of the population (and doubled if using a generational GA). With small populations, the memory occupied by the code can also be important.

D.8.2 Speed

A number of trials on both machines were made using the MAX problem. In this problem the population will be dominated by + and 0.5 primitives, as both of these require only trivial floating point calculations we expect the run time to be dominated by the time to interpret the GP programs and so Table D.2 gives an indication of the performance of GP-QUICK on the two machines. The top two rows of figures are obtained by dividing the total time by the number of individuals or primitives evaluated.

GP-QUICK supports a FASTEVAL pre-processing step which is aimed as increasing performance when GP individuals are evaluated multiple times. In the MAX problem individuals are only evaluated once so a modest saving might have been made by removing the FASTEVAL step.

An estimate of program evaluation time was made by evaluating individuals multiple times. The bottom two rows of Table D.2 were obtained by dividing the increase in total time by the increase in number of individuals and primitives evaluated. The lower two rows can be used to estimate the extra runtime caused by multiple evaluations, e.g. due to multiple fitness cases.

Due to the cache structures on the two machines individuals can be re-evaluated very quickly, leading to very fast times in the lower part of Table D.2. On problems with large numbers of (or complex) functions or terminals the cache may not perform as well and longer run times are expected.

D.9 CODE

Most of the source code used in the experiments described in this book is available on an *as is* unsupported basis, for research and educational purposes, via anonymous ftp node cs.bham.ac.uk in subdirectories of pub/authors/W.B.Langdon/

- The C++ code used in the experiments described in this book (except propriety code for the South Wales problem, cf. Appendix C) is available via ftp from sub-directory gp-code

  Additionally a copy may be found at ftp node ftp.mad-scientist.com in directory pub/genetic-programming/code

- The test cases used in Sections 7.1.4, 7.2.4 and 7.3.4 are available via ftp sub-directiory gp-code in file file GPdata_gp96.test.tar.Z

- The simple GP system used in the example in Section 2.3.3 is available via ftp sub-directory gp-code/simple in file gp-simple.c

- The program used to calculate the number of different trees of a given size with given terminal and function sets [Alonso and Schott, 1995] used on page 16 is also available via ftp sub-directory gp-code in file ntrees.cc

- C code for the demonstration four node problem and C++ code for QGAME (Appendix C) are available via ftp from sub-directory ga-code

- Finally an interactive on line demonstration of the four node problem written in Java can be found on the Internet at http://www.cs.bham.ac.uk/~wbl/four_node.demo.html

Index

Bill Langdon has been both a research officer in the electricity supply industry and a software engineer with Logica. His software is used to control the supply of gas to millions of people. In this book he shows how some of the lessons of software engineering can be beneficially used within genetic programming with the ultimate aim of using computers to automatically generate programs.